FEASTING ON MISFORTUNE
Journeys of the Human Spirit in Alberta's Past

Feasting on Misfortune

Journeys of
the Human Spirit
in Alberta's Past

DAVID C. JONES

The University of
Alberta Press

First published by
The University of Alberta Press
141 Athabasca Hall
Edmonton, Alberta, Canada T6G 2E8

Copyright © The University of Alberta Press 1998

ISBN 0–88864–301–2
A volume in (cuRRents), an interdisciplinary series. Jonathan Hart, series editor.

Canadian Cataloguing in Publication Data

Jones, David C., 1943–
Feasting on misfortune

Includes bibliographical references and index.
ISBN 0–88864–301–2

1. Frontier and pioneer life—Alberta. 2. Alberta—Biography. 3. Hubbard, Elbert,
1856–1915. I. Title.
FC3655.J66 1998   971.23'02'0922   C97–910728-8
F1075.8.J66 1998

∞ Printed on acid-free paper.
Printed and bound in Canada by Friesens, Altona, Manitoba.

The University of Alberta Press acknowledges the financial support of the Government
of Canada through the Book Publishing Industry Development Program for our
publishing activities. The Press also gratefully acknowledges the support received for its
program from the Canada Council for the Arts and the Alberta Foundation for the Arts.

COMMITTED TO THE DEVELOPMENT OF CULTURE AND THE ARTS

To the Fra

Contents

Acknowledgements

I THANK MANY FOR THEIR KINDNESS AND COUNSEL—
Doug Francis, Bob Stamp, Tad Guzie, Sarah Carter, David
Leonard, John Gilpin, and Paul Voisey. I am grateful to those I
spoke and corresponded with, often at length—Carl Anderson,
Lois Valli, Ted Valli, Gilda Valli, Angela Valli, Eileen Ross,
Gordon Albright, Frank Brown, Neil Rutherford, Patricia Jones,
Keith Stotyn, the gracious staff of Glenbow Alberta Archives and
Library and the Provincial Archives of Alberta. Pamela Hannan-
Wamboldt and Jo-Anne Deane helped immeasurably in
translating Father Culerier's diaries. Finally, I salute unknown
reviewers of this press for their tolerance and wisdom and the
Social Sciences and Humanities Research Council for its aid.

Prolog

THIS IS A SAGA ABOUT THE SEARCH FOR HUMAN FULFILLMENT. The paths to that state seem as diverse as humanity itself, and from the faint markings left it is clearly dangerous to judge the motives or meaning of other lives.

All parts of each journey seem somehow necessary—the meanderings, the indecision, the dead-ends, the delights, the triumphs, even the mistakes and the misery. Every experience, every event, even the worst, offers value. It may, for instance, be necessary to oppress another to learn that oppression is abuse, or to hate another to see that hatred affords no resolution, or even to write a book to learn what is better left unsaid.

What seems consistent in each life is some form of opposition, some constraint, some adversity. Without resistance, the sense of accomplishment is stillborn, the realization of self, stunted. A kite flies high against the wind—it is pushed aloft in its struggle to be what it is, and it must be confronted to reveal its nature.

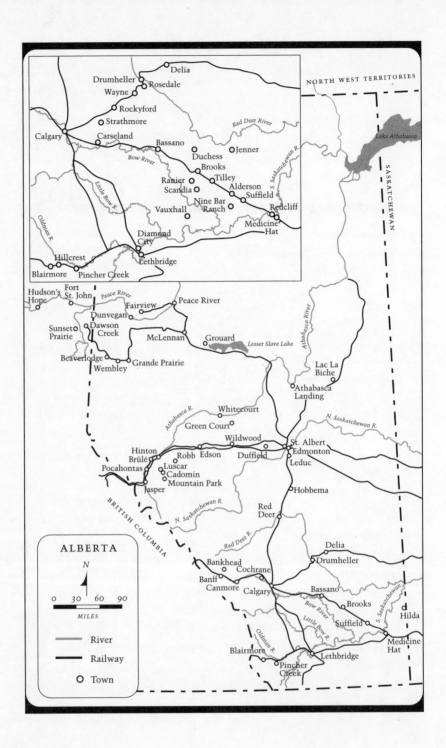

Confrontation, constraint, adversity bind together the disparate, sometimes faintly related stories that follow.

Chronic constraint or adversity is but a step from misfortune. And what does the human spirit do with misfortune?

It feeds on it until the spirit grows or sickens. It feeds on adversity until the spirit becomes strong or weak.[1] And what determines which it will do? I think not so much what happens to it as what the spirit thinks of itself.

There is a state spoken of in the literature on the self wherein the self becomes acutely aware of its power, capable of withstanding the crash of worlds and the break-up of all we cherish. Some say this indestructibility is our real nature, a nature we have somehow, in the millennia of time, either suppressed or forgotten.

The test of the strength of the self is what it does when sorely tried, and so, sooner or later, it must face its demons. Those who would become serene within, even disappointment-proof, must confront their fears. And the external world is ever filled with things to fear, and obstacles to overcome, and calamities to meet.

Shortly after its birth in 1905, the fledgling province of Alberta was neck-deep in trouble—the settlement of the Peace River country reached dangerously too far; the southeastern dry belt disintegrated in drought; irrigation projects teetered in crisis; colliers agonized over life and limb, exasperated by the overexpansion and overproduction of an industry that satisfied no one. Men of the cloth serving hundreds of new communities and outposts were stretched to the breaking point, without solace or comfort, in a mission that was well-nigh insupportable.

Who are my actors in this troubled setting? With supporting cast— Donald Albright, Lois Valli, Willet Trego, Carl and Lee Anderson, the entangled trio of Frank Moodie, Harry Smith and the coal spy, Father Louis Culerier, The Office Cat, and Elbert Hubbard.

Donald Albright was the Apostle of the Peace River country and a Burnsite, a member of a break-away sect from Methodism that sought their dreams by accessing directly the guidance of the Holy Spirit. For this simple hope and other creedal indiscretions, Burnsite leaders were tried in Ontario for heresy. In a sense, their trial was everyone's trial and their search every soul's search, for it was about humanity's relationship with God and man-made churches and their rules into heaven. It was also about the quest for freedom and fulfillment and the great elusiveness of these qualities in the new land, or anywhere else. Primarily, it was about human nature and its link to the source of resolution to its problems; so, crucially, it concerned the deepest of inquiries—*what a single human soul might accomplish*.

Lois Valli was a downcast ranchwife, eight miles south of Alderson, a ghost town-in-the-making, in the forsaken dry belt. There she wrote poetry about her place in the sun, snow, wind, and dust, and she looked into the great emptiness to find herself.

Willet Trego and Carl Anderson struggled to rehabilitate that wasteland, to fill it with progressive farms, fed by life-giving irrigation. The gargantuan feat of moving the rivers the Canadian Pacific Railway had already done; now, moving the railway would be even harder.

The colliers—Frank Moodie, Harry Smith and the spy—fought a brother's war; and the saint, Father Louis Culerier, fought a civil war, the spirits of the former in deadly conflict with each other, the spirit of the latter in deadly conflict with itself.

There is suffering in this book, and feuding and spite, and not always as a prelude to peace. "Suffering is not ennobling," a master surgeon once said. "Recovery is."[2]

Some players here, recovered, others I cannot say.

The Office Cat, I believe, mended himself. He is a composite of characters appearing, usually anonymously, in one of Canada's best humor columns, from the *Medicine Hat News*. The Cat is every man and woman at every stage of cosmic awareness, and so he may be interpreted as one pleases. At diverse times, as he grew up, he seemed cynic, a misogynist, a misogamist, a misanthrope, a grouch, but I have left him with only traces of these immaturities, for they are hopeless ways of seeing the world.

Rather I have seen the Cat after he became wise, or what I take for wise, and I have seen how he found himself, how miraculously he dissolved misfortune.

Elbert Hubbard, warmly known as "Fra Elbertus," is my philosopher. Born in Illinois in 1856, the Fra was "the sage of East Aurora," New York—a Renaissance man interested in philosophy, oratory, art, music, literature, religion, education, business and metaphysics. Spring to fall, he rode the lecture tours of America, even to Winnipeg and Edmonton, addressing audiences of hundreds, sometimes thousands, in what many considered a communion of souls. From roughly 1895 to 1915, his literary output was staggering—twenty-eight volumes of *Little Journeys* to the homes of the great; forty-one volumes of his periodical, *The Philistine*; another journal, *The Fra*; several novels and shorter pieces, and a book of mottos.

Beauty and expression were dear to him. His Roycroft shops in East Aurora were inspired by William Morris's Kelmscott operation in England. Employing five hundred people at its peak, Roycroft made oak furniture—rocking chairs, writing desks, and magazine pedestals—sculpture, pottery, hand-woven rugs, and hammered silver, copper and brass chandeliers, lamps and ornaments. All are collectibles today. The Roycroft Press produced classy and costly books, many hand-illumined, leather and suede bound—the modeled leather edition of Thoreau's essay on "Friendship," for example, sold for $250 a volume. Even cheaper $2 copies, still pricey, were lovely, and the Fra's creations won red ribbons at international shows and were called "the most beautiful books in the world." Good paper was nine-tenths of a book, Hubbard believed, and Roycroft parchment is as radiantly strong and white as a century ago, unlike the acid pulp combusting on shelves today.

In 1899 Hubbard wrote "A Message to Garcia," a slight, four or five page essay. Hardly the best piece of so masterful an essayist, it was read like Scripture, and perhaps 80 million copies were printed by 1940. The demand was immediate and incomprehensible. Two hundred newspapers and magazines carried the message, two movies were made of the main character, and every member of the U.S. Marine Corps and the Boy Scouts of America received a copy. It was translated into twenty foreign tongues. All Russian railway employees received it, and during the Russo-Japanese War the Japanese found it on Russian prisoners. Impressed, the Japanese rushed another translation into the hands and minds of their own troops.[3]

What did it say? It was simple enough. Just before the Spanish-American War, President McKinley called Lt. Andrew Summers Rowan to contact General Garcia, leader of Cubans opposing Spain. Rowan offered no excuses, no delay, no questions—he simply *acted*. Landing in Cuba by night, he crossed a jungle, sidestepped hostile bands, and found Garcia. "It is not book learning young men need, nor instruction about this and that," said Hubbard, "but a stiffening of the vertebrae which will cause them to be loyal to a trust, to act promptly, concentrate their energies, do the thing—'Carry a message to Garcia.'"[4]

The essay appealed to those in authority and berated the "insane suspicion" of some employees that their employers were "oppressing, or intending to oppress" them. Alas, only a fragment of Hubbard's philosophy inhered—for oppression he *did* oppose; indeed, he seemed a throwback to one persecuted for his thoughts. Group sanctioned dicta and mass hypnosis he abhorred—anything that tore sane consideration and sacred choice from people. The methods and constraints of medieval and modern religion he scorned, and mind-closing he slew at every turn.

His clash with Billy Sunday, premier evangelist of the era, was typical. To him Sunday was the crown prince of printed authority, however unbelievable. He preached human worthlessness, and he controlled through fear. A mesmerist he was.

When Sunday thundered that the Fra was "exactly the same kind of man as Voltaire, David Hume, Thomas Paine, Thomas Huxley and Robert Ingersoll," Hubbard smiled.

"A great compliment has come my way," he mused. "I might have wished it had come from another source. However, they say that your enemies are the ones who tell the truth about you. Friends are given to flattery.

"What the Reverend Billy Sunday says about me ought to be true. The sad part is, it isn't quite.

"However, he has set me a standard, and like Billy's constituents who thought the doctrine of total depravity a good thing, 'if only you lived up to it,' so I have something to live up to."[5]

Sunday may have been more religious than Hubbard, but scarcely more spiritual. Hubbard's *Man of Sorrows*, the life of Christ, was as beautiful as anything else he wrote. But he would not be told what to believe; he would find out himself.

And what he found he expressed in epigrams, many imperishable:

The goal of evolution is self conquest.
Success is the realization of the estimate which you place on yourself.
To lose your self respect is the only calamity.

All laws, creeds and dogmas are of transient value, if of value at all. And should be eliminated when they no longer minister to human happiness.

Orthodoxy is that peculiar condition where the patient can neither eliminate an old idea nor absorb a new one.

All separation of society into sacred and secular, good and bad, saved and lost, learned and illiterate, rich and poor, are illusions which mark certain periods in the evolution of society.

I doubt the wisdom of being too wise; and I see much wisdom in some folly.

Nothing is so fatal to integrity as pretense.

All suffering is caused by an obstacle in the path of a force. See that you are not your own obstacle.

The only sin is unkindness.

We gain freedom by giving it, we hold love by giving it away.

Love is all. I say to you that man has not sufficient imagination to exaggerate the importance of love.

In 1889 Hubbard met his soul mate in Alice Moore, teacher at East Aurora High School. A divine discovery—save that he was wed. One of his lectures, Alice attended: "Suddenly my eyes looked straight into the eyes of a Personage. She was twenty-nine in June, I think, or thereabouts—rather tall, plain, but with a face that beamed intelligence, insight and good nature. She was not coy, affected nor abashed and she smiled the frankest kind of smile of welcome.... I smiled back.... It was all in an instant, but we had met, this fine, strong woman and I in a soul-embrace, and there was a perfect understanding between us."[6]

In 1894 Elbert Hubbard fathered two daughters—one with his wife Bertha, the other with Alice Moore. Painful years later, the story came out, disgrace descended, and Bertha sued for divorce.

Then the self-righteous, clerics and all, closed on him in a feeding frenzy. "He became the center of a cataclysm which it seemed…would break hearts, and inflict wounds that a lifetime could not heal," his sister remembered. "He was to meet averted faces that had been kind and friendly, and to see hands withdrawn that had joyfully clasped his. His own flesh and blood was to deny him, and recriminations and vituperations were to be heaped upon him." In agony, he cried, "The Catholics are right, there should be no such thing as divorce."[7]

To his parents, Hubbard wrote: "I am deeply gratified to know that in my hour of bitterness you have stood firm and held your peace. It is not necessary that you should endorse all that I have done; neither is it for you to exonerate me. You have simply loved me....When calamity lowered and disgrace seemed nigh, what a humiliation if you too had deserted me and denied me."

"*It is the whole that counts*," he told his mother. "My heart is right and I am in the hands of God....If I go down it will be because I deserve it, but look you, *I am not going down*."[8]

One does not know what lies in store, and one can scarce think that all this could be for some greater good—but Hubbard saw it so.

Later, after the Fra was again loved by scores of thousands and shortly after his tragic death, Billy Sunday was preaching one day when he noticed Elbert's aging mother in attendance. Finishing, he rushed to her, embraced her, and whispered emotionally, "Nobody felt worse than I did."[9]

"We are all sailing under sealed orders," Hubbard once said, and as he opened his to the light, he accepted his lot with grace.

Even then, thinking of his life and in some sympathetic, intuitive way of all our lives, he sensed the part each plays in destiny. Murmured he, awed, "No great spiritual event befalls those who do not summon it."[10]

"The soul knows all things, and knowledge is only a remembering," says Emerson. This seems a broad statement; yet the fact remains that the vast majority...know a thousand times as much as they are aware of. In the silent depths of subconsciousness lie myriads of truths, each awaiting the time when its owner shall call it forth. And to utilize these stored-up thoughts you must express them to others; and, to express well, your soul has to soar into this subconscious realm where you have cached these net results of experience.

When you reach the heights of sublimity, and are expressing your highest and best, you are in a partial trance condition. And all men who enter this condition surprise themselves by the quantity of knowledge and the extent of insight they possess.

But what think you is necessary before a person comes into possession of his subconscious treasures? Well, I'll tell you: It is not ease, nor prosperity, nor requited love, nor worldly security— not these, dearie; no.[11]

Fra Elbertus

The Peace

1   Burnsites

THE TRIAL

THE CHARGE WAS HERESY. The time, November 27,

1893, at Tilsonburg, Ontario. The defendant was Reverend Albert

Truax, a fading Methodist preacher, now high officer of The

Canada Holiness Association. His accusers—a tribunal of the

Methodist Church.[1]

Because Truax was one of several ministers astray, his trial was really the trial of many.

"What had he done?" J.W. Cooley, the reverend prosecutor, asked. On cue, witnesses, long-standing Methodists, pastors and Sunday School Superintendents, spewed out their censure.

Truax depreciated the Bible as simply a history, like any other history, and parts of it as anything but the word of God.

He disbelieved the immaculate conception of Christ.

He doubted if Paul's writings held any greater authority than his own.

He said he would just as soon go to hell as to believe everything in the Bible and if he did go, he could get out, if he wanted to. Hell, he asserted, was not the Eternal Punishment of God, but the self-imposed remorse of one's conscience.

He could walk before God as Christ did, he said, he could know the will of God as Christ did, and he was just as much a son of God as Christ was.

He disparaged the doctrine of the atonement that dictated that Christ died to appease a riled Father who accepted the sacrifice as the cost of his love for humanity. This notion Truax called "monstrous."

He denounced all creeds as insufficient and arrogant presumptions of God's nature and plan.

Most frighteningly, he upheld as the highest authority *individual guidance by the Holy Spirit.* And he declared, "Following the Holy Spirit as the only absolute law of life, leads one to examine any creed or dogma in a fearless common sense manner; and leads him to accept any logical satisfactory conclusion at which he may arrive; and this too without the slightest regard for the antiquity of the dogma, and in spite of the numbers who may subscribe to the creed."[2]

In South Cayuga, Ontario, Truax bade a convention pledge itself in anthem to the Holy Spirit as the primary guide. A stanza of the foul hymn rang out:

The sacred book though held most dear
Never with Thee shall interfere
All pious rules though Bible taught
Before Thy Word shall be as naught.

All these aberrations flew in the face of established Methodist doctrine, as Truax well knew. Indeed, he admitted, "there are men in the Niagara Conference who would cheerfully pile fagots around my roasting body if they had a chance." But to the charges Truax responded not; nor would he—because he was absent, preferring to preach that night. This was not his first trial, nor would it be the last spawned by the holiness movement and its impulse to encourage human perfection.

*Inspiration of the Christian
Association—Nelson Burns—
communer with the Divine
Mind. NA 493–18, GAA.*

"I frankly admit teaching Christian righteousness," Truax wrote his inquisitors,"—that is that men can be as holy as Jesus, and know the will of God concerning themselves as well as He." All other charges, he asserted, were "side issues."[3]

Stern-faced, the inquisition pronounced judgement. One might teach righteousness, it agreed, but to expect Christ-like righteousness of a creature innately sin-ridden, even to aim at it, was hopeless. Hopeless too, was Truax, and *guilty*.

At the next Niagara Conference Truax was expelled from the Methodist Church. That same year, 1894, the President of the Canada Holiness Association and Truax's chief counsel and inspiration, Nelson Burns, was turfed from the Guelph Conference.

Five years before, Burns's tract *Divine Guidance or the Holy Quest* had set off the long brewing crisis. Burns preached the import of seeking and accepting holiness. Divine guidance was available to anyone, prelate or pauper, and it needed no intermediary, no dogma or doctrine. The guidance, he said, was an "intimation to our consciousness by the Holy Spirit whereby we know we are taking that course in all things, from moment to moment, which is the best possible under the circumstances and is therefore pleasing to God and satisfactory to ourselves."[4]

Intimation of what kind? Dreams, visions, intuitions, suggestions, scripture—the ways of the Spirit were many and impossible to contain. Confirmation that a request for right thought or right action had been answered was simply a knowing within.

Simple, indeed, but horrifying too to the established church, *any* established church. For too little could be counted on to be confirmed by so many parishioners relying on their separate intuitions. Would they all know within that the articles of faith and the doctrines of the church were true?[5] Would they all welcome what pastors had been preaching since John Wesley? Would they all accept the sometimes extraordinary claims of holy writ? Would they be of one mind, would they agree on *anything*? What kind of church could be built on such fluff?

For institutions, these effervescences of the spirit are destined to alternating moments of extinguishment and rekindling, because it is difficult to form a church that has boundaries so elastic and indeterminate, that seeks truth beyond creeds, or even believes there is one.

Worshippers do demand stability in their relationships with the Infinite. But what Burns and his lieutenant objected to was the freezing of belief patterns into immovable, non-growing molds. What they sought was liberation from old patterns and old trammels fitted by others. They knew that the discovery of God can lead to very unexpected places, beyond the careful confines of creed.

The Burnsites carried with them the thought that one might be guided by a higher intelligence and that in the process the creature might merge with its Creator. If it were true that men and women could be like Christ, what vistas would open, what hidden power would be released, what self-esteem might be enhanced, what dignity restored. The potential may have been too chaotic and too uncertain for some, but for Burns it was exciting and ennobling.

Most institutional churches set nets around themselves so that their members might see clearly the limits of the church's understanding of God and people. Of course, most churches take *their* limits to be *the* limits. When an individual's understanding passes those limits, he leaps over the net and into the vast beyond. There he will discover the nets he has placed for himself at the edge of the waves on his horizon.

Bull Outfitters upset en route to Eden. A 2531, PAA.

A MUDDY HELL HOLE

Some years later, in one of the communities where the Burnsite heresy had spread, Elias Smith told a congregation that he had received God's word to go West where believers might fashion an agrarian civilization. Many listeners accepted this guidance implictly: a message had come from the Eternal—they were to leave Toronto the Good for Alberta the Better. Out of Methodism they leapt, a school of them together.

On March 16, 1909, five families of Burnsites, with others, left Toronto aboard a colonist coach, heading west. In Edmonton they met others of the faith, the Gaudins and Drakes, and determined to trek to the Beaver Lodge River Valley where they might settle in a block. Over land and water, the trip was five hundred miles.[6]

For comfort, Amos Sherk bought a small streetcar, dubbed "the Car," which seated ten adults. Fourteen wagons they loaded and hitched to thirty-six oxen who gave the expedition its name—the Bull Outfit. In late afternoon on April 20, they rolled out of Edmonton and camped at the outskirts.

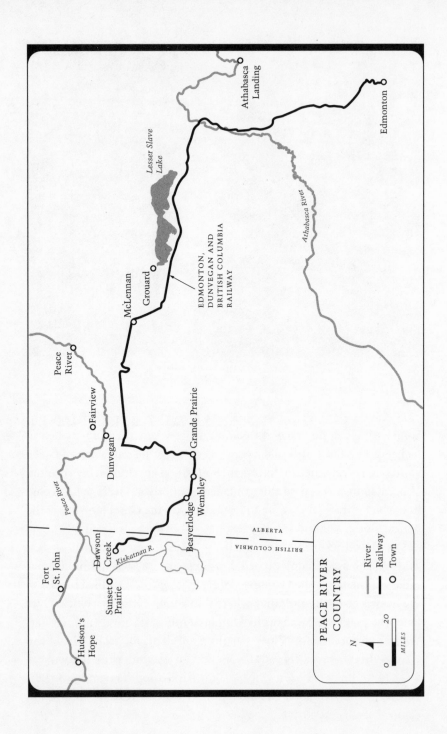

PEACE RIVER COUNTRY

N

River
Railway
○ Town

0   20
MILES

Athabasca Landing

Edmonton

Lesser Slave Lake

Athabasca River

McLennan

Grouard

EDMONTON, DUNVEGAN AND BRITISH COLUMBIA RAILWAY

Peace River

Fairview

Dunvegan

Grande Prairie

Peace River

Wembley

Beaverlodge

ALBERTA

BRITISH COLUMBIA

Fort St. John

Dawson Creek

Kiskatnau R.

Sunset Prairie

Hudson's Hope

Next day, thirty-one settlers-to-be pried the wagon wheels out of the freeze and headed north against a cold wind. Elias Smith was named trail boss, Mrs. Smith, food boss.

They reached Athabasca Landing in a week where they left "the Car" behind as a mobile home for some trapper. Its low clearance made travel over stumps and through wallows a nightmare. Too heavily laden now for the tough slogging ahead, the expedition shipped six tons of freight to the west end of Lesser Slave Lake.

Still, as the convoy approached a series of three hills on May 2, it took three hours to cross. Down one icy slope they locked the brakes and slid, out of control, the oxen slipping down on their knees and haunches. Near the infamous bald hills, a two-mile gully took two days to pass. With water everywhere, mud two-feet deep, and upsets aplenty, Gaudin, the official secretary, damned the place as "the hilliest, muddiest hell-hole I ever got into." The heavier loads took four teams to budge.

Delay followed delay, and food was running out. So Mrs. Smith resorted to rationing, and she meant it. Once she noticed Mrs. Sherk give some tidbits to her famished boys, and to halt the extravagance, she cut Mrs. Sherk's portion! Meanwhile, Mac Miller, with false teeth that couldn't cut it, had to smash his hardtack with a hammer on a wagon wheel.

When the pack trail around Lesser Slave Lake was reported to be impassable, the remaining wagons and freight, the women and children and older men were shipped across to Shaw's Point, near Grouard. The rest then led four oxen apiece along the shoreline looking for the trail which they found halfway between faint and invisible. Through the trees for ten miles the oxen pointed, one this way, another that, tangling the lines and tormenting their handlers. Lost and exasperated, the seekers returned to the starting point and determined to cut a trail themselves.

In the rocks and boulders on the north side of the lake, the wagoners tried to protect the feet of the oxen with gunny sacks. But oxen have a remarkable overreach, and their hind legs stepped on the sacks of the front feet, tripped them, and tore the sacks off. Gritting their teeth, the men chopped their way through forests and churned great spans through two feet of water. Somehow they staggered into Shaw's Point ahead of the boat.

A Burnsite gathering near the time of Albright's arrival,
Beaverlodge, 1916c. NA 493–15, GAA.

As "the Northern Light" chugged into port, the men ashore, beaming and expectant, waved banners of welcome. But the vessel brought only the Lossings and one other. Tons of freight and too many passengers, too much for the little "Light," had been left behind and would not arrive for two more weeks.

Cooling their heels, the overlanders, chopped wood for the steamers, awaited the next boat, then pressed on. On the fourth of July, heading south now, they reached Dunvegan, and were the happy first settlers to cross on the new ferry. Joy was short, however, as squadrons of the legendary "heavy" Peace River mosquitoes now strafed them—darting even through face nets and momentary clearings in the clouds of stinking, near fatal (to humans) smoke from smudge pots. One sweltering night, Amos Sherk, layered with hat and gloves, parka and mosquito veil, was so pestered and lanced, he broke from his tent yelling that the bugs could never be as bad outside as in.

On July 14, the troop entered paradise, the beautiful Beaver Lodge River Valley, where hay was half up the backs of their faithful beasts. Then they fanned out seeking the choicest parcels of land which they staked in readiness for the surveyor even now portioning out God's country.

Most of the hardy lot were comfortably settled when Donald Albright and his wife Eva, daughter of the Lossings, joined them three years on. Albright was on a great mission, though the veil covering his awareness of it was only partly lifted.

Born in 1881 in South Cayuga, Ontario, of Pennsylvania Deutsch extraction, Albright never tired as a lad of the daring and romance at the top of the globe. He first wetted his appetite with his grandfather's *The Polar and the Tropical Worlds*, a three-inch thick cyclopedia, fine printed and thin folioed, and weighty as stone. Northern Canada was his focus—Resolution, Chipewyan, Providence, and Dunvegan—and he wondered how flesh and blood could survive at 60 degrees below zero.[7]

Later, possibly as part of an Ontarian's manifest destiny, he wondered how the land might be possessed—by Canadians and not Americans.

At the Ontario Agricultural College in Guelph, Albright absorbed its deep rural bias. For general proficiency he won in 1903 the Governor General's Prize. That year he became editor of *The Maritime Farmer*, and in 1905 he went over to *The Farmer's Advocate*, London, Ontario, where he edited the paper and managed its farm until 1913.[8] At Beaverlodge he became superintendent of the experimental station.

All his life, Albright walked his own path inspired by his own muse. As a teenager, he tasted whiskey, realized he liked it, and renounced it forever—an unusual script for anyone, let alone an adolescent, which marked him as indomitably unorthodox.[9]

His open-minded theology and long adherence to the Burnsites bore him the same brand. What drew Donald Albright to their dissent was the freedom of its thought, the complete rejection of the imprisonment of the mind in dogmas and doctrines, and the conviction that truth-seeking was a progressive enterprise. Divine guidance was ongoing, unbroken. And it was revealed a sparkle at a time in response to the asking and in keeping with the wisdom of the asker.

How much grander this scheme was then the pinching, puerile doctrine of original sin, of humanity's ghastly depravity and separation from God. How simple, how liberating and empowering the scheme was. And how appropriate for a man destined to uncover the secrets of nature in one of the world's last great agricultural preserves.

2 The Apostle

SETTLEMENT INTO THE MIGHTY PEACE RIVER
country flowed and ebbed like the tide. Led by the "Bull Outfit"
that trekked 550 miles from Edmonton, the first major influx
coincided with the height of the prairie settlement period and the
infilling of the southern dry belt. It lasted from 1909 to 1913,
when war and depression stanched it before the second wave
began with the chimes of armistice.[1] From 1921 to 1925, depression repossessed the land, and dispirited pioneers tumbled
southward as if caught in the torrent of a spring freshet.[2] In 1926
the third wave began.

By early summer 1928, there were ten thousand of them grinding and grunting along the trails north of McLennan. Bounding through the ruts, their model T's, McLaughlins and Essexes threw up clouds of dust discernible for miles on several serpentine byways. Said someone, "This is the greatest land rush in Canadian history."[3]

One more bumper harvest in 1928, British Columbian oracles pronounced, and '29 would see thirty-thousand landseekers in the Peace. "The Peace River country can and probably will have a population of 2,000,000 in twenty years time," beamed the euphoric *Edmonton Journal*. "It may be far-fetched....It may sound ridiculous."[4]

But not so, judged John Imrie, managing director of the *Journal*. Four times in the past seven years had he forayed into the region, and each time he emerged more certain than before that here lay God's ultimate prize to stewards of the land. The wheat yield of 1927, he reminded doubters, was double that of the whole province when it was formed.[5]

Speedily, Imrie dispatched correspondents to the new Israel. Two, H.F. Mullett and George Murray, itinerated as the last great prairie boom peaked, and they were as able propagandists as ever confused good land with heaven.

In 1923 there were just twenty-two grain elevators in the Peace; on March 1, 1929, there were 120. The total grain harvest in 1924 from an area in crop of 160,000 acres was 3.8 million bushels; in 1927, the area in crop was 354,000 acres, and the yield 10.8 million bushels.[6] There were reports of 78 bushels of wheat an acre and 100 bushels of oats.[7]

Fort St. John, B.C., had reached 4,000 strong and was doubling every year. Someone dreamed that Wembley would become a second Winnipeg, Hudson's Hope, a second Pittsburgh, Grande Prairie, a second Chicago.[8]

For the avant-guard half a continent from steel, the wheat belt went on forever. "The settler north of the Peace, 'going it blind' in the face often of sage advice to remain nearer the old centres of settlement has proven the possibilities of the new north," effused Murray. "He has stampeded ahead of surveys and railways. And he has in almost every instance made such a success that he himself has been astounded."[9]

As a doctor reined in at a settler's shack on the fringes of civilization, a woman shrieked in anguish.

"How long has this been going on?" the doctor asked.

"A day or so," answered the calloused husband.

The mother was half through a childbirth she could never complete, for the baby was twisted and lodged in the birth canal. It was one of those nightmarish "malpresentations" that ripped a woman to pieces and bled her dry, and that husbands knew nothing of except its horrors. The doctor arrived in the nick of time.

"There are...many families up here now who are a good deal nearer to starvation than any I've ever seen in England," Dr. Mary Percy Jackson wrote at year-end 1929. "And as for housing conditions— well—two families (6-10 people) living in a one-roomed house 10 x 12 x 7 is not even considered overcrowding." The entire community had eschewed money and relapsed into barterism.

For two- or three-hundred children of school age scattered over 800 square miles on the margins, well north of Grande Prairie, where Jackson spent much of her time, there was a single school—for thirty pupils. The average retardation of the lucky thirty was four years. "So that the adults of this district in the next generation," said Jackson, "will have the education of children of 10."

By early spring, Jackson was counting the toll of winter. "I'm up to my eyes in work," she wrote on April 11. "I've been up three nights running and done 78 miles on horseback in the last 48 hours too!" Comatose and freezing, with her horse footworn, she lumbered home at midnight anticipating the boon of sleep. At her doorstep was an anxious caller ready to guide her twenty miles into the muskeg to a woman on deathbed.

The way was an impossible sea of mud and mush, crisscrossed by bridgeless streams in frigid flood that had to be swum. Two miles from the homestead, a frantic rider met them and urged the greatest speed. "So," said Jackson, "I did the last two miles of a 45 mile day at a dead gallop."

Bursting through the door at 4 AM, she found the woman "cold, clammy" and "pulseless." With great effort, she rekindled the life. She

kept watch till 6 PM the next day, and then confident, she returned through the mush traps. Four hours later, she staggered home, tended to her faithful mount, fed herself, and toppled into bed.

At 1 AM, as sleep finally held her, a voice jarred from outside the window. Could she come? The man's wife was sick. It looked like appendicitis. Immediately Jackson dressed, packed her satchel and left.

As before, the trail was broken and navigable only by steed. When they arrived, the diagnosis proved correct, and the good doctor speedily arranged to cart the woman to hospital at Peace River. That very moment, another wild-eyed settler raced up asking if the doctor might come at once—another wife was on the brink of death.

In the eight days before April 16, 1930, Jackson rode 180 miles on horseback and managed just one and a half nights in bed. Once in a blinding snowstorm she had to evacuate another acute appendicitis case by caterpillar. For seventy miles to Peace River, she drugged the woman with morphia while she herself neared insanity listening to the maddening trat-a-tat-tat of the cat.

One Sunday in this hectic tour of duty, she nearly drowned crossing a raging Jack Knife Creek. Her mount got in, but could not climb the almost vertical bank of mud on the other side. They plunged back in and swam up current before escaping to the same side they had left.

A farmer on the other side was loading hay with a team that had almost drowned the day before. He hauled Jackson's horse over with a rope, and then he yanked Jackson across on two thin poplar poles, like a bobcat on water skis. Half way, the poles rolled over and dunked the doctor again. On terra firma, Jackson, soaked and freezing, remounted and galloped four miles against the wind to her next patient.[10]

WANDERLUST

Donald Albright never doubted Doc Jackson. As the premier historian and agricultural scientist of the Peace River Country, he bewailed for half a lifetime the insanity of its settlement process. Nothing could still his tongue, for he had seen too much.

"There may be a more chaotic way of settling a new country than by giving the land away as homesteads but it is not easy to think of one," railed Albright in 1930.

"Few of the highly placed business and public men who parade their early days on the homestead show any great anxiety for their sons and daughters to attend the same school. Recollection hallows home-steading—from a safe vantage. Even the fortunately successful seldom choose to repeat. The ne'er do wells may. And what of the victims strewn along the way, filling lonely cemeteries, rusting in detached communities, occasionally incarcerated in asylums, but more often forsaking the frontier as poorer, sadder and wiser men?

"And what of the women and children? Grant if we will the right of a man to immolate himself on the altar of misguided ambition, has he a moral right to sacrifice his wife and family on the same altar?"[11]

How long O Lord, and how many times must it happen, Albright winced. How it reminded him of the Sunset Prairie fiasco.

About 1920, a remote satellite of the British Columbia Peace River Block was thrown open to returned soldiers. Sunset Prairie, as it was aptly called, was available at the edge of the world, a mere 135 miles from steel and 35 miles from the nearest post office at Pouce Coupe. If thirty men could be drummed up with a stake against seen and unforeseen costs, a cool one thousand dollars each, the outpost was theirs.

Cynics in the throng of thirty scoffed at such a loose stipulation and prided themselves in the ease with which they could subvert it. Again and again, the lie was repeated, and the same one thousand dollars was used over and over "like a baton in a relay race."[12]

At Grande Prairie they marshaled in a cavalcade of binders and bunglers, shorthorns and greenhorns. The parade of inexperience creaked westward almost without dust or notice, for some swore it was not moving at all. Inching four miles a day, it took a month to reach Sunset Prairie!

Incessant rain was partly to blame. Fording the swollen Kiskatinau River, the party lost three horses including the community stud. After the crossing, they camped in a mudhole. Out of feed and with only bushes to tether the horses, they allowed the livestock to forage freely. When the settler-apprentices awoke on the morrow, the beasts were gone, having easily reswum the river in the night without the handicap of human guidance.

Completely befuddled, the trekkers decided to walk the last twenty miles to Sunset Prairie. On leaving, they met a trapper who somehow tricked the steeds on the far shore into a third crossing.

In the weeks before their first winter, the tenderfeet hurried to put up hay, but in bush the gathering was a straw at a time. Bad weather hit in October, and it was still snowing next June.

The experience, according to one, was proof positive that "the Almighty had reserved this country for moose and Indians." About half the Sunset settlers concurred, and over the next few years left.[13]

"What happens under a free homestead policy is this," said Albright. "Lured by some whim, notion, or fancy a landseeker will trek twenty-five, fifty, a hundred, two hundred, four hundred or eight hundred miles from steel and pick a quarter section. Another does likewise several miles away; another and another, all well apart.... Gradually the land between is taken up in straggling fashion. By the time the intervening ones have arrived some of the originals have got 'fed up' and pulled out. Ere the last of the land is taken the second and third and perhaps the fourth waves have thinned out and Heaven only knows how long it will be before the population is thick enough to support schools, churches, resident doctors and dentists, stores and other facilities. Thus the pioneer stage is dragged out indefinitely."

Albright's solution was to divide the Peace into three—farmlands; ranchlands; and timber, game and mineral reserves. The farmland he parted again—that close to rail and mostly clear, that close to rail but unclear, and that remote. The first category only, the Class A lands, should be thrown open.

The Apostle W.D. Albright,
holding the first apples grown
at Beaverlodge, 1929.
A 6988, PAA.

"Wanderlust," Col. J.K. Cornwall, protagonist of the high latitudes well declared, "is a fine spirit, but it should not be allowed to lead a man away to some nice creek or high mountain on which to starve."[14]

NATURE'S EXHORTER

Donald Albright's function in these latitudes was to reveal truthfully nature's storehouse in the Peace. It was a sacred charge carried out as faithfully and steadfastly as any servant ever managed a worthy trust.

In thirty years, Albright and his minions at the Beaverlodge experimental station drafted and dispersed a mountain of mimeographs, shot a thousand slides and four to five thousand photos, and wrote perhaps one hundred thousand letters. Each annual report was tome-thick. In his last dozen years, he delivered 409 lectures in every hub and hamlet of the Peace and Athabasca. To reach these, he lurched through mud and ice, sleet and snow, sometimes speaking every night for a week, five or six hours an evening before turning in at 3 AM.

By the 1930s, halfway through his tour of duty, he had "shuttle-cocked" forty thousand miles through every rut in the Peace and had visited twenty thousand settlers. The totals at his retirement in 1945 were anyone's guess.[15]

Albright pioneered alfalfa growing and was the first to grow standard sized apples in the Peace. He generated forage crops and early maturing vegetables and cereals and helped adapt hundreds of varieties of ornamental shrubs and trees.

He even dabbled in apiculture, though his successors in the Dominion Service at Beaverlodge would demonstrate his vision here. Before long, Peace River honey production would lead the world. European production averaged 35 pounds per colony; Canadian, 75 pounds; and the Peace—150 to 200 pounds. The quality—No. 1 water white. In time, there would be sixty thousand colonies in the Peace, producing 12 million pounds a year, standout colonies averaging 305 pounds.[16]

Successful agriculture in the Peace, Albright soon divined, required above all, the gentle cultivation, less of the land than of settler's *minds*.

In the post Great War depression, he penned "In the Trough of the Wave." It had greater effect than anything else he ever wrote. The essence of the depression was not the general hard times, not the transportation snafu, not drought, but rather the inflation of hopes and values—expressed in nirvanic immigration propaganda, rampant townsite speculation, predatory wheat mining, and sky high interest rates.

The snarl-up was jointly the fault of bankers and entrepreneurs, the Soldier Settlement Board and the Department of Agriculture, and, of course, the settlers themselves. So pleased was the Bank of Commerce that for once it was only 20 percent to blame that it rushed Albright's article into special edition.

The real culprit was a frame of mind, a way of thinking, and the real war was the age-old one between optimism and pessimism. "Optimism strengthens purpose. Pessimism paralyzes effort," Albright intoned. "Both are infectious. To a large extent we make times good or bad according as we view our case with courage or despair."[17]

The chapfallen and the quitters had to heave the lemming mentality, to cast out the chaos of demoralization, and to recompose themselves. Take heart, mobilize the inner self, and realize that answers will come, Albright cheered.

When the Great Depression struck, there was Albright with the same messages in all the weeklies of the North. "Timely Hints," he called them, and they were as much spiritual as agricultural: "One of the most valuable sciences any one of us can learn is the science of doing without"; "The triumph of life lies not in the felicity of circumstances but rather in the way trying circumstances are met."[18]

The great de-energizers of the mind were fear and fretting, the farmer's second cousins. In summer 1935, Albright characterized these trouble-makers as largely illusory:

When it snows, snows, snows, snows,
Seems as if the ground would never get bare again;
When it rains, rains, rains, rains,
Seems as if 'twould never dry up again.

When it blows, blows, blows, blows, blows,
Seems as if 'twould never get calm again;
When it's dry, dry, dry, dry,
Seems as if it never would rain again.
But it does, it does, it does.
Why worry?[19]

Even misfortune had a lighter side. "The depression," said the exhorter, "was only doing without things our fathers never knew." In the dreadful price pit of 1938, one cynic delighted that it was "a good year in which to have a poor crop." "When worst comes to the worst," Albright added, "it takes about six men, standing in a row telling hard-luck stories, to keep each other cheered up."[20]

3 The Disorder

A HOUSE DIVIDED

IT IS THIS PICTURE OF DONALD ALBRIGHT WE
HAVE BEEN GIVEN. It sets out his legacy as if he were
primarily a dauntless visionary. That he was unmistakably—but
he was infinitely more complex, and rather more star-crossed
than legend suggests.

Albright's dominant impulse was to establish order on the Peace
River frontier, and that frontier included the experimental farm
and his own family. He was a reformer, and all reformers are in the
process, whether conscious or not, of discovering the limits of
their own self-assertiveness. Most need less to impose their
reform than to nourish their own patience.

Albright always spoke his mind. That he would be sincere, no
one doubted; that he might be discreet, fewer expected. When he
was editor of *The Farmer's Advocate*, he blessed reciprocity seven

days a week, while four-fifths of the paper's business came from farm machinery monopolists protected by the very tariffs he ranted against. By 1913 these firms had forced him out.[1]

During the Depression, he advised a cut in wages, was noticed by an irate union man, and nearly punted off a Northern Alberta Railway coach.[2]

On a third occasion, he was summoned to Ottawa to edit a volume commemorating the Dominion Experimental Farm Service. The vassals assigned to him had not experienced such regimentation since a previous incarnation as galley slaves. When his task was done, mercifully in short order, the East was even happier to see him go than the first time.[3]

The experimental farm he dominated too, but because the best of his men were hand-picked and sworn to his ideal of rolling back the frontier, the dominance was less over-bearing and surely less resented. They accepted his leadership and did his bidding. No one who saw his daily devotion to work doubted his high-mindedness. None who read his motto—"It is a pleasure as well as a duty to serve"—ever questioned his dedication.

Yet he expected even the peons of the experimental farm to share his enthusiasm, and doubtless he exacted as much from his civil servants as has ever been willingly or unwillingly vouchsafed by their class. In argument, he could be ferocious, and an erring subordinate he could render speechless.[4]

A flunkey at the farm once told Eileen Albright, "your father is so straight, he is bent over backwards!"[5]

To the outside, he was always respected but infrequently revered, often lauded but less loved. Settler Clyde Campbell delighted in his encouragement, but noted a broader, uncharitable sentiment that resented his knowledge and possibly his inordinate will to bestow it.[6] There was in him a strong urge to remake others in his own image.

His wife Eva was emotionally fragile and despondent in marriage. She was a teacher of remarkable acuity who wrote faultless English, a math whizz, a pianist, a paragon of impeccable memory. "Mentally she was a lighthouse," son Gordon thought, "but emotionally a wreck." In a later age, her keen mind might have sent her soaring to the skies, but in this more primitive time, constraints, some self-imposed, dogged her every step. Gordon claimed he never knew her.

The Albright Clan: Albright's parents, Eva, Donald, with young Gordon, Eileen and Bruce, left to right. NA 493–17, GAA.

But said he, "A mother she was not, a homemaker she was not, a housekeeper she was not, a pioneer she was not, and yet these were the roles that fate ordained her to be in."[7]

Donald answered this malajustment and its ensuing despair with rigidity and finality. He was a drill sergeant of perfectionists in that household—meticulous, precise, fastidious, even finical and always demanding. Photographs usually revealed a tautness in his face, an unglad demeanor with a mark of impatience. Marshalled with his family, he appeared cheerless. Not given to much waggery or small talk, he was, of course, not humorless, but much too serious. He did not dote on his children, and his boys often found him unyielding and unpleasable. Said Gordon, "his standards were not of this world."

At times Eva concurred. Once, referring to Donald's many speaking tours, she confided to Gordon—"I was always so glad to see your father go."

Eva craved a simple, caring companionship, a single soul to cherish—and that soul came in her elder son Bruce.

For younger Gordon, though, life was oppressive. To him his father was a powder keg of emotions and his mother an impenetrable maze of dejection. "There was no cooperation, no we feeling, no love, no harmony, nothing—it was a desert," he said. "There was no place in the world that I would rather not have been than in that home. It was untenable."[8]

No one doubted Gordon's discontent.

His sister Eileen, ten years older, was cast from a very different mold. Her judgments were softer, her sentiments, more accepting. She knew her mother's heartache and felt sorrow sooner than anger, and she understood her father's nature and felt admiration and no disrespect. While sometimes questioning his strictness, she was grateful for the virtues he instilled; she trusted him and believed that he acted with his children's interest at heart.[9]

A single anecdote best highlights this difference of perception. Everything one sees is witness to the outlook one accepts as true.

Eileen knew that honesty was a precious possession to her father, but Gordon judged that he paid too much for it. The one saw honesty as a foundation of character; the other saw that a virtue over-stressed becomes a vice—honesty itself, run rampant, hurts; it turns callous and cruel. Now Donald Albright was a very honest man, but interestingly, he deemed *punctuality* a form of honesty. It was a small but significant sign of how pervasive the concept was in his mind.

At any rate, when time came for Eileen to marry, Donald just had to tell fiancé Bill Ross—honesty demanded it—of an old family taint, genetic, lingering, and in the works, as it were. And Eva's recurrent depression was not the primary evidence, though Donald must have counted it. The defect was on Eva's side all right, but its manifestation was more serious—the "confirmed" lunacy of an aunt.

Though Eileen showed no signs of disturbance yet, Bill might look forward to a scary outbreak, anytime after the nuptials.

Gordon saw in the incident his father's distortion of a virtue; Eileen and Bill just saw father, and laughed.

Progressively, Gordon sought refuge in the comforting presence of his brother Bruce, nine years older. The two were in tune and seemed to know each other's mind. Though hardly faultless, Bruce was a serious lad, as his father put it, sensing some spiritual fineness in him that Gordon instinctively turned to.

The day Bruce went off to war the two brothers shared an inner knowing. Gordon knew that Bruce would not return, Bruce knew, and Bruce knew that Gordon knew. But no words were spoken.

Returning from a massive air raid over Essen, Germany, one frightful day in 1942, F. Bruce Albright was shot down.

OLD BURNSITES

By the late thirties, the Christian Association had fallen on hard times. All along it opposed clerics and creeds and favored instead direct revelation of the Spirit. This revelation was so direct that there was no need for formal prayer. Routinized petitions to God were clergymen's crutches, imposed rather than spontaneous, parroting rather than communing.

At Association meetings, various vessels of God's grace channeled his word to the others, and a form of group-sanctioned righteous living resulted. To the extent that it worked, it was revealed in the fruits of the spirit of members such as I.E. Gaudin, E.A. Smith, Robert and Mary Anne Lossing, and at times Donald Albright.

Despite its beacons, the Association had always exhibited a tension between contacting God or the Spirit personally and telling others what God had in mind for them. In the personal contact, Nelson Burns and his followers had grasped one of the great truths of the kingdom— that religion was essentially a personal and individual relationship between man and his Maker. In relaying God's message for others, the Burnsites had unintentionally inserted the herald of the Word between God and his individual sons or daughters ranged round the room. It was the equivalent of adding a cleric, or more properly, a cloister of clerics.

As with most churches, this cloister began to dictate acceptable belief and behavior, and the dictation could be uncharitable. Again and again, Albright's children recalled their mother, grandmother Lossing, and others departing from meetings in tears, pummelled for failings, wracked by guilt, criticized to the core.

By degrees, harmony with the group overtook as the supreme goal, guidance by the Spirit. At times, it mattered little whether such harmony had anything whatever to do with spirituality. Shortly after the election of Aberhart's Government, the surviving Burnsites, some grim and grudge-bearing, stalked to the meeting place. When they arrived, they glared meanly at old man Lossing as if they had tracked him to his lair where the hounds could rip him.

As usual, the meeting began without prayer, though one might have been uttered for Lossing. Then for half an hour torrents of abuse poured down on the old man, and he *was* old—fifty-six when he came with the Bull Outfit, now eighty-two. How he had betrayed the group, what thoughtlessness, what depravity was his, what personal disgrace he had cast on all the Association, what a model he was of dissent and disharmony! Judas had done better!

The cause of Lossing's public scourging was that, after decades with a group of Liberal, Conservative and more latterly United Farmer leanings, he had just voted for Social Credit!

The tirade troubled Robert Cromwell Lossing not a whit. Though scarcely an Association leader, he was an example of what Burns had revealed in himself, which was the potential of all Burnsites. Lossing possessed an inner knowing that made him impervious to what his neighbors might say, and he was living proof of the peace engendered by communion with a higher mind. Find harmony first within, then it will exist with others—such was his course.

Lossing had his own higher connection, and it appeared especially in his love for horses. One of his favorites was the plug "Bobbie." They were as one. "Robbie and Bobbie" they were called, and rarely has there been such love between these two orders of creation, so literally did it shine between them. The two would trundle down from the old town of Beaverlodge to the new site on the railway, bearing saplings. These they planted on what became Lossing Boulevard.

Several months after the Social Credit castigation, Lossing became ill. In this stint, grandson Gordon, now fourteen or so, kept clear of the upstairs bedroom, having no fondness for death. In time Lossing rallied, and Gordon screwed up his courage to visit his aging grandfather with whom he shared genuine affection. At the height of the stairs, the signs were propitious. Grandfather Lossing was eating his favorites—apple sauce and home-made bread—and his jouncing jowls always made his false teeth click. It was the comforting "click, click, click," that beckoned Gordon.

Gordon assured him that his recovery would soon be complete. Death had passed him by, and life would shortly resume, as always.

Old Lossing halted the clicking, listened intently, and then replied:

"Well, Gordon, I thank you for what you say, but it is not to be."

Taken aback, Gordon repeated his good cheer, adding even more pleasing images of hope.

Then his grandfather spoke again. "I would like to be here because we are about to embark on one of the most interesting times a human being can witness. But it is not to be. I'll be gone in three days."

He spoke so quietly and with such authority that Gordon couldn't quibble. For two days, he stayed in the pink of health, clicking away with his dentures in perfect peace. On the third morning, he slipped, and in hours he was gone.[10]

THE DRUMMER HE HEARS

While Lossing's death naturally meant more to his daughter Eva Albright, than to Donald, it was for Donald part of a painful transition. With both the Lossings dead, I.E. Gaudin dead, Nelson Burns long gone, and his successor gone, Albright sensed the deterioration of the Association, and he was well aware of its failure to replenish itself. None of his children were held by it. Bruce and Eileen felt stigmatized, Gordon was repulsed by the weekly run of character assassination he perceived, and Eileen left for the United Church at age 14. On occasion, Donald's brother, a United Church minister, wondered aloud why God could speak to Mrs. Albright only through the mouth of Mrs. Smith.[11]

Doubting his own authority as a Burnsite leader because of the family disaffection, Albright was further disenchanted with C.H. Partridge, an iron-willed successor to Burns of the central body of the Christian Association in Toronto. Donald would not submit to Partridge, nor Partridge to him, and as a result, like his children before him, Albright broke ranks with the Association.

The act cut him from a lifetime circle of friends. It moved him even further from his wife who remained loyal to the group and who in her own manner expelled her frustration and despair in the tears she cried. For both of them, Nelson Burns's photograph of tranquility aglow in the family album was constant reminder of a fond but faded ideal.

The Great Depression brought other clouds. Both Eileen and Bruce were university stock, but times were hard and funds were scarce, and other walks were eventually taken. When Gordon came of age, later, Donald offered to help him—but Gordon wanted no part of university and soon left.

Eileen became a stenographer in Edmonton, and if Donald ever desponded in her choice, he never said so. When he visited, he invariably took her to dinner and displayed an honest affection for one whom as a babe he had once saved from an eagle.[12]

Bruce went into business developing the Monkman Pass, west of Beaverlodge, but a colleague absconded with the funds, leaving him neck deep in debt.[13] Not long afterward, he joined the Canadian armed forces, now at war with Germany. The enlistment pleased his father who knew that soldiers were protected from predatory creditors and that Bruce might better settle accounts while in the service or after. Likely, Bruce would have enlisted without the thought, but when he was killed, Donald assumed a measure of guilt.[14] Devastated by the loss of the one she was most able to love, Eva was inconsolable. And grief strained every discomfort.

Donald fell into his work, meanwhile, running himself ragged. As usual, his effort in agriculture was only the start. By the late thirties, he had played countless roles—pushing for the extension of the Edmonton, Dunvegan and British Columbia Railway, organizing a twelve-hundred name petition, animating the United Farmers of Alberta, boards of trade, boards of education, and others; advocating the setting aside of Saskatoon Mountain as a public park; pushing for better roads; and always, always, writing about the Peace. He was chair of the local advisory committee of Saskatoon Island and Saskatoon Mountain Parks, president of the Beaverlodge Board of Trade, initiator of the Associated Peace River Boards of Trade and chair of that general council. On and on it went.[15]

While the endless speaking engagements gave outlet for Donald's energies, they wore him thin. Eva instinctively knew the dangers.

"Don, if you don't learn to handle your work compulsion," she told him, "your health is going to break early, and when it does, it will be disastrous."

Albright looked at her and quietly answered, "Yes, Eva, I guess you may be right."[16]

Some hint of how this prophecy might be fulfilled had appeared. Decades earlier Albright thought he had "nerve trouble" plugging for exams. Later he thought journalism would tax his nerves. And he suspected if he toiled after supper he might break down.[17]

As the Great Depression drummed itself slowly out, the defeated pioneers on the fringes brought up the rear. While the Rowell Commission on Dominion-Provincial Relations sat in Winnipeg, an old captain of the agrarian guards, Premier John Bracken, spoke of keeping settlers off inferior lands. Albright shook his head at the thought: "For nearly twenty years I have been hammering at this idea, but as a voice crying in the wilderness."[18]

He had written until his pen ran dry. He had told politicians, department gurus and underlings, half the Peace River settlers personally. He had cheered the progressive, inspired the novices, admonished the lapsers, rallied the dispirited. But the results displeased him. It was as if in his quest to make the Peace livable, it were his own fault if some should find the margins unlivable. And not just the margins were hard.

There were so many complexities, complications, constraints and *knots*, so many *questions*, and all seemed so very personal—how to reconcile a family with a dead son, a disaffected son, and a despairing wife? How to revivify a search for inner guidance that had stumbled on thorns? How to avert the accidents of settlement—how to turn settlers from their own misery, why they must have that misery, and what lessons has sorrow?

It is humane to say tragedy must not recur, but it is enlightened to know precisely how far one can stop it in other lives. Such enlightenment marks the natural limit of what any reformer might accomplish.

Albright had two sets of problems—his own and those of others—and he concentrated on some of the latter, the ones beyond home. As he internalized them, he may well have concluded with Elbert Hubbard that "if you lend a willing ear to any man's troubles, you make them your own, and you do not lessen his."[19] Such a conclusion about one's principal effort in life saps and dismays.

Albright's health began to slip. By 1940, the debilitating Parkinson's Disease had its hand on him, and by bits his nervous system disintegrated. Photographs of the Apostle in his last years show an advancing hollowness—his trousers loose, his jacket hanging, his hand behind his back to conceal the shaking.

The man who does
too much for others
leaves himself
underdone.[20]

Fra Elbertus

"The two things most plentiful
are trouble and advice to farmers."

The Office Cat, May 31, 1930

The Desert

4 Birth of a Ghost Town and Despair

WEMYSS'S LOVE LETTERS

WEMYSS COTTER WAS TIRED OF ONTARIO.

An officer of the Metropolitan Bank in Bridgen, he wrote in August 1908 to darling "Teedie," his fiancee: "My time is drawing to a close here, and I am anxious to get away and get going. I have stayed here [long enough] to know every man, woman and child in the place. The evenings are very quiet and all seldom stir out of the house once the lamps are lit. I can truly recommend Bridgen to anyone requiring a rest cure."[1]

Both Wemyss and his brother Arthur abhorred the slavery of office work. "The free life of the West appeals to us," Arthur told Teedie. "The country is being opened up in all directions, and it has a bright future before it. A person does not require a great deal of practical experience to enable him to take up the kind of farming that is carried on in the West."[2]

Following Wemyss's wedding to Charlotte "Teedie" Mason, he traveled to Calgary in spring 1909. Never known for his patience, Cotter chided his beloved when she balked at moving west and when the constant flow of her love letters broke for a second. "Wake up, old stocking, and don't allow my memory to fade so quickly. You will find that life is not all sunshine before you are through with it and that there are other places on the globe besides Toronto."[3]

Ontarians were everywhere, he told her, though almost all were male. "Ask them if they ever mean to go East again and they laugh at you," he said. "Everyone tells you that they have done twice as well here."[4]

At May-end, Wemyss, who fortunately came to be called Bill, went to Langevin, a little station house in the newly opened Alberta drylands between Brooks and Medicine Hat. Four miles north, he picked a half section—"the finest land that one could get," he crowed.[5]

In the next fortnight or so, Cotter complained to postal authorities and to J.S. Dennis of the CPR that too many places sounded like Langevin, one especially, Langdon, east of Calgary.[6] The real problem was that Cotter feared the misdelivery of Charlotte's love letters.

Some obligor soon changed the name "Langevin" to "Carlstadt," and between June 20 and 30, five perfumed epistles came directly to the spot—an efficiency that more than justified any trouble mapmakers and sign-changers were put to.

Still, citified Charlotte wondered about homesteading. "You sweetheart, you speak as if you dread coming here," Wemyss wrote on July 21.[7] He was right: Charlotte hated bugs and worried about water. The wind blew away mosquitoes, Bill told her, and farmers everyplace were digging and "getting good water," he fibbed.[8] They could have all the water they wanted, and if they needed more, they could come to town or go to Suffield. "So don't be afraid of the water question," he assured her.[9]

He did not mention that Suffield was twenty miles there and back, and he did not know that Carlstadt would *never* have decent water.

Nonetheless, he continued an unabashed boosting which would have pleased the railway, owner of the townsite, no end. Absolutely

Wemyss Cotter's new railway station, Carlstadt, 1911 c.
Medicine Hat Archives.

vitalizing, were the fresh air and the lovely, cool nights in summer. Said he, "it is only people who are closed up in offices in the city who get nervous prostration."[10]

Charlotte, however, was certain she would contract it on the farm. Perhaps sensing truth in her intuitions, Wemyss promptly arranged an indoor job in Carlstadt—in the post office.[11]

In a few months, Charlotte arrived, and Carlstadt grew like Topsy. On Dominion Day 1910, Wemyss addressed the citizens of the new metropolis: "Our city will be what our citizens make it, morally, financially and religiously. We are laying the foundations for a city, a city which in days to come will make its influence felt and its name known all over the great Dominion."[12] In the same breath, Carlstadt might be whispered with Toronto.

At the acme of the boom, Elbert Hubbard visited the Prairie West and declared it the "paradise" of promoters—the world's premier place, despite progress aplenty, to make "foolish investments." "Most of the real-estate boomers are Yankees—some of them Damyankees," he said. "Townsites, ports, terminals, are mostly too good to be true."[13]

Wemyss Cotter lived the rest of his life in Carlstadt. During the Great War, the "city" of two or three hundred was renamed Alderson, at Charlotte's suggestion. It was then devastated by the long drought of 1917–1926, and almost completely depopulated in the swirling dust storms of the 1930s. On November 16, 1935, Wemyss carted a heavy pack of mail from the railway station, and inside the post office, his heart seized, and he fell to the floor dying.[14]

Down to half a dozen citizens, Alderson ten weeks later was disorganized as a village forever. Once called "the Star of the Prairie," it was now in the centre of the worst farm abandonment in Canadian history.

No fewer than five commissions of inquiry examined the wreck. Wandering through the ruined civilization of southern Alberta, beginning in 1921, pollsters counted bodies—those still abiding and those gone. By 1921 losses were terrible, over the next three years, horrendous. From 1921 to 1926 the best off of 138 townships across 3.2 million acres lost 55 percent of its population. Part way through the debacle, in late 1924, Russell and Snelson of the Interior Department examined these same townships—one had 65 resident farmers six or seven years before and now 11; another 55, now 14; another 40, now 2; another 93, now 10, one more, 12, now none.[15]

By then rural muncipalities were in debt to their eyeballs and were owed a fortune in seed grain and relief extended to farmers already gone. In towns like Alderson, Suffield, Grassy Lake, Youngstown, Jenner, Retlaw, and Richdale the local treasury was open and bare, lots were vacant by the hundred, owners wishing to repudiate ownership, weary reeves and village secretaries not knowing who was was still on the tax rolls, where they all were, or even how to find out.[16]

One observer reported the whole of the Goose Lake line from Hanna to Oyen along with the line south to Steveville, sown to Russian Thistle, tumbling mustard and Russian pigweed.[17]

Of the farm, a woman said, "I swear it was the last thing God ever made, and He didn't finish it."[18]

William G. Wenbourne of Taber summarized the general experience when he labeled himself—"a man that came, saw and has not conquered."[19]

Halting homesteads in the area, the governments, federal and provincial, arranged with the railways the evacuation of the destitute.

Then Alberta lumped the wastelands of the southeast into no man's lands called Special Areas.

It is hard to capture how far Cotter's hub and its agricultural hinterland had fallen, but one incident in one family symbolized it well.

In spring 1938, Ace Palmer of the Dominion Experimental Station in Lethbridge asked Tracy Anderson, fresh from high school, to supervise some crested wheat grass seeding experiments in the badly eroded dustlands. The assignment required living with selected farm families.

East of Alderson, near Bowell, Anderson stayed with a Scandinavian couple who appeared somewhat elderly to his youthful eyes. The haystack for the horses was Russian Thistle, not unusual, for the thistle if green made passable forage. One supper time, they discussed the hardships imposed by soil drifting, drought and depression.

The woman invited Anderson to the food cellar dug into the basement. Through a trap door, they crawled into an earthen compartment, the walls of which were lined with shelves of preserves.

She fingered a dozen quart jars on one level, smiled, and stated— "They ate our crops. We had to eat them."

The jars were filled with pickled grasshoppers.[20]

GOING CRAZY

Between 1934 and 1938, Lois Valli lived on a ranch south of decaying Alderson. Life in the barrens on the edge of Alberta's first special area amounted to captivity.

Using labels off flour sacks and bits of paper, Valli began to write poetry. Her whole world was a great "Empty Land":

There it lies, stretched flat under the bleached sky, looking innocent, almost benign.

Burnt light brown, no color relief in the scorched miles of emptiness.

It holds my gaze, though it offers no solace for my need.

The silence is broken only by the whir of the windmill.

When the snowy blanket covers all, it appears to sleep in the sun.

During the long dark hours the mercury shrinks, timbers groan and crack.

The feeble glow of the oil lamp casts a meager ring of comfort on the table,

The dim unfriendliness reigns beyond.

When the savage wind lashes the sand or the snow, all bend, turn, seek shelter.

Some find it and those who do not are swept away like leaves.

None dare defy such power.

Why must man pit his silly feeble wit against its elemental strength.

Why am I in this merciless place?

The windmill is the only reply I hear.[21]

Silence oppressed her, and depression gripped her, and she fought a mortal battle for her own self respect. In "Nine Bar Ranch—1935," she penned:

December, and dark comes early
Loneliness fills my heart,
I think of my friends and parents,
We are many miles apart.
I busily tend to the fire,
The men will expect a hot meal,
But my mind is not on the cooking.
I can't stifle the sadness I feel.
I am not alone in this ranch house.
My husband and children are near
But now I hear no more music,
That's over for me now I fear.
No piano for me to play on.
My fingers are roughened and sore.
What music is the choir singing?
I want to play for them once more.
But I know those times are over.
The crew expects to be fed.
I must concentrate on the present
From now till I go to bed.[22]

Eight miles from doomed Alderson, she could hear the silk trains roaring through on the main line of the CPR. Bearing raw, Oriental silk which deteriorated rapidly, they tore from Vancouver to Ft. William fifteen hours faster than the quickest passenger train. En route to eastern markets, their precious cargo had priority over all other rail traffic. Said Lois, "They didn't stop, and they went at a great fast rate, and they whistled frequently. It almost tore my heart out to have to stand there to hear that train going. And there I was—no way to get away, and I was going crazy there almost by myself."[23]

She wondered how her life had come to this.

5   A Woman for All Seasons

"THE HALF SUCKED ACID DROP"

WHAT A SIGHT HE PRESENTED TO HER, the perfect

portrait of Latin dash and charm as he sauntered down the streets

of Brooks that spring of 1927. He wore a fur hat, a buckskin coat

with long fringes and the highest riding boots she had ever seen.

He had a guitar under arm, and he was dragging a huge Police dog,

named Gene Tunney.

"Where are you going?" nineteen-year-old Lois Pinder asked, half amazed, half amused, and completely taken.

"Ssh!" answered he with a twinkle. "I'm on the trail of the half sucked acid drop!"

It meant nothing, it was just a saying, but it was the beginning of courtship.[1]

Mario Angelo Valli disported his lineage well. Forbears had migrated from Spain to Italy as mercenaries for a principality near

Bergamo, and beginning in 1745, the family record was kept in the monastery of Pontida. In the next century, two brothers marched with Napoleon to Moscow. The daughter of one was Maria Valli who married the son of the other, her first cousin Oswald.

Oswald fashioned grandfather clocks, cabinets and inlaid tables which the upper classes, even royalty, coveted. A grateful King Victor Emmanual conferred upon Oswald the title of Cavaliere, gentleman.

The cousins had six children, then a respite of eight years, long enough to assure Maria that her birthing days were over, when Mario was conceived. Vexed, the mother repaired from England whence the family had emigrated and deposited Mario in the motherland at Pontida, on June 15, 1904, leaving the unwelcome babe with peasants.

Four years on, Cavaliere Oswald tired of lounging around the Society of Garibaldi and Mazzini of which he was president, and he ordered young Mario back into the fold. Crossing the channel, Mario's sister fetched him from the serfs. But what none had foreseen was the trauma the lad suffered on being uprooted from those who truly loved him. In Britain he was unmanageable at home and school.

Mortified, Maria and Oswald redelivered Mario to his surrogate parents and enjoined him to regroup. Again he was summoned to England, but again he was a misfit. Fiercely resenting the domination of mentors, nuns and family, he temporarily escaped this problem when he emigrated to Canada after the Great War.[2]

TURNING ON THE TAPS IN REDCLIFF

Lois Pinder was born in southern Saskatchewan, near North Portal, in 1908. Not till fifteen years later, when she visited England, did she understand the transition her parents had made to the raw prairie. "Pavement everywhere not a blade of grass visible except in the cemetery," she saw. It was near Nottingham City with its rows of attached, stoney buildings outfringed by coal pits. "On Sundays, everybody put on their best 'bib and tucker,' went to church and then walked miles to get into the country," she observed. Some grew gardens in the "allotments" far from their homes. Many spent all their lives in one house.

In Yorkshire, Lois met her father's mother, living in Napoleon Square with its community oven in the centre. Behind each house was a garden that grew mostly flowers. "Dad's Uncle Joe showed me the little stone 'pig sty,' long unoccupied at the end of his yard," Lois recalled. "It was all so small and crowded," so unlike the bald and limitless plains.[3]

Lois's father, Henry Pinder, had mined coal before advertisements of the wonders of the Canadian West caught his eye. Like many other pitmen, he became a farmer, and though resourceful, a farmer he was not. He made the door to his new home open outward, until it was snow-drifted in one day. He bought a team of horses, grazed them on spear grass, and they died. The cow meandered off, calved in the bushes, and coyotes devoured the newborn before he could find it. A cyclone blew out one crop, rust ravaged another, and drought parched many more. Whenever they did have a crop, threshing crews were too far afield to help in time.[4]

But Pinder took it all in good humor. Once while being towed across a field by ornery oxen he was "directing," he finally blurted, "All right, go anywhere, you buggers, it all has to be ploughed."[5]

Pinder worked hard and hopefully, plowing, fencing, seeding, harvesting, building, and gradually adjusting, and he was happy. His wife Lydia regretted the whole homesteading venture, wept copiously, and pined for the cement walls of home.

"My father was a small, unassuming man, but to me he towered above almost all other humans," Lois said. "I never had occasion to change that opinion. The love and care he gave us was always there, never wavering, never dulled by temper or emotion."[6] He took Lydia's frequent tantrums with patient resignation. "He never expected 'Ma and the gels' to lift a finger outside of the house," wrote Lois. "I know now that my mother was a very spoiled woman."

Lydia was indelibly scarred by the winters, by people freezing to death in blizzards. Recurrently, she remembered the mother and child they found frozen, like grotesque ice sculptures, the babe's nose pressed flat against the mother's breast. The corpses waited thawing for some time before they could be "laid out."[7]

The nearest doctor was twenty-four miles away in Estevan, so the women were undertakers and midwives and medicine-givers, as the need arose. For the sick they bought antacids, antiseptics and ointments—ginger root, Minard's Liniment, Carbolic acid, and Zam Buk. By degrees, Lydia responded to the demands put upon her, and in crisis, her courage bloomed, and she comforted many.

But Lois's primal bond was ever with her father. One winter, when her mother was off midwifing for a relative, Harry walked with Lois to Talorton to escort mother home. Shortcutting over a hill, they plodded hand in hand in the dark over ground understrewn with mining shafts and caves. When they walked across a thin crust, Harry broke through with a shout. Lois held on with all her might, bracing her foot on the edge. Fear stricken, her father clambered out. Later he said that without Lois he would have disappeared, perhaps died.[8]

When Lois was five years old, the cow dried up and the canned milk ran out.

"I can drink my tea without milk," asserted her dad.
"So can I," affirmed she.
Neither ever put milk in tea again.
"I wanted to be just like him," said the little admirer.

As a child, Lois possessed a sixth sense—a kinship with other orders of creation, with flowers and animals. She knew when the neighbor's cat had died, and when other things were not right.[9]

Eventually the family gave up on droughty southeastern Saskatchewan and in 1918 moved to Redcliff, Alberta, several gradations drier. But here there were services. "In Redcliff we could turn on the taps, and that was the biggest thing that had happened in our lives, my sister and I," said Lois. "And we kept running to the tap to turn it on just to see the water flow, because we had pumped water in Saskatchewan by hand. My mother had to make us stop…because she couldn't stand to see water running away being wasted when we'd been short of it all our lives."[10]

Harry quickly found work in the coal mines where he amazed fellow laborers with his prodigious output.[11] But chopping at seams underground was dangerous, and Lydia fretted constantly about her children's welfare, should father be hurt. One day in the early twenties, the thought materialized as Harry flailed at a coal lump with his pick. Like a flint arrowhead, a black shard flew into his right eye, blinding it.

Workers' Compensation awarded him $9 a month for life. The pittance he carefully invested in three houses that had gone back to

Miss Lois Pinder, 1925 c.
Photo courtesy of Lois Valli.

the Town of Redcliff for nonpayment of taxes. He refinished and rented them, and his forethought brought a new stability to the family.[12]

In Redcliff, Lois nurtured her considerable musical talents. The children were brought up on classical music, and brother Stanley played violin and later flute and piccolo with the Medicine Hat Symphony Orchestra. Lois played the church organ for the Nazarenes, the piano for itinerating evangelists and the junior and senior choirs of the United Church. She was also pianist for her brother's local dance band and for Masonic, Robbie Burns and other functions. At the tender age of fourteen years, she even played for the silent movies. Given a chart of the action and the mood demands, she chose her own music. Her Redcliff sojourn was a period of intense joy.[13]

She might have stayed there all her life, save for an inner knowing that she would not. She graduated from the Garbutt Business School in Medicine Hat in 1925, the year an orchestra needed her in Brooks. There she found work in the CPR land office.[14]

Lois and Mario, or "MA," as she called him, "Val" as other women knew him, "Buck" as the rest dubbed him, were wed in the Pinder home in Redcliff on January 4, 1928. In time, the marriage brought many surprises.

Like many before and since, both anticipated bliss—he in the capture of one so talented and popular, and she in the continuation of the harmony that now suffused the parental home in Redcliff. Lois wanted, perhaps even expected, a man like her father: she hoped for companionship and consideration, a mate more given to selflessness than self-service, more a partner than a manager, more accepting than directing, one who would see the world through warm eyes. It was the hope of many, the lot of few. And she was not the first to wish to marry a soul almost too majestic for this world.

Because Lois had been the church-goer and Buck not, they agreed that a United Church minister might preside at the wedding. Said she, "I did not know that in two weeks a stern little French priest would appear from Medicine Hat to announce that we were living in sin." Buck was directed to confession, and Lois was handed a document to sign, promising to bring up any children Catholic. Leaving tomes for her enlightenment, the curate urged her swift conversion. Shortly thereafter, he married the couple properly.

After Buck moved into the Schuler-Hilda area to sell insurance, the couple resided six months in the Hat. There they did not regularly attend St. Patrick's, the resplendent Gothic cathedral with its copper roof, oak doors and round rose windows from France. When they did go, the ceremony and the incense much impressed Lois, but the droning Gregorian chants did not. True to the promise, Gilda, the first-born, was baptized a Catholic in this sanctuary.

Later, the family returned to Brooks. When time came for the baptism of son Ted in 1932, Buck announced that his mate would now join the church. Lois wanted more time, so Buck set the date.

At the appointed hour, a baptismal contingent arrived—a black robe from the Hat and two lady witnesses from the local parish. Buck was out, and Lois wished to await his return. "At last," said she, "the ladies wanted to go home, the priest had to get back to Medicine Hat, and the ceremony went ahead to baptize a very unwilling subject." When MA finally arrived, his convert was in tears.

Afterward, the resident priest visited every week to allay her concerns. But in a reverse inquisition, under constant bombardment of questions about the necessity of regularized confession, the presence of Christ in communion wine, the need for priests as mediators between God and woman, the point of fasting, and other matters dear to Mother Church, Lois so exasperated the long suffering priest that he finally told her that she had to "FORCE" herself to believe! This she would not do.

By the Great Depression, Buck had difficulty selling insurance against the worst that life might bring when it had already brought it. The family moved to a farm house on the Duke of Sutherland's estate, where the Pinders provided a cow and 100 lbs of flour and other staples. But the relief was stopgap, and the strain on Mario and Lois intensified. Finally, on February 8, 1934, Buck procured work as manager of the Nine Bar ranch, under an old employer, John J. Bowlen.[15]

By the early 1920s, Bowlen had the largest herd of horses in Alberta. He also had the biggest herd of Shetlands. These he crossed with Welsh ponies to produce pit ponies for the coal mines of the Drumheller valley.

A future Lieutenant Governor of Alberta, Bowlen was elected a Liberal to the Alberta legislature in 1930. He became Leader of the Opposition in 1936 and had a field day with Aberhart's flounderers. All the while, he tended many fires, though his ranches were perhaps his first love.[16]

The Nine Bar extended from the South Saskatchewan River north almost to Alderson and embraced a fiefdom of seventy-six sections. It was in the southern half of the Tilley East country, devastated in the drought and destitution of 1917–1926. By the latter date, the whole region had been almost completely depopulated, and 2400 farm families had dwindled to fewer than 500.[17]

The Nine Bar was a cluster of buildings—a farm house, bunkhouse, barns and corrals, arrayed round one of the few good wells of the region. Once a horse ranch, it was by the thirties primarily a sheep camp. On the margins of Alberta's first special area, the wastelands of the Tilley East country, the Vallies worked out their future.

In her outpost, Lois rose at 5 AM to start the fire which burned old railway ties by the cord. In lambing and shearing seasons, she fed

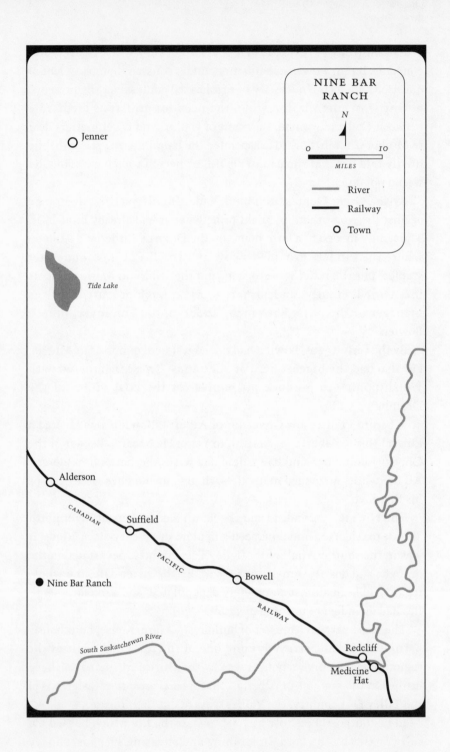

NINE BAR
RANCH

N

O ———————— IO

MILES

——— River

——— Railway

○ Town

○ Jenner

Tide Lake

○ Alderson

CANADIAN

○ Suffield

PACIFIC

● Nine Bar Ranch

○ Bowell

RAILWAY

South Saskatchewan River

Redcliff ○

Medicine
Hat ●

twenty or more toilers three times a day. She churned butter every day until Bowlen finally got her a larger churn, and she made bread by the batch for the ranch hands and for herders living in wagons on the range. One old-timer taught her to make sour dough hotcakes and scones, and the sheepmen gave her recipes for muffins and biscuits.

Her stove Bowlen had bought in Medicine Hat. The salesman stood on the door to demonstrate its strength, rather like headbutting a bumper to demonstrate the worth of a car. Bowlen said it had a "malleable" steel top, but he did not know what that meant, and neither did Lois.

Washday was a "holy horror." Lois had a copper tub for heating water, a scrub board, two galvanized wash tubs, and water so hard it curdled the soap. She kept huge bars of soap, and she dumped lye in the salt-ridden water to make bubbles. The hundred weight of water she lugged herself from the well, as Buck would not spare the men for housework.

Cleaning the old house was impossible. "The wind blew in one door and out the other," said Lois. "It filled the house with dirt, and I don't mean dust, I mean dirt. You could shovel it under the windows. And the window sills were piled with dirt."[18]

Her wrists swelled, and her feet ached.

And Buck was not always a comfort. That he was colorful, she well knew. His nickname Buck was an abbreviation of "Buckshot" which he had earned after he took a shotgun to shoot ducks and bagged an antelope! How, was a mystery, though he always fancied fast horses, and perhaps shot the fleeter antelope at a gallop.

In the early twenties, Bowlen had magnificent thoroughbred and registered mares, and Buck always rode the best. "Riding one of them I thought I was higher than the King of Caracticus," he effused, inventing a mythical satrap. It was the comparison with the commoners that impressed him—those who loped around with their "club-footed Clydes."[19]

Cowboy life attracted Buck, and he could toss a lariat like Will Rogers. Once he even lassooed a coyote pup. A picture of him on horseback reminds one of a Texas ranger or the warden of some preserve.

At parties, he did the Charleston in a tear, approximated several other dances, and bellowed energetically off key to the tunes of his guitar. He was loud in every way. His mind worked as he danced—spontaneously, demonstratively, and unrestrainedly. He was glib, charming and handsome, but always better in a crowd.

He guffawed at gross things, though he was also witty. When asked if he could remember stories of hardship or destitution that were particularly difficult, he answered—"Well, the worst of them was the one I suffered." When queried about his appointment to the Nine Bar, he replied—"Eating regular appealed to me, so I stayed with it." [20]

Compromise was not his forte, softness not a gift, unless daughter Angela, born twenty-two years after Ted, found and nurtured it. Against opponents, ridicule was his weapon, intolerance its origin. Brash, abrasive, and assertive, he was bright but distinctly averse to self-criticism, especially from Lois. He believed that men were "the lords of creation," as he put it.

It was Buck's misfortune that he married a woman who was indomitable, that he bred in those times a son the same and a daughter the same. It was hardly a misfortune, but he took it that way, and he sipped the bitter cup of opposition most of his life.

His experience was filled with any number of instances wherein he sought to overawe and over-control those around him, and just as importantly, it was peppered with antagonistic personalities the most resolute a man can face. He had many run-ins with the towering Carl Anderson, and he probably lost them all. When once he threatened Anderson with a news article citing the number of times he had been tossed bodily from Anderson's Eastern Irrigation office, Anderson responded that the next issue would have an article explaining *why* he had been thrown out. [21]

It was said he was fearless, but that was not altogether true. He feared disobedience and insubordination with a passion. He feared the uncertainties of life, and he clung like a barnacle to his monarch J.J. Bowlen.

Buck's great problem was how best to harmonize the conflicting demands of Squire Bowlen and the subsistence farmers surrounding Bowlen's domain. He was motivated partly by his unflinching loyalty to Bowlen and partly by fear of his master's judgment on him. His failure in the insurance business deeply hurt him, and that setback, indeed his very existence in that fraternity revealed in him a consuming and, in the times, an understandable urge for security.

When the Vallies finally left the ranch in 1938, Buck still sought the comforts of Bowlen's overcharge.

Now the range-short settlers never could bring themselves to believe that poaching, in the form of grazing on CPR or Bowlen lands was wrong. Both landlords, they thought, were as rich as King Croesus and would hardly miss a few bellyfuls of grass. Those bordering on Bowlen's estates expected Sheriff Valli to turn a blind eye to their "harmless" raids of the Squire's larder.

Valli might have been more lenient had Bowlen not been in the habit of springing surprise inspectoral tours. So he made a hard decision to round up all strays he found and to convey them to the nearest pound. For those who had to pay for their release, his actions were infuriating. But he persisted, and when his approach was neither gracious nor discreet, he made enemies.

Returning from the pound one evening, he stopped at a neighboring ranch for supper and conversation. Other ranchers were present, some of whom had suffered from his rigid enforcement of Bowlen's boundaries. An argument ensued and tempers flared. In high dudgeon, Valli strode to the barn, now dark, to get his horse.

He stepped inside and was knocked senseless by an unknown assailant who bludgeoned him about the head, shoulders, and ribs with an iron bar. Battered and bloody, he crawled to his mount, somehow flopped onto the saddle, and gave rein to the horse.

As the hour crept on, Lois, sensing mishap, anxiously watched the dark horizon through her window. At last the mount walked in with its semi-conscious cargo.

The beating did not dissuade Buck, and he responded with violence, verbal and physical, of his own. Once he punched out a hired hand for what he called Buck's own "self respect sake."[22] "A dog is no good until he's been run over once," was one of his mottos, and he applied it to more than dogs.[23]

Increasingly, for his sensitive helpmeet, harmony suffered, and lacking a confiding temperament, Buck could not restore it. "Loneliness is not in being alone," said Fra Elbertus, "for then ministering spirits come to soothe and bless—loneliness is to endure the presence of one who does not understand."[24]

It would be wrong to say that Lois played no role in her discomfort. Daughter Angela remembered incessant arguing years later, her father "loud and adamant," her mother "self righteous and defensive," in disputes ranging far and wide that might be resumed months later.[25] Neither sought quarter, nor often gave it, and neither could be coerced. If there was a difference in their circumstances on the ranch, it was that MA was able to leave the ranch regularly; Lois was not. While he was off to Alderson or Tilley in slow times, or supervising herders, she found herself pinned down and isolated.

A SONG FOR THE FLOWERS

The experiences of isolation were proof enough for this generation, if not for all, that social separation was unnatural and destructive.

In one family east of Tilley, a brute abused his wife and daughters like thralls. He would not allow them to use sugar in breadmaking. He hated waste, so their worn out dresses he ordered cut into strips and braided into rugs. When he needed a new coat, he sent for Mackinaw cloth, and after it arrived, the girls used the old one as a pattern and made him a new one. Once the wife had to walk ten miles to have the cow bred. Oppressed at every turn, she finally snapped and fell insane.[26]

Joe Millfight, a disturbed bachelor near the Nine Bar, shot at everything that moved. And Buck Valli's successor on the Nine Bar shot every owl and hawk in the township. "In the spring the gophers were so thick," said Buck, "it looked like the ground was moving."[27]

Old Mailman sat in his barn and serenaded his beloved horses with his violin. When his favorite died, he buried it. His chickens he forgot. Shut up in their coup, they pecked pebbles until they starved to death.[28]

South of the South Saskatchewan River, T.L. Duncan wrote about the gathering gloom in his torn community. There were three bachelors all living alone, all miles apart, and far from settlements. "The mental state of these settlers is certain to deteriorate under this isolation, and in some cases no doubt has already fallen away to a point that may take years to overcome under more favorable conditions," wrote Duncan. "No estimate can be placed on the great value that lies in human contact, human associations and relationships that have been lacking in this community for the last fifteen years. No church, no organized social activity, school struggling for existence, bachelors living alone—these do not lead to normal existences."[29]

With these sentiments Lois Valli had no quarrel.

She survived because of an innate trust in her own inner resources. It was an ancient and effective mode of confronting adversity—turn the mind from what dejects and dispirits it, and dwell on what engages and invigorates it. Part of the process was the gradual discarding of her "poor me" poetry. In her own way, she sensed that self-pity was a crutch in the hands of a whole person soon to be sick. Self-pity paralyzed the inner resources. It was ever self-respect, dignity itself, which armed and mobilized those resources.

To shorten her brooding, Lois said, "I wrote funny expressions, strange to me, that I heard the men say. Their personal stories I stored in my mind, never able to talk to the men openly. This was my 'fantasyland,' and nobody ever knew about the envelopes stuffed with bits of my soul, hidden in my dresser drawer."

One might think it was a denial of reality, but it was really a focus on the sunlit aspects of a dreary life and a reshaping of her irrepressible artistic and creative impulses. It was also a restirring of a child-age ability to create a reality and to live it.

Sensing how the monotony can exaggerate troubles and how over-regulation grates on an artist, she began to act, and the positive movement, bit by bit, overrode her resentment. She turned to her children.

Most schools of the Tilley East region had been sealed for ten years. None of the remnant was near the Nine Bar, so Lois taught Gilda and Ted herself, using the Department of Education Correspondence courses. Each grade they finished before lambing season in May.

She propped the words, "Bread" against the breadbox and "Water" against the water pail. "We tried the sight reading method used by the Department for one day, and then mom switched to the phonic method," Gilda remembered. "We argued about the sounds 'ch' and 'sh.' I said, 'How come?' and 'Why?', and when mom stated very firmly that was how it was, I gave in."

"I remember the exact moment I learned to put the sounds of the letters together, and from then on, my refuge was in reading everything I could find. By the time I was ten, I had read the adult version of *Tom Sawyer* four times, all of Longfellow's poetry, *The Swiss Family Robinson*, and many more of my parents' books."[30]

A handsome family: Buck Valli, Ted, Gilda, Lois, 1937.
Photo courtesy of Lois Valli.

To keep her mind above the soapy water, Lois recited poetry to the children—"The Rime of the Ancient Mariner," "The Charge of the Light Brigade," and other long narrative poems she had memorized. "I acted it out with great fine gestures, and they thought that was just great. And then I made up stories about Mike the Muskrat and Bertie the Bunny. And stories about young mice and what their lives were like." Sometimes she spoke in a broken German accent, or in the Scottish brogue of the sheepherders.[31]

Gilda recalled her mother making a Christmas doll house for her, using a pull-out in the English magazine *The Home Chat*. The little rooms her mother pasted on a cardboard box. "It was the most magical doll house any small girl ever had," Gilda exulted. Another Christmas, the Vallies took the children to a school southeast of the Jorawsky place, also owned by Bowlen. There each received a net bag of peanuts, rock candy, and a "Japanese orange." Said Gilda, "words cannot describe the delight for Depression-era children."

The youngsters' innate and sharp interest in the natural surroundings helped rekindle Lois's love of the same, and her love heightened theirs.

"There was an enormous amount of physical and mental space on the prairie," Gilda observed. "When I was a child on those ranches, we were the center of a world that stretched for miles to the horizon on every side. Ted and I walked the prairie by the hour, often with our bottoms up as we leaned down to look at the tiny prairie mosses and flowers, the cactus, the grasshoppers and beetles, the animal droppings, the skeletons of cows, sheep, gophers...."[32]

Rattlesnakes especially interested young Ted. Once J.J. Bowlen treated the stripling to a ride to the river. When they got back into the car, Ted brought a rattler, apparently freshly dispatched, dangling it limp by neck and tail a few inches from Bowlen's face. Calmly, Bowlen answered the kid's questions about snakes, and then he asked him how he'd killed it. "Kill it!" exclaimed Ted, "I haven't killed it yet!"[33]

On a walk with his mother, Ted once sat on a rock to rest. Intuiting danger, his mother bade him be still, and a sidewinder slithered from under the stone. Another time, the lad saw a rabbit being eaten by a rattler in a stubblefield. After the family returned to Brooks, Ted often spent summers on the ranch. One time he skinned a diamondback and, like an Aussie snake hunter, stuck its hide on his belt and around his hat. But the skin did not dehydrate as expected, and soon smelled gangrenous. One of the sheep dogs tracked the belt down and ate it.[34]

Lois also found fascination with the ranch hands and herders. Most of the herders hung around the Assiniboia Hotel in the Hat waiting for a call from the government employment office. Experienced, they wanted $20–$25 a month; novice, they could get $15. They would take the train to Alderson where a wagon would meet them.

Lois saw the humor in daily turmoils. In "Depression Help—1932" she recalled the "little white lie" of the inexperienced:

Some were asked, "Can you milk a cow?"
The answer was "Yes," tho few knew how.
Many men swore they had worked with sheep,
But their ignorance sometimes made us lose sleep.
"Taffy" from Wales worked nights in the shed,
Every night called the boss from his bed.
Sandy from Scotland knew nothing of sheep,

And he lost the herd while enjoying a sleep.
Mike was a Pole who got lost in a fog,
While the sheep found the camp and so did the dog....[35]

In "Sheepherder's Code," she wrote:

Be good to your dog, give him plenty to eat.
You might have to pull cactus thorns from his feet.
You're a team, he's with you awake or asleep,
And it takes both of you to outwit a sheep.[36]

"Ranch Work" was about a new man, "Shorty," just five-foot-three,
who thought he was to haul hay. Said Shorty,

After breakfast next morning I go out with the crew.
A fellow named Pete tells us all what to do.
He says to me," 'Shorty,' go saddle that bay.
Bring the team from the pasture and feed them some hay."
I say, "My name's Elmer, I don't ride very good.
That bald faced bay horse over there—the stud?"

I go get a bridle which gives baldy a clue.
And I try to catch him—with advice from the crew.
The horse and I circle then go round again.
Pete cheers for the horse. Howls from the men.
I'm so mad at that horse I wish he was dead.
I lash out with the bridle and it catches his head.
As soon as the leather rests on his brow
He stops dead in his tracks, like a gentle old cow....[37]

By degrees, Lois recaptured a playful spirit, and found meaning on
the Nine Bar. She anchored herself to Mother Nature and spoke of the
secrets of the breeze.

To know the burden of the wind
We must be finely tuned.

Every key in perfect harmony
Each rebellious branch be pruned.[38]

In "A Lesson from A Flower," the earth was the common mother: "You must respect all forms of life/ Tho humble they may be."[39] The consciousness in all life forms she felt deeply.

But these feelings had always been with her. When she was five, the family moved from the homestead to a rented farm with a double row of poplars. "I had never before lived where there were trees, and I felt a kind of magic when I played under them." All her life trees comforted her. Once when she saw wild strawberries, currents and plums growing along the banks of the Souris River, she ran amongst them and had to be forcibly brought back to the buggy.

"When I was a very young child, I got out of bed one morning and looked out the window," she remembered. "The sun was burning away the fog, and the ground was covered with crocus blossoms. I ran out the house in my nightgown, without shoes and threw myself down in the wet grass to get close to the flowers. I could never forget that feeling of ecstasy. Another time, I found some wild lilies in bloom. I sat on a rock and sang to them." [40]

6 Water

Survival concerned others in the south in

those years too. If the place were almost a desert, surely

water could be brought to it, and with water, crops would grow

and people would return, and normal relationships would resume.

The thought was both magnificent and misleading, magnificent because it was a spark of human ingenuity that would transform an empire of dust, misleading because it put too much store in material change, and it diverted attention from the way adversity can bring people the realizations they most need. As a solution to life's problems, even the region's problems, irrigation might be a start. But only that.

And what an abysmal start it was...."The history of irrigation development in America has been one long record of losses to the promoters and very frequently disaster to the settlers," said the great dean of agrarian editors, C.W. Peterson, in early 1936.[1] In Alberta alone there was enough proof of this assertion, for everything that could go wrong had gone wrong.

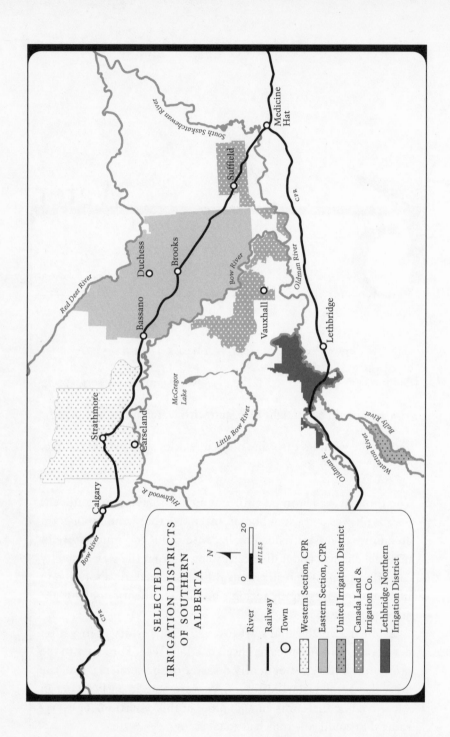

SELECTED
IRRIGATION DISTRICTS
OF SOUTHERN
ALBERTA

N

0   20
MILES

River
Railway
Town

Western Section, CPR
Eastern Section, CPR
United Irrigation District
Canada Land &
Irrigation Co.
Lethbridge Northern
Irrigation District

Medicine Hat

Suffield

South Saskatchewan River

Red Deer River

Duchess
Brooks

Bassano

Bow River

Vauxhall

Oldman River

Lethbridge

Strathmore

Carseland

McGregor Lake

Little Bow River

Belly River

Waterton River

Oldman R.

Calgary

Highwood R.

Bow River

CPR

CPR

CPR

Birthing the Lethbridge Northern Albatross, 1921. NA 230–1, GAA.

THE LETHBRIDGE NORTHERN MILLSTONE

Two-thirds through the construction of the massive Lethbridge Northern project, in February 1922, Alberta's new Attorney General J.E. Brownlee apprised the Legislature that eastern financial houses had written off southern Alberta as irreclaimable. To save itself, the province would have to pursue irrigation. It might have to guarantee the bonds covering costs, and it might even have to pay interest on the bonds for years.

At that very moment, government whip J.C. Buckley fell off his chair with a loud thud. Before the government was through with the project, every member would be on the floor.[2]

In 1919 and 1920 the Lethbridge Northern millstone was established, and by 1923, it was completed and ringed round the necks of its sparse and unwary settlers. The capital cost was $5.4 million. The big winners were the contractors who raked in 10 cents a yard on the continent of dirt moved by subcontractors.[3]

In its first year of operation, floods blew out the headgates and immobilized the project the whole season. The next year, 1924, was drier than parchment, and before farmers could ditch their fields, the crops scorched to death. Watered at last, some of the grain made second growth in time to be frozen by mid-September. In fall 1925, the heavens opened, and the floating grain sprouted in the marshy stooks. Three years later, a hail storm that beggared description hammered crops to pieces from the Albion Ridge east to Turin and Iron Springs. Two hundred and thirty quarter sections were wiped out, and nothing was insured.[4]

After just two years, the Mormon irrigation specialist, John Widtsoe, was ushered in to help. At every turn, he found wrong thinking.

Some settlers harbored the hope of sufficient rain and did not irrigate until too late. In 1924 only 20 percent of the total irrigable area of one hundred thousand acres was irrigated—which meant that settlers paid irrigation land prices and then lived as if they were on dryland. Many refused to diversify. Several went too far into sugar beets, which demanded armies of hired hands, loads of managerial skills and coffers of capital. Almost none went into alfalfa, despite the fact that it yielded well, fertilized the soil and fed the stock. Most planted too much wheat. In 1924, 72 percent of the total irrigated area was in wheat, a practice which contributed to the worst weed infestation since the region had emerged from a prehistoric sea.

Several cultivated too much land and could not release a drylander mentality. Almost 30 percent of the one hundred thousand irrigable acres were held by owners in oversized blocks of from 480 to 2560 acres each. Eighty to 100 acres, said Widtsoe, was reasonable. Also, more than half the irrigable lands were held by nonresidents.[5]

By 1932 the capital loss was $5.4 million, and of 1203 separate parcels of land, well over half were in the hands of the Colonization Manager, either unsold or forfeited.[6] The dispossessed were replaced, and the replacements were dispossessed.

In 1934 a moratorium on capital debt was declared till 1936.[7] The white elephant was "getting whiter every day," quipped an opposition member in the legislature. The cost of project was approaching $12 million, and half the land lay under a vast canopy of Canada Thistle.[8]

One of the biggest bugbears of the Lethbridge Northern was the crazy way it was sold. Unlike virtually every other project in the province, the land was sold with the water right *not* included.

The Wilson Commission of 1930 compared costs of two quarter section farms, each with one hundred acres irrigable—one in the Lethbridge Northern project and the other in the CPR's Eastern Irrigation Section. In 1951 when the Eastern Irrigation man got clear title, the Lethbridge Northern man still needed $6755 to pay out. If the former invested at 5 percent an amount equal to the latter's payment, he could bank over $31,000 before the Lethbridge Northerner got title. "He could purchase a second quarter section and have clear title when the Lethbridge Northern man still had thirty years to continue paying on his first quarter," said the commission. "He could then purchase a third quarter with 80 acres irrigable and get clear title before the Lethbridge Northern man was through paying off his first."[9]

FLEDGLINGS AND MAMMOTHS

Other projects hung by a thread too. The Little Bow Irrigation District comprised bottom lands along the Little Bow River. It was a small operation, under 10,000 acres with 2600 acres irrigable, established in the early twenties to stabilize ranching and mixed farming by guaranteeing pasture.

In 1932 the Highwood River changed course and inundated settler lands to a depth of three feet, causing a large damage claim. Up to 1930, landowners paid their water rates, but by 1934 many had left, and those still around were broke and could pay no more.

The most striking fact about this tiny irrigation enclave, L.C. Charlesworth of the Provincial Irrigation Council informed Premier Brownlee in late 1933—"None of the landowners in the District have ever irrigated"![10]

In 1919 the United Irrigation District was formed in the southwest, close to the mountains, in the area of the Old Cochrane Ranch. No sooner were the works finished in 1922 than the locals began to realize that it did rain a lot in these parts.

In 1927 from May 1 to September-end, 26 inches of precipitation fell, and the people rejoiced at the ditches so painstakingly dug, for they were perfect drainage culverts. Settlers persisted in straight grain growing, and weeds so polluted the fields that agricultural production was a faction of potential.[11]

The Canada Land and Irrigation Company, an amalgamation of earlier ventures, started construction in 1909. The plan was to divert

*Waterless ditches of the
Canada Land and Irrigation
Company, near Suffield, 1990.
Photo by D.C. Jones.*

water from the Bow River near Carseland and to run reservoirs and canals south, then east toward Vauxhall and Suffield. After investors spent $6 million on construction that included a diversion dam, head-works, the filling of Snake Valley and the creation of Lake McGregor, the war broke the flow of capital. The company thereupon turned to the Dominion Government for a loan of $355,000.

By 1922-end, the main canal and its connecting reservoirs were 192 miles long, and there were 110 miles of laterals. The irrigable acreage: 202,650 acres; the total investment: over $14 million. Handiwork of British investors, the mammoth had a grand total of sixty-four water users by 1922, daubing just 9,809 acres.[12] Miles of canals never touched a drop of water, and some still stretch empty across vacant, burnt space, seventy-five years on.

Completely unable to attract settlers or to exact payments in the agricultural downturn of the early twenties, F.W. Hanna, manager of the Canada Land and Irrigation Company, was the picture of misery. Of 520,000 acres for sale, 500,000 remained unsold by 1925, a sales record the envy of none. The company's property was assessable for

Irrigating the CPR Western Section, 1914. NA 2179–22, GAA.

taxation under ten acts, including the Corporation Tax Act, the Educational Tax Act, the Wild Lands Tax Act, the Village Act, the Noxious Weeds Act, and the Municipal Hospitals Act.[13] "The Company is called upon to finance annually about $40,000 in interest, about $75,000 in tax, about $2,000 in reservoir leases and about $9,000 in bridge maintenance, totaling $126,000," moaned Hanna on the eve of a sorrowful departure. It was, he averred, a "dead load."[14] Ten years after the Dominion loan of $355,000 the company still owed $368,000![15]

Here was a portrait of an irrigation company completely unable to perform its duties, castrated and confounded. Conditions were so abysmal that it could not even lease the land under agreement that the lessee pay just the taxes for the year. Taxes could not be paid without selling the land, and the land could not be sold because taxes were too high. In February 1924, the giant fell into receivership, and after April 20, it ceased trying to collect what was owed it.[16]

By far the biggest irrigation promoter in Alberta was the Canadian Pacific Railway. Comprising 100,000 irrigable acres, the Lethbridge Section, had started under other auspices in 1900. Centred on Strathmore, the Western Section of 220,000 irrigable acres had begun in 1906. Headquartered in Brooks, the Eastern Section of 250,000 irrigable acres started in 1914. By late 1934, the first of these huge enterprises had cost $2.1 million; the second, $5.5 million; and the third, $13 million.[17]

That year Gus Griffin, the railway's chief engineer, said of the Western Section—"twenty years' effort to get farmers to use the water which ran past their farms has been generally unsuccessful..." In the previous decade, operation and maintenance costs were one and one-half to three times possible earnings.[18]

In spates, farmers surrendered their water rights, asserting that the water was either useless or harmful. At the same time, many of these same cross-grained toilers would suddenly demand water when the railway had trouble with delivery, and if it were not forthcoming, would lay damage claims.[19]

Disappointingly, even in the drought of the early twenties, 75 percent of the land on which water rights were being paid was being cultivated as dryland.[20]

Surveying its massive projects in mid-Depression, the railway determined to unload it all. By then, it had staggered through a dozen nightmares, some of its own making, some not.

7 In the Toils of a Huge Octopus

SEVERAL ASTONISHINGS

IN THE DEAD OF WINTER, ON JANUARY 19, 1923, a cabal of malcontents met in the inner recesses of the United Farmers' convention halls in Calgary to resume an old pursuit. Their complaint was the recession, their target, the Canadian Pacific Railway. Their leaders were Glen L. Carpender, an Irricana farmer who took the chair, and W.D. Trego, a Gleichen settler, who became chief scribe. The most dangerous to the railroad was Trego, an old nemesis.[1]

In days to come, one by one of the CP hierarchy was informed—P.L. Naismith, manager of the Calgary Department of Natural Resources, Sir Augustus Nanton, executive advisor in Winnipeg, J.S. Dennis, chief commissioner, and E.W. Beatty, president in Montreal. When all heard that Trego was at the bottom of another revolt, none rejoiced.[2]

With alarm, the malcontents viewed the railway's vast dominions, the so-called irrigation blocks between Calgary and Tilley. The economic downswing after 1920 had pressed their friends and loved ones to the wall. Of all afflictions, one stood out as eminently remediable—their principal obligation, the CP contract for the land beneath their feet. The first step of this unofficial United Farmer committee was the ringing of protest up and down the line, followed by demands for relief. Such venting required little orchestration at first, for it was the season of protest.

From the Western Irrigation Section, Frank Kelly, representing two hundred settlers, petitioned the railway directly. "The continued fight against blizzards and hard winters and dry summers is discouraging, and the [recent] wet summer with its hordes of mosquitoes, nose flies, flying aunts [sic], early frosts and hail damage is something that neither the Easterner nor the immigrant can understand," he wrote. "When the settler undertook these lands, he thought of only making a home and a living. He now finds that he is called on to build a nation, pay for the bloodiest war ever fought, build schools, roads, hospitals, exterminate grasshoppers and gophers, fight mange, submit to all the extortions of profiteers, pay for law and order and all the million of small things that go to make civilization." These struggles were enough, but now his very babes were starving.

Should the railway disbelieve this tale of woe, "we are willing to outdo the socialistic principle of giving you a fair share of the profits each year," Kelly announced. *"We offer you all the profits during the past three years*, and ask for a receipt for three years interest."

Joseph S. Bonham, fronting another mass meeting of sorrowers at Rosemary, in the Eastern Irrigation Section, bypassed railway overlords altogether and appealed directly to the Governor General. "This is wild, rough prairie sod land, very expensive to break, ditch and level," he moaned. "In this locality it is very heavy clay, bordering on gumbo soil. Much of the land lies low and is sloughy, other parts are higher and knolly. Heavy levees have to be constructed for long distances across lowlands to convey water to the high lands, then irrigation is ineffectual until considerable leveling is done of the surface."

The great weight was not so much these conditions as those of the CPR contract. Costs of $50 an acre for irrigated land at 6 percent interest with $1.25 water rental per acre per year for the whole irrigated tract, whether irrigated or not, had been set in better times and were now insupportable.[3]

On June 23, Trego and Carpender petitioned the railway for reductions, which it politely declined. Mindful of the distress and not entirely ungenerous, it did offer to extend the contract period from 20 to 34 years.[4]

Trego was completely unsatisfied. As well as the slickest CP propagandist, he understood the workings of publicity. Upgrading the pressure, he sent full reports of the disaffection to 103 dailies and weeklies across the continent.[5]

That summer and early fall, momentum gathered. Communities everywhere clamored to join the revolt—sixty-eight in Alberta, from Cardston in the south to High Prairie in the north, even the coal town of Wayne. Requests to affiliate came from twelve towns in Saskatchewan and from individuals from Owen Sound, Ontario, to Vancouver, British Columbia, from Michigan to Alaska.[6]

At Nolan's Hall, Calgary, on October 30, 1923, the insurgents massed. One delegate wondered if the railway could seize his grain as payment on his contract.

"I think I'll start hauling my grain tomorrow," he said. "If I get rid of that, they are welcome to take the farm and everything left. I'll never be able to pay for it if I live [another] 50 years."

A second muttered glumly, "We seem to be in the toils of a huge octopus, and there doesn't seem to be much chance of getting free."

Trego was resolute: "We have $12,000 that has been subscribed by the contract holders to see this thing through, and we will take it to the Privy Council if necessary."

The insurgents' demands were simple enough—cancel all interest charges since 1918, defer all payments on principal till spring 1925, apply all installments since 1918 to principal, slash the cost of irrigable parcels from $50 an acre to $25. And on first hint of alkali, regardless of the farmer's tillage practices, refund all payments.[7]

If the demands were excessive, it was exactly how the UFA (and their Aberhartian successors) thought the moneyed interests should be handled. Cancel the law of contracts and institute a celestial order of perpetual outflow from the haves to the have nots.

The next day, P.L. Naismith, manager of the railway's Department of Natural Resources, telegraphed Sir Augustus Nanton, high counsel in Winnipeg, saying that about a hundred heard "considerable Bolshevik talk by several agitators." The message in secret code conveyed the railway's anxiety better—*"About one insufferably all told boldness meeting massacre night and miscarriage to deadness bolshevik unspeakable by several of astonishings!"*[8]

Two days later, Trego warned the executive committee of the rail line—"The disgruntled emigrant is the worst advertisement we can have."[9]

Exasperated, the upper echelon of the CP left no stone unturned in seeking to discredit Trego. But the muckraker was not a contract holder at the time of the dispute, and he was hard to hurt. For lands he had purchased from the railway, he had paid nary a cent after the down payment, and after eleven years of delinquency, as he fought the company tooth and nail, he gave the property up. He claimed he would never pay another cent until he got a "reasonable adjustment."[10]

When the CPR filed a writ asking for all owing on contract, roughly $8,000, Trego filed a counter claim for a paltry potato crop that the railway had been unable to irrigate and that he valued on two past harvests at twice that much.[11] When he dumped his rail property in 1917, he promptly bought Indian lands from the Interior Department. Again, he made the down payment, and by mid-November 1923, had remitted nothing more.[12] The municipal district of Dinton also attested that he owed $1300 in unpaid taxes.[13]

By his son's admission, money was his weakness. But Trego was consistent—if it meant less to him than to his creditors, he did not intend it to mean much to his debtors either. He loved to travel to Victoria, Phoenix or California for winter, and he would invite other children along as playmates for his own.[14] To the railway, he resembled the eastern stereotype of western farmers who crabbed forever, shunned their obligations, and cruised to warmer climes at first snowfall.

But there was much more to Trego than this. He was also a reformer, one of a long line of determined and dreaded opponents that, despite every protest to the contrary, the railway desperately needed in order to curtail its own excesses. Like all reformers, he possessed an iron resolve, but unlike most, he was patient. More than was warranted, railmen mistook this patience for perversity.

His wife said he had the patience of Job, and who would know better? One scorching day, he and son Leslie drove twenty-seven miles from one farm to another and suffered no fewer than eleven flat tires. Never once did he lose his temper. Each time he jacked the car, removed the tire, sat on the running board, and patched the tube—all the while singing or telling tales of Idaho, his former home.

Another time, young Les saw a fly light on his father's face. Reading, Trego let it be, so the fly toured his visage at will—to his ear, his mouth, his nostrils, his eyes, everywhere.

"How can he stand it?" the boy whispered to mother.

"It is his way of testing himself," she answered. "He would never let a fly get to him."

There was also a softer side to Trego's temperament. Always kindly, he hated violence. Once when he was hiring muleskinners to haul grain at harvest he saw one carrying a bag.

"What's that?" he asked.

"A black snake," the muleskinner answered, meaning a thirty-foot bull whip.

"I don't allow whips here," spoke Trego.

The muleskinner said he needed the whip for certain mules, to get their attention, and he offered to demonstrate. Just then one of the mules acted up, and the skinner snapped his black snake inches above the head of the obtreperous one. Instantly, the mule quieted.

The skinner was hired on the understanding that the black snake was never to touch flesh.[15]

Hired hands and animals Trego treated with respect, and with both he held a special communion. The men he paid better than most and sheltered in real houses, with plastered walls, attractive beds and dresser drawers. His commissary he opened to them at cost. The animals he protected as he did farmers, and he could walk into a stall with an unbroken stallion without fear or mishap. He could do more with a look than most men with force.

Generous, he helped the widows of soldiers fallen in Flanders, carting milk, cream, eggs and meat to their saddened homes. Children loved him and trailed him in downtown Gleichen, holding his hand or coattails, and he gave them candy and ice cream, and they called him reverently "Pop Trego."

This gentler nature made the confrontation with the railway more difficult for him than anyone knew. That he would eventually fall into the excess of reformers must have troubled him afterward. Not perfect, he was still farther along than most. Contemplative, he seemed always in deep thought; quiet, he spoke when it was time to speak; tolerant, he hated no one. It is safe to say that the Canadian Pacific hierarchy did not know him, and could not divine his motives.

Claims were made of him, mostly unprovable now, which still measured the man—that he was *the* pioneer irrigationist of Idaho; that he shipped the first alfalfa seed west of the Mississippi; that he brought the first combine into Alberta; that, according to cattle baron Pat Burns, he was the best judge of livestock in the province; that he set individual records for grain shipment in Canada in 1915 and 1916, with ninety carloads, when he farmed the land of Idahoans not yet in place.

He experimented with mules as a source of farm locomotion, with grain stackers to replace bundling and stooking, with deep tillage implements that allowed for moisture penetration into the subsoil but left the surface intact. Crucial in the early days of the United Farmers of Alberta, he rose to the vice presidency.[16]

Trego was raised a Quaker, and there was similarity between that faith's first objection to the Church of England and his own quarrel with the CPR. The authority of an established corporate colossus meant little to him—here he was brother to the Burnsites and Fra Elbertus. He would find the truth himself; then he would do his all, for whatever span, to have it honored.

Trego was a collector of grievances and injustices which he kept a long time. He was meticulous, logical and convincing, unstinting in effort and relentless. In a single issue of *The Farmers' Tribune*, published in October 1914 at Carlstadt, he unleashed 27,000 words flailing the CPR.[17] According to the railway's own informants, his voice was even, emotionless, and undramatic. His writing was the same—not colorless, but a controlled form of scolding and suspicion.[18]

He waged a personal vendetta with Colonel J.S. Dennis for fifteen years. He so irritated P.L. Naismith, a veteran of bitter coal strikes around Lethbridge, that Naismith suggested inducing the Department

Coloradans briefed by anti-settlement agent Trego, Bassano.
NA 3060–1, GAA.

of the Interior to eject Trego from his Indian lands, as if this were the business of the Canadian Pacific.[19]

On December 19, Trego reported that at least a third of the settlers in the eastern irrigation block were leaving, and he wasn't far wrong. He advised the *Albertan*, which took pleasure in smirching the iron road darling of the *Herald*, that he would now escalate the campaign. He would megaphone to the planets the disturbing details of his previous dispute with the railway.[20]

As a foretaste, he reminded everyone of the Bassano incident. When the railway tried to settle the Bassano colony in 1914 with Coloradans, it expected over two hundred families. Trego sailed a missive to the *Denver Post* that was more than faithful to his jaundiced view of the railway. At Bassano on the red letter day, the colonial coach lurched to a halt, and out trickled just twenty-two families.

Among the greeters was Trego. The incomers told him the no-shows all had money, unlike themselves, and had scattered like quail when they read his report. The arrivals were so penurious and the railway so desirous of saving face, that it did not, perhaps could not, extract even a down payment, and more, it had to loan funds for seed, fare and freight. All would try irrigation for a year or so, and if it flopped, they would leave.[21] And that is exactly what they did.

THE FARMERS TRIBUNE

"BACK TO THE LAND,--BUT TELL THE TRUTH"

VOLUME I, NO. 1   TUESDAY, OCTOBER 6, 1914   PER COPY, FIVE CENTS. PER YEAR, $1.50

IRRIGATION A SUCCESS!

IN THE RIGHT PLACE--YES! BUT A FAILURE IN WESTERN C.P.R. BLOCK EAST OF CALGARY CLAIM FARMERS WHO HAVE TRIED TO USE IT

Trego flails the CPR, 1914. From The Farmers' Tribune, October 6, 1914.

IRRIGATING BUFFALO WALLOWS

In the old dispute Trego was one of several actors.

He had left Iowa in 1885, arriving in Blackfoot, Idaho, on August 1, at age 19. Interested in irrigation, he was elected in time to the board of directors of the Danskin Canal Company and became one of three irrigation commissioners who divided the Snake River among sixty-odd canal concerns.[22] His many contributions to early irrigation in Idaho led him to believe that he could do the same for Alberta.

In 1906 he bought land east of Calgary, near Gleichen, and in spring 1908, he began to settle Idahoans in Alberta's new western irrigation block, as an agent of the Canadian Pacific Railway.[23]

Early in 1911, Trego warned Colonel Dennis not to enter into the eastern irrigation project until the western was fully operational. In bone dry 1910, irrigation had failed in the western section. Water was short.

"Oh, don't worry, Trego. We will make a success of it," said Dennis. "You men have not been here long enough yet to understand our conditions."

If the flow lacked, Dennis advised Trego and others to pool their water allotment and to combine three irrigation heads at once.

Dubious, Trego answered snidely, "Do you mean that each one should irrigate our lands once each three years or to irrigate one-third of it each year?" In no year had more than 1 percent of the so-called irrigable land had actually been irrigated, Trego charged.[24]

While he blamed the company for shortages in a dry year, he wondered if in normal years irrigation of cereals was necessary or even helpful at all. In 1909 he irrigated 300 acres. *"When harvest time came on,"* he emphasized, *"I had oats which stood fully 6 feet high, but when they should have been ripening they stayed green week after week until frost came, and I never threshed a single bushel...."*[25]

With these experiences and others, dawned the realization that the railway had misrepresented the region. Quoting a pamphlet entitled *A Handbook of Information Regarding Canadian Pacific Lands*, Trego wrote, "Conditions for the raising of barley are almost perfect in the irrigated block.... In fact, irrigated barley from the Bow River Valley is of such a superior quality that the farmers in the irrigated block have a standing offer from the grain buyers of 10 cents a bushel in excess of the prevailing market price...." The book lauded John McEwen of Gleichen with the record yield of 1907—91 bushels an acre.

Trego could see McEwen's land from his own window. "Mr. McEwen," he intoned, *"has never used a drop of irrigation on his farm."* Trego himself had never taken advantage of the premium mentioned, had never even heard of it, and had never raised any barley because the market had never justified it.[26]

Trego soon struck an alliance with Henry Sorensen, farmer from Strathmore, erenow civil engineer. In December 1909, Sorensen provided none other than C.W. Peterson, former Territorial Deputy Commissioner of Agriculture, founder of the *Farm and Ranch Review* and current director of the Canadian Pacific Irrigation Colonization Company, with the details of his operations. Answered Peterson, "We have taken the liberty of changing your letter to a certain extent, as, for our purpose, it seems inadvisable to refer to frosts. We propose making exceptionally good use of your letter in our new Public Opinion pamphlet."[27] This modification the usually straight and steady Peterson surely later regretted.

A few years on, Sorensen was chairman (and Trego chief secretary) of the vaunted Farmers' Combined Irrigation Committees. To the ear of E.F. Drake, federal Superintendent of Irrigation, he disclosed his own grave and mounting troubles.

In London, England, he had paid CPR agents $5,000 down for four sections of land, half irrigated, half dry. Before embarking, he discovered that the railway had already sold pieces of the same tract. Someone then gave him four other sections. But these were not put under irrigation for two years; in fact, CP men did not even start digging the ditches for a year after Sorensen's arrival.

In June 1911, the CPR published a circular that praised Sorensen as the settler *parfait*. "What success he has achieved," it stated, "can be shown by the fact that he has paid for his land...."

"*Subsequently* to that statement," fumed Sorensen twenty-two months on, "the CPR have sued me for payments on my lands!"

The railway had promised that the raising of grain and grain alone would bring success. Sorensen had pumped $60,000 from Norway into his operations without a cent of return. He assumed that the railway had "thoroughly investigated...the climatic and soil conditions" before palavering its poppycock to the world.

"I do not believe it will ever be beneficial use to put water upon these lands with their heavy non-porous subsoil," said he. "Inasmuch as there is plenty of moisture for our western farming in this western section of the irrigation blocks, this artificial cold watering will sour and deteriorate the land and cause alkali to work its way up to the surface....But above all the cool nights and short seasons are against the scheme." The first retarded growth, and the second terminated it. "With the exception of 1910, the dry year, when I had no water at all," he echoed Trego, "the trouble has been too much summer moisture for the grain."

Sorensen sought to implicate the Department of the Interior in his predicament. "Had the CPR been some ordinary wild cat undertaking, or even an ordinary land selling company, I am fully justified to state that not one quarter of the emigrants from abroad would have listened to the statements of the company," he snarled. "It was the pleas of the integrity of the CPR with the full sanction of the government which did the work."[28]

Others howled the same. Frank Sugden of Cheadle noted that the railroad had boomed the area for winter wheat. So Sugden planted a section of it in 1908 and lost every acre to frost. After two wet summers, he wheeled in an expert to demonstrate the irrigation art in the dust of 1910.

"From a ditch which was supposed to irrigate close on 800 acres, I could irrigate an acre a day, and no one but myself was using the water," snapped Sugden. With anyone else on the line, he might as well have used a pail and a water gun. The expert allowed that he needed triple the water to succeed.

Then Sugden hammered the general classification of lands. Again he called in experts—CP watermen and surveyors. "I showed them some of the worst parts—alkali flats, high rocky points and a deep coulee over half a mile long, all of which was classified as irrigable," he said.

"I asked how could I irrigate a steep coulee and the low alkali places which would almost bog a duck."

Drain the alkali land, *then* irrigate it, one expert answered.

He had not come 8,000 miles from Australia to buy drainage land, Sugden huffed.

But all land below the point of delivery, according to contract, was irrigable, said another technician.

"If it was so," shouted Sugden, "see the injustice of it! Sloughs, lakes and coulees, rocks, etc. classified as irrigable land and charged [accordingly]!"

As the dissidence gathered, other dupes of the railway contributed their stories. A.L. Blunt wrote the Minister of the Interior from Chicago. Half his 240 so-styled "irrigable" acres at Strathmore were "too low and wet to ever need irrigating."[29] In normal seasons, his farm resembled a rice paddy.

J.B. and B.W. Hall bought a section near Langdon, 607 acres of which, according to the railway, were irrigable. On the east half section, there was "land counted as irrigable on ridges." The entire west half was part rock and part buffalo wallows. "It becomes half a section of lakes from 3–10 feet deep," the Halls deponed from Mt. Sterling, Kentucky. "These holes hold water like a jug. It is as necessary to be able to get the water off the land as it is to get it *on*."[30] A travesty it was—trying to irrigate with the land submerged!

*Col. John Stoughton Dennis,
Chief, CPR's Department of
Colonization and Immigration,
during his fire fight with W.D.
Trego, 1914 c.
NA 2430–1, GAA.*

All this deeply frustrated Colonel Dennis in the Calgary CP offices. In February 1913, in three Calgary newspapers, he counter-attacked the main complainants led by Sorensen and Trego. Of the 1,630 contractors of irrigable land in the western irrigation block, 231 filed complaint, 18 did not own irrigable land, and 7 did not own any land, leaving just 206 who complained and 1,424 who did not. Of the carpers, 191 were in arrears one to five years in water rentals and land payments.[31]

Sorensen responded that many were supporting the irrigation committee secretly to avoid CPR reprisals, and that at least one water-master was promising seed grain to farmers who spurned the rebels.[32]

The confrontation reached a boil in February 1913, and the combatants were hauled to Ottawa where they exchanged discourtesies.

Minister of the Interior W.G. Roche informed the railroaders that their classification was improper and that the Department itself would resurvey and reclassify the land. Then he ruled that no water license would be issued to the company until its works were functioning satisfactorily. Thirdly, while his own men were painstakingly resurveying the western block, the railway was to desist in collections of rentals and payments for irrigable land.[33]

Nemesis of the CPR, Willet Trego, 1916 c. NA 627–1.

The farmers' victory was well nigh complete. Jubilant, the irrigation committee of the UFA now sought to induce Roche to repudiate the entire western irrigation block scheme as fraudulent and untenable. This the good minister would not do.[34]

When the reclassification was done, roughly 140,000 acres, formerly classed as irrigable, now were not. The legitimately irrigable portion sank to roughly 223,000 acres.[35]

Speedily, the company offered new contracts based on the reclassification and amortized over ten years, as before. Again the farmers objected, and with reason. Pressed by settler difficulties, the railway had begun offering to new settlers new contracts amortized over *twenty* years. The old boys thought they deserved the same. Because of the trouble they had been put to and the bad years they had undergone, they also thought the first installment should come due after a year.

The farmers deputized Trego, F.M. Black, President of the Calgary Board of Trade, and H.W. Wood, president of the UFA, to wait on Colonel Dennis in his Calgary sanctum. Since relations between

Trego and Dennis were at an all time low, Trego voluntarily restrained himself in a nearby hotel.

The other two met Dennis at 10 AM, and an hour and a half later, they returned to Trego, rebuffed. Trego stirred them up and launched them at Dennis again at 1 PM. Some minutes later, they returned, again foiled.

Trego told them he was through, that the farmers would leave, and that the railway could forget about settling its lands, as every jerkwater hamlet with a newspaper in America and Europe would carry the whole rotten saga in ten parts. Flung again at Dennis at 9 PM, Trego's men made one last assault. Near midnight, the CP chief, bleary-eyed and barely conscious, folded and accepted their entire proposal.[36]

8 Bloody Bolivia!

REVOLUTION HABIT PROVES UNPLEASANT

THIS VICTORY TREGO RECALLED AS HE CUDGELED THE RAILWAY ANEW TEN YEARS ON. He did not mention the great price he himself had paid for the endless tension—

a heart attack.

Still unstoppable, he barely took Christmas 1923 off before swooping down on the stricken eastern irrigation block. When unforeseen circumstances forced him to ride out to the Bow Slope Community Hall with a carload of CP men, the rail boys took measure of both his discomfort and pluck.

In this meeting, in others, and in the *CPR Contract Holders' Bulletin*, Trego dredged up the past and explained his gradual conversion into an anti-immigration agent. He was on softer ground this time, however, and the Interior Department did not support him.[1] The railway had already redressed its mistakes, and by re-introducing them, Trego seemed to demand second payment. Less called for now, his recollections would lead him by degrees into the very errors he so damned.

Now he offered his 1924 New Year's Resolutions—every farmer in the irrigation blocks should write friends and news organs back home about the impossible conditions exacted by the railway. Then they should all put out "For Sale" signs.[2]

If the railmen should scoff at the threat of departure, Trego was prepared to state the destination. And nothing could have surprised more. Alter the contracts, ordered he, or an army of dissidents would leave—for *Bolivia*!

In this final phase, the drama turned to farce, and the irony was complete. Until their faces ran blue, the Tregoites had scored the railway for misrepresentation, deception and fraud. Every form, every shadow of falsity in the irrigation propaganda, they floodlit; every bald-faced lie, every misstep, every misstatement they reiterated with disgust and loathing. Now to promote the Bolivian option, Trego stooped to the same fare.

In March 1924, Robert "Klondike" Jones representing the Bolivia Colonization Association, spoke, upon invitation, to the insurgents. Though it came close at times, nothing the CPR had done in half a century outdid these two masterful hours of arrant distortion.

Klondike's realty held a concession of 864,500 acres in Bolivia which it proposed to sell for $2.50 an acre. Jones himself had toured the country for three years and had apparently settled comfortably in some villa. A neighbor on one side, he said, owned 31,000 acres and 2,000 head of cattle; another to the west had 46,000 acres and 2,000 head. Of the near million acres of land, there was not one acre untillable. Klondike had never seen rocks and no pebble as large as a pea. When someone asked how colonists could build roads without stones, Klondike told him to scrape up the dirt anywhere, and it would pack like a cement highway.

Grass was green year round, and cows with their fatlings wandered through it up to their necks, too full to stand up or lie down. Cattle and hog disease were unknown.

Peach trees flourished everyplace and were apparently sown broadcast. Blessed with 48 inches of rain a year, timber was lush, and ox carts were solid mahogany, the axles hickory. Sugar cane popped up everywhere on stump land and thrived unattended for seven or eight years running. Corn prospered the same way—throw seed into a hole and stand back, Klondike counselled. Like shade trees, the stalks propelled themselves skyward, ten to twelve feet high. For all these products, eager markets beckoned just down the way, in the mining sector.

Happy workers hired out at 16 cents a day, or deluxe, with ox and wagon, at 40 cents. If these wages suggested a standard of living below sea level, Klondike was quick to point out a cowman who had sold 4,000 head at 69 cents each—and profitted nicely!

There was no building tax in Bolivia, and even if one were imposed, doubted Klondike, there were no tax collectors. Anyone with anything taxable was supposed to tell the authorities, and if he failed to do so in this laissez-faire elysium, no one would bother him.[3] There were no poisonous snakes, no fevers, no malaria. The closer one approached this paradise, the fewer the flies. In fact, screens on doors and windows were unknown. Summarized Jones, "we feel safe in saying that it is not only the *best land*, but in the *best location*, in the *best country*, with the *best climate* and with the *best markets* on earth...."[4]

The glee of the pro-railroad *Calgary Herald* was unbounded. "If a quarter of what was stated was true, then Bolivia is 50 gardens of Eden all rolled into one," it chortled. "The picture painted of Bolivia entirely put in the shade any attempt that ha[s] ever been made in land booming in Canada."[5]

When Trego and his cohorts awoke from their Klondike trance, they would proceed immediately to build a city in the middle of nowhere. The name "Los Angeles," Bolivia, was suggested, and later changed on a whim to "Alberta," Bolivia. A map appeared in the contract holders' *Bulletin* with measurements taken from the flagstaff, presumably flying Bolivian colors, in the plaza. Each land buyer would receive free a 50 x 142 foot lot. Adjacent to the residential palaces would be market gardens, then quarter, then half, then full section farms.

The next week's project was to establish sawmills to supply lumber, then flour mills to grind wheat for the Bolivian mining metropoles. Then someone would need to lay a railroad between Alberta City and the markets, estimated at 150 to 280 miles. Since

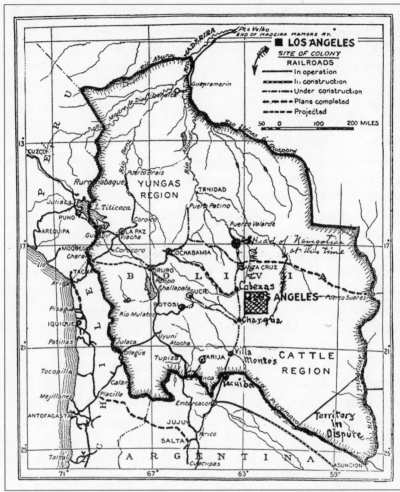

Trego's city of gold—Los Angeles, Bolivia, later aptly renamed Alberta, Bolivia. CPR Contract Holders' Bulletin, *1924.*

according to the CPR every settler produced $746.33 annually in freights (one of the few CP figures Trego trusted), the Bolivians would naturally rush completion of the line.

What fiestas there would be when Bolivia and its new colony celebrated the nation's 100th birthday on August 6, 1925. What contributions to Hispanic civilization these Anglos would make! "Bolivia is seeking immigrants from North America of the frontier type," exclaimed Trego, "knowing that they are empire builders[!]"[6]

For days after Klondike's blathering, Trego found it easy to pipedream. He began to think that his committee might strike a separate deal with La Paz. If they sold the first 100,000 acres at $20 each, they could bank $2 million, enough to build the mills, curing plants and packing houses. Then they could hike the price to $50, or five times what the CPR was charging for nonirrigable estates in late 1924. If they sold the next 100,000 acres at $50 each, their take would reach $50 million, and then they could buy every railway in the country.

"Would we yield to the temptation to own the railways so we could boost the freight rates and passenger rates on the poor mining interests who would be bearing all the burden of taxation?" Trego mused. "Could we stand the prosperity?"

There it was—the monopoly, the hopeless exaggeration, the discounting of climatic problems, cultural problems, language problems, the neglect of the influence of world prices on agricultural success, the etching of paradise itself. Every vestige of the hated CP system Trego now embraced. Possibly he saw the dangers of his own course—of becoming what he so reviled in his enemy.

As Trego prepared to dispatch envoys to South America to confirm everything, H.F. Willoughby Greenhill, an old UFA man from Didsbury offered his farm to the committee to dispose of at best advantage to him and the committee.[7] Unbeknownst to Trego meanwhile, seven farmer-speculators jumped the gun and bought land in Bolivia. One from Rosebud picked up four sections.[8]

Then came shocking news. On April 3, 1924, the *Calgary Herald* interviewed the still shaking M. Froschmeier who had just escaped from Bolivia after a personal reconaissance. After fifteen years in Alberta, he had left Calgary on New Year's Day, travelling via Portland and San Fransisco. He sailed to Arica, Chile, and caught the train to La Paz which disappointingly ran but once a week. Despite assurances from Klondike Jones's Bolivia Colonization Association in Portland that he could buy land at $2.50 an acre, when he reached the capital, he discovered the government had not passed the necessary legislation.

A day after Froschmeier's arrival, a revolt broke out in La Paz that so delighted the *Herald* that its coverage featured the subtitles— "Revolution Habit Proves Unpleasant," and "Disagreeable Revolution." Moreover, the American consul advised Froschmeier that insufficient capital ensured that there would be no railway for years. Consequently, grain hauls—at 300 miles a round trip—could be fatiguing.

Fearing for his life, Froschmeier fled to Arica. For three tense days, he awaited evacuation, and just as he neared normalcy, an earthquake struck. By the time his vessel touched off from the tottering port, his Alberta press release was sealed—"I saw all I wanted to and I'm not going back."[9]

Thus the infamous Bolivian threat died its absurd death—at the very moment, most ironically, that the railway gave in. Eyes open and ears cocked, the CPR soon confessed obliquely that Trego's original contentions were more than accurate. Conditions were depressed beyond recognition. As the worst year in dry belt history wore on, farm abandonments in the southeast multiplied like cutworms. The shadow of drought darkened the whole south, and cries for relief reverberated to Montreal.

Buffeted by calamity and sick of criticism, the company wrote off five years' interest and three years' water rental, and it dropped the price of dryland farms in irrigable areas from $25 to $10 an acre. Still settlers were strapped, so the railway again reclassified its irrigated lands in 1927. Good irrigable land near rail lines remained at $50 an acre, while the poorest was priced as low as $10. The price of nonirrigable land was dropped to $5 an acre, a fifth of what it had been a few years earlier.[10]

These horrific reductions would have felled a weaker corporation, certainly one that had not been given the land in the first place. Yet they reflected favorably on the railway, and, of course, its critics.

Trego's methods in the end were more than curious, but curiosity does draw attention. His first fight was the natural result of the monopoly the railway had been granted to colonize the irrigation blocks, for monopolies are prone to offend. Expected to direct the massive reorientation of life of a huge sector of the southern prairies, the railway quickly took matters into its own hands, formulated widespread policies, and became a law unto itself. There was always danger that this law might lack common sense and justice.

Thus Trego claimed that the CPR colonization plan had been misleading, even fraudulent. Doubtless, it was misinformed and misdirected, and certainly in the classification of lands, arrogant and cavalier.

By the time of the Bolivian revolt, though bad odor remained, things had changed. Now the Eastern Irrigation Section was involved as much as the Western, and the postwar depression and settlement failure had rendered almost any contract for land and water impossible to honor. Now Trego claimed the railway had been less fraudulent than unfair, even unfeeling.

The farmers' paladin knew there was a morality that transcended the law of contracts, and this principle he advanced with the full force of his irrepressible personality.

One who had signed Trego's threat to depart for Bolivia would now take the stage.

9 Hell and The Sage

A CHRISTMAS TREE

Despite the railway's adjustments, conditions did not improve. From 1918 to 1921, 1500 settlers entered the eastern block, and by 1928, 800 were gone, broke and disillusioned.[1] In 1926 the railway recorded 443 abandoned farms there, and of 780 current contractors for land, seven years on, only 146 owed less than when they first signed, fourteen years, on average, before.[2] Fifty of the worst delinquents had surrendered their contracts and reverted to renting.[3]

S.G. (Sam) Porter, manager of the Department of Natural Resources of the company, reported that from 1931 to 1934 the Canadian Pacific forgave over $6,226,000 in interest due from land holders.[4] On its grazing lands, it charged 3 cents an acre and paid

10 cents in taxes.[5] From 1925 to 1935, it shelled out $2.5 million in taxes on behalf of settlers, writing off over half.[6]

When all is said, it cannot be concluded that the railway was a harsh creditor. It made repeated adjustments of contracts on principal and interest—credit on arrears of interest, waivers of interest, reductions of every mark. Despite Trego's revelations and others to come, the morality of the company was probably on a par with its clients'.

One exceptional light was the Superintendent of Operations and Maintenance in Brooks, Gus Griffin. No one who dealt with him ever forgot his stewardship. A modest version of his idol Luther Burbank, the California horticultural phenom and creator of hundreds of varieties of vegetables, fruits and flowers, Griffin contributed much to the area's beauty and esthetics.

The peas, beans, onions, sunflowers and fruits he imported and adapted were favorites of the CPR dining car chefs and won many honors at fairs.[7] Along the arid banks of the Red Deer River, he collected chokecherries, bull berries, gooseberries and strawberries. Waterton mock orange, Strathmore crab apples, Jumping Pound cherries, and Brooks sandcherries were all his offspring. Native plants and shrubs he gathered and improved, and Brooks and Griffin poplars he bred. Like Donald Albright of the Peace River country, he answered hundreds of inquiries with the same zest and gratification. With Burbank, he exchanged cuttings and insight, and if Burbank were a saint according to the spiritual giant Paramahansa Yogananda, Griffin, as the following story attests, was akin.[8]

Near Christmas 1918, J.A. Hawkinson and young Carl Anderson hauled wheat into Brooks, then went shopping. Hawkinson wanted a Christmas tree like ones in Minnesota, his former home, but finding none, he complained to the CPR—where all ills of whatever order, were laid.

At 4:30 next morn, the two men rose, harnessed the horses, and headed south. Freezing, they walked beside the teams to keep warm. Half way through the still empty expanse, Hawkinson glanced in the wagon and was shocked. "You shouldn't have done it, Carl!" he blurted. "You shouldn't have!" Puzzled, Anderson stared at the load and discovered in amazement a lovely four-foot green spruce.

Still wondering how the tree had come, Hawkinson proudly presented it to his family. Now came another surprise—the wife and children did not want it! While father was at Brooks, they had rounded up some Russian Thistle—tumbleweeds—stacked them in the corner, and crowned them with ornaments. It had a strange, holy land appeal, and its starkness attracted. From that day till Christmas trees became readily available, wives of settlers in the region decorated tumbleweeds instead. The story ended long after, when someone discovered that the real tree had been secretly stowed by Gus Griffin.[9]

In hard days ahead, the human sympathy of railway people was seldom noted. Even the good the Canadian Pacific did, including the planning and building of its vast and costly irrigation system was undervalued—and without that, viable agriculture in the sector would have waited a century.

HARDLY IMPASSIVE

Nonetheless, there was something deeply wrong with the irrigation project, and the heart of the problem was paternalism. In secret code, the CPR once called its irrigation ratepayers "cozened impassives." It was half true—they were cozened, but not impassive.

Every time groups are coddled and pampered and removed even a single soul-width from their responsibilities, so that others decide for them, trouble ensues. It is, quite frankly, unnatural for people to surrender their will for extended periods. By fits and starts, they will come to their senses and demand control of their lives, then agents who resist must stand aside.

The Eastern Section by the 1920s had created a class of bureaucratic Brahmans—panjandrums of the railway, favored and feted, until a red line ran down the streets of Brooks, separating the preferred from the great unwashed. Houses of rail employees sat in the exclusive Evergreen Park—"rotten row," some called it.[10] A chauffeur would pick up a lady there and drive her to the station where she would board a train for Calgary, shop the day, and return. The cost: two wrist flexes flashing a free pass, one going, one coming.[11]

Headed by Sam Porter, manager of the CPR's natural resources, the engineering branch in 1933 was crowded to the gunwales with superintendents, canal superintendents, assistant canal superintendents, watermasters, assistant watermasters, levelers, inspectors, ditchriders, draftsmen, garage foremen, farm formen, machinists, mechanics, mechanics' helpers, clerks, accountants, stenographers,

"Rotten Row"—Nesting Houses of CP mollycoddles, Brooks, 1919.
NA 4389-5, GAA.

storekeepers, blacksmiths, carpenters, gardeners, dam masters and dam tenders. There were eighty-one employees attached to just the engineering branch. Yet this swarm was nothing compared to the over two hundred employed a decade earlier.[12]

It was the solution to these problems, and especially, the recapture of personal responsibility, that so animated Carl J. Anderson. At age nineteen, he and his father emigrated from Omaha, Nebraska, to the CPR's Eastern Irrigation Section, south of Brooks where rail propaganda had limned the area as a celestial oasis. At Scandia, north of the Bow River, in 1918, the two prepared for the arrival of family and helped found a Swedish-Canadian colony. Soon they were disappointed with the iron road that had promised a branch line into their estates to supplant the thirty-mile haul north to Brooks, or the seventeen-mile lug south to Vauxhall, across a treacherous river. With mounting impatience, they waited and waited—for ten years, before steel came.

Every misery, Willet Trego, of course, had spotlit. Supporting him, the United Farmers of Scandia, led by Carl Anderson, voted to a man to sell out—before sailing for South America.[13] Penniless, none had the slightest inkling of going, but all opposed the railway.

Even the CP agricultural experts were disrespected. "They always told us how well they did," Anderson noted, "but they never said if they made any money."[14] In 1922 specialists told him to grow sunflowers, to cut them for silage, and to feed livestock—so he slaved away building corrals, troughs, pit silos and sheds. He jammed the unruly ten foot long bundles into cutters, chopped away, and with silage at last, he staggered to the bank for a loan to buy livestock to eat the feed. A bad year for feeding it was, they said—and that was that.

Then experts bade him grow corn. Turn lambs into it, and they will gain twenty-five to thirty pounds, they said. So Carl seeded thirty acres of corn in 1926 and cultivated it so devotedly that he quit going to baseball games. Then the corn froze, and the lambs feasted on their own misfortune. In the dry thirties, ducks landed in the cornfield by the millions, so Carl turned sheep into the field to get ahead of them, but the quackers were ravenous. Because the locals were too poor to buy shells, he finally imported hunters from Medicine Hat to shoot the ducks. In the end, the bombardment failed, and the ducks won.[15]

Perhaps then Lelia Anderson, Carl's wife, entered a poem in the family Bible:

The farmer knocked at the pearly gate
His face was scarred and old.
He stood before the Man of Fate
For admission to the fold.
"What have you done?" St. Peter asked
In accents loud and clear.
"I've been a farmer, sir, all my life
For many and many a year."
The pearly gate swung open wide
As St. Peter touched the bell.
"Come in," he said, "and choose your harp.
You've had your taste of Hell!"

MAJESTIC PETITIONS

For a good while, Anderson had been eyeing a piece of land near his Scandia homestead. Boasting an excellent house, it would complement his present holdings, providing space and feed for his expanding

Carl Anderson on the eve of his calling, 1926. Photo courtesy of C.J. Anderson.

sheep operations. Time came when he thought he had it secured through the local CPR land department.

Not long after, a wagon rolled up to his door. It bore a sixty-year old man with one arm cut off near the elbow, and beside him was his wife, veteran of an uneasy life, her dress ripped to the waist, showing men's long johns underneath. The man said a CPR boss in Brooks had awarded him the contract for the adjoining land—the piece Anderson thought was his. The amputee asked for the key.

Anderson stiffened, and an animated discussion followed. Now Anderson was six-foot-two and weighed two hundred pounds; he was a big man with big voice. More force resided in him than would occur again in a single personality in the entire region in a hundred years.

Anderson's spouse Lee took in the scene and called him aside. Her sympathy ran to the handicapped and unyoung couple, and she knew they had nowhere to go, so she advised surrendering the key. She and Carl would manage without the extra land.

Anderson thought a moment, then went for the key.

Lelia M. Anderson was a gentle woman. Once a terrific hailstorm pounded the family sheep mercilessly, and the pelting iceballs split open the heads, faces and hind quarters of the little lambs who bled profusely. When the storm lifted, the ewes would not have fifteen of them because of all the blood. So Lee took them, fed them with

Lee Armstrong, 1923, before her marriage to Carl Anderson. Photo courtesy of C.J. Anderson.

nipples and bottles, loved them, and became the mother they never had. As they grew up, each one was named after a neighbor, and each assumed a special, affectionate personality. Lee raised them until they weighed sixty pounds, Carl fattened them in a feedlot until they were a hundred, then came time for their final journey.

Easily led, sheep follow anything, even to a slaughterhouse. On this occasion, Lee brought up the rear, gathering strays, talking to the woollies, and the lambs that were her children recognized her voice and ran to greet her. Seeing their trusting nature, Lee said sadly, "I feel like a murderer."[16]

Lee Anderson was the leaven in Carl's life. Coveting no recognition, she acted quietly, behind the scenes, and led as an agent in right thinking. There was a beauty in her soul, unarguable, unassailable, and Anderson leaned toward it instinctively. "She calmed me down, she kept me straight, she had a wonderful influence on me," he recognized. "My father taught me good Christian tenets; my wife taught me how to live them."[17]

Lee knew when he had become too angry, too bull-headed, too demanding. She knew what could be accomplished and what not. She knew the difference between courage and rashness, between constructive change and disorderly, ruinous change. And she understood the human effect of an overarching personality. But remarkably she could overpower his force with her own serenity, and just as memorably, he in his best moments could recognize her confident, affectionate presence and the rightful place of calm over conflict. He was the first to admit that most of what he achieved was due to her.

A Baptist of Scottish-Irish extraction from New Brunswick, Lee was descended from British Empire loyalists. A teacher before she married, she read Elbert Hubbard's books avidly and was drawn to the beauty of his counsel on human relations. Hubbard was an evolved thinker who spoke of divine laws and eternal matters. The first few pages of his famous *Note Book* said these things—

Soon or late I know you will see that to do right brings good, and to do wrong brings misery, but you will abide by the law and all good things be yours. I can not change these laws—I can not make you exempt from your own blunders and mistakes. And you can not change the eternal laws for me, even though you die for me.

I believe that no one can harm us but ourselves; that sin is misdirected energy; that there is no devil but fear; and that the universe is planned for good.

No greater insult was ever offered to God than the claim that His chief product, man, is base at heart and merits damnation.

I believe that men are inspired today as much as ever men were.

The race is one, and we trace it to a common Divine ancestry.

The big man at the last is the man who takes an idea and makes of it a genuine success—the man who brings the ship to port.[18]

It was all very simple, very positive, though much of it would have reaped damnation in certain sects. Akin to Burnsism, it carried God's revelation beyond the Bible, it rejected the innate sordidness of people, and it explicitly raised modern "saints," like Henry Thoreau and Walt Whitman to the grand heights Ezekiel and Elijah had held millennia ago.[19]

More inspiration flowed from Hubbard than from a score of seminaries. No book of memorable quotations even now can be gathered without some seed of his thought. The most positive human force of his era, he was called, and perhaps rightly. He spoke like a prophet commissioned in mists before time to call an entire tribe together, to remind them who they were, what they might become.

"I am not widely known," he wrote modestly—"but everywhere are the Elect Few who Understand. I express for these the things they know....All those who think as I do, whose heads are in a certain stratum, who breathe the same atmosphere—these know all I know.... Life is a search for our own—for those whose hearts beat in unison with ours—who respond to the same vibrations....Our own are those in our key. And when this is struck, we answer back out of the silence."[20]

In answering, would we know what wisdom was? Yes, we would sense it when once we heard it—then choices would follow. The enlightened man, said Fra Elbertus, "believes in all religions and in all gods. He sympathizes with every sect, but belongs to none. He recognizes that every religion is a reaching out for help, a prayer for light, and that a sect is merely a point of view. He recognizes that there is good in all, and that a man's 'god' is the highest concept of what he would like to be—his god is himself at his best, and the devil is himself at his worst.

"Yet the wise man does not cavil at the multiplicity of beliefs and strife of sects. For himself he would much prefer a religion that would unite men, not divide them. Yet he perceives that denominations represent stages of development in the onward and upward spiral of existence. There is much clay in their formation, and all are in a seething state of unrest; but each is doing its work in ministering to a certain type of mind. Birds moult their feathers because they are growing better feathers; and so in time will these same 'orthodox' believers gladly moult the opinions for which they once stood ready to fight.

"The wise man not only believes in all religions, but in all men— good, bad, ignorant, learned, the weak, the strong. He recognizes that night is as necessary as day; that all seasons are good; and that all weather is beautiful. The fierce blowing wind purifies the air, just as running water purifies itself. The winter is a preparation for summer.

"Each and every thing is part of the great whole. We are brother to the bird, the animal, the tree and the flower. Life is everywhere—even in the rocks...."

Nature made no mistakes, and even the errors of humanity were but stepping stones to a better life. A wise one neither blamed others for anything nor punished them for their blunders. Never did he enslave them, for that was to enslave himself. Influence them yes, educate them, yes, but only with their consent.

"[A sage's] life will be one long pardon; one inexhaustible pity; one infinite love, and therefore, one infinite strength."

"Anchorage is what most people pray for, when what we really need is God's great open sea," Hubbard continued. "The command, 'Sail on, and on, and on, and on!' comes only to those...in...the stage of enlightenment."

On these oceans of adventure, a sage learned to meet each swell, each surge, with equanimity; after all, what is there is there, and he has come to see and feel and know it, tempest and all.

"It is almost too much to expect that the period of insight and perfect poise should be more than transient," said Elbertus. "Yet it does exist, and there is no reason why it should not in time become a habit of life. Most free souls who have reached this state of 'cosmic consciousness,' will testify that insight came first as a thrill, and the periods then gradually extended as mastery became complete. It was a matter of growth—an evolution. Yet growth never proceeds at an even, steady pace, either in the realm of spirit or matter. There are bursts and bounds—throes and throbs—and then times of seeming inaction. But this inaction is only a gathering together of forces for the coming leap—the fallow years are just as natural, just as necessary as the years of plenty."[21]

A short space cannot capture the sweep and sensitivity of any sage, let alone the Sage of East Aurora who wrote ten thousand articles before his untimely end. Suffice it to say that so many answered Hubbard's call there is a searching for him still.

A Chicago writer said Fra Elbertus had "more near, dear, personal and loving friends than any man in America." Friends met him everywhere—in hamlet, village, town and city. At the trains they met him and saw him off; at the theatres they met him in droves. And when they came to him in thousands, in East Aurora, in the Roycroft hotel, he often greeted them at the station, even carried their bags to the inn.

That he also had enemies Hubbard admitted. He had indeed spoken of lawyers unmoved by truth, of doctors more interested in curing illness than preventing it, of churches whose creeds still imprisoned, of schools and colleges whose curricula still relished dead languages, irrelevancy, and repression. Yet even dross Hubbard strangely valued. "Repression," he wrote, "is invariably the first ingredient in the recipe for evolution."[22]

There were differences between the Fra's friends and enemies, but the differences were transient. "The friendships, for the most part, are real, substantial and lasting," he said. "They are built on positive qualities, while the enmities are a vapor that only awaits the sunshine, when it will be dissipated into nothingness."

Hate and harmony lived so far apart, Hubbard wondered if it were "worthwhile to hate anything, even sin."[23] Anyone who "indulges [hate], who feeds upon it, and hugs it to his heart," faced real danger. "Hate is a toxin: it poisons the well-springs of the soul. Its end is madness and the grave. Hate hurts most the one who hates. To be hated may be annoying," he allowed, "but to hate is a calamity."[24]

The Fra, however, was rarely too serious: he laughed hard and often, with a comic's instinct. The famous "Essay on Silence" he counted his best work, and a tastefully bound volume lay on a coffee table at Roycroft—in it, a swatch of blank pages. His critics' curses of himself Hubbard reproduced in his magazines, but he resisted answering everything. "On my barn door I find written in my absence the word 'rascal,'" he said once. "Evidently some gentleman has called, and, having forgotten his card-case, left his name."[25]

In 1907 Hubbard penned *White Hyacinths*, a book which reconciled all but the bitterest back snipers of his divorce. Like his epigrams, it could never be paraphrased, for it was a tribute to Alice: it may be the most beautiful tribute from a man to a woman in the history of the language. Three thousand letters had he written to her, and she to him. Hyacinths recalled the sorrow they shared before their wedding. The dark markings of these flowers were once construed as an exclamation of grief—the blood of Hyacinthus, a youth accidentally slain by Apollo. Richly aromatic, hyacinths flower early, in spring. The whiteness of Hubbard's variety perhaps symboled Alice's inner nature, one that had overcome grief, one in which only purity of intention remained.

"I have seen her in almost every possible exigency in life: in health, success, and high hope; in poverty, and what the world calls disgrace

The elegant and accomplished Alice Hubbard—a guiding light at Roycroft. From The Selected Writings of Elbert Hubbard.

and defeat," said the Fra. "But here I should explain that disgrace is for those who accept disgrace, and defeat consists in acknowledging it.

"She...realizes that the mother is the true teacher: that all good teachers are really spiritual mothers. She recognizes the divinity in all of God's creatures, even the lowliest. She is the magic mirror in which I see the divine.

"What she will say and what she does will be regal, right, gracious and kindly—tempered with a lenity that has come from suffering...."[26]

More than Elbert saw her character. Said a former female pupil of hers at Potsdam State Normal School, New York: "I remember Miss Moore as a very charming person with a dignified, sincere friendliness toward each member of her class, which left with you the impression she was your friend and that your progress meant much to her. She was good to look at, tall and slender, with a lovely creamy white complexion, naturally curly hair, and she always gave the impression of being very well dressed. The ambition of the young women of her classes was to be like her. She had the faculty of implanting self-esteem, often singling out individual members of the class and talking with them on general subjects as well as the work of the classroom.

Part of the wisdom of Elbertus—
his rural roots. From The Selected
Writings of Elbert Hubbard.

Dr. Stowell...head of the school, said...she did not live on the plane with ordinary mortals."[27]

At the peak of anguish over his long liaison with Alice, the Fra asked, "How can sin be sin if through it I rise to heights unguessed?"[28] The thought was no amoral justification of his acts. Hubbard saw God expressed everywhere, in everything, even sadness. And when anyone wants to see only His expression, that is all one sees. The result is acceptance, benevolent understanding, patience, and a recognition that everything works for good, at its own pace. Little wonder Hubbard was never despondent for long, never sick in his life.[29]

What did Carl and Lee Anderson see in Elbert's *Note Book*, a best seller of the 1920s? A man who touched people in a throng as if he spoke to them alone. A man with common sense enough that he could have been a farmer (indeed, he was, too,) one whose faith in the individual neared Infinity.

Like Lois Valli, Lee Anderson could recite poetry for hours, and one of her favorite poems, which she wrote into Hubbard's *Note Book*, was "You."

"Your task—to build a better world," God said.

I answered, "How? This world is such a large, vast place, so complicated now! And I so small and useless am—there's nothing I can do!"

But God in all His wisdom said, "Just build a better you!"

Lee also highlit lines in Hubbard's *Scrap Book*, a collection of apothegms the Fra loved:

Arthur Brisbane's—"No matter how well you are doing, do better."

John Altgeld's—"Two voices are calling you—one from the swamps of selfishness and force, where success means death, and the other from the hilltops of justice and progress, where even failure brings glory."[30]

In the family Bible, Lee inscribed the memorable prayer of Saint Francis: "O Lord, give me the serenity to accept what I cannot change, courage to change what must be changed, and wisdom to know the difference." This majestic petition, the prayer of the reformer, she in a gentle way set about to impress on her doubly energized husband.[31]

10 The Bargain

AN OFFER

FOR A LONG WHILE, ONLY THE UPPER LEVELS KNEW.
Besieged by dropping revenues, farmers defaulting on everything
defaultable from land contracts to water contracts and taxes, the
president of the Canadian Pacific Railroad in 1933 ordered a
complete study of the tatters of the once proud Department of
Natural Resources in Calgary. The report was a shocker—
continue the abandonment of the Western Section and prepare to
hand over the Eastern Section to the farmers.[1]

In fall 1933, George Walker, solicitor and *grise éminence* of the CP
hierarchy, nabbed Carl Anderson alone one day in Calgary, and leaked
the intent. "If you farmers were willing to take over the district," he
whispered, "you'd be surprised at the deal we'd give you."

Walker was acutely aware that of the 108,000 acres sold in the Eastern Section, only 8,000 had been paid for in full, and on the remaining 100,000 acres, payments were so anemic that tillers owed more than when they had started.[2] Now the railway had a dimmer view of its oasis. Seventy thousand acres, it reckoned, were poor, and another 150,000 acres, classified as irrigable for most of the life of the project, it now declared unirrigable.[3]

If for Walker settlers were on the brink of valuing delinquency, for Anderson they were on the brink of despair, valuing it not at all. But both knew the old order was collapsing. Walker's suggestion Anderson incubated awhile, then he went to his own UFA local in Scandia with the revolutionary idea.

"They laughed at me," he said. "So I went to Rainier, and they laughed at me in Rainier." After all, if a great corporation like the CPR could not run the project profitably, what could business-blind farmers do? As the ridicule dampened Anderson's ardor, an old man rose and said, "Let's give the kid a chance."

The meeting ended with converts, so the thirty-six-year-old kid drove back to Scandia and admonished his own. "I've been your secretary and your president, I'm shipping your livestock," he howled, "but you won't trust me here." An honest appeal, fiery as Anderson's persona, it was.

With the southern locals on side, Anderson rode into Brooks in March 1934 where railmen and pro-railway businessmen again derided him—many thought him daft; local CP men shouted "Bolshevik!"[4] Two mass meetings of hard up farmers turned him down—more concessions they wanted, not a new deal.

Taunted and reviled, Anderson reached a personal crisis. For six months, it seemed, his sole support was Lee, and even she felt the barbs of carpers. Wading against a conservative torrent, he wondered; then a family sorrow visited.

Childless, Carl and Lee had taken in an orphan girl, aged ten, after their marriage in 1928. The girl, Minnie MacNichol, had lost her parents in New Brunswick where Lee's folks had first cared for her. For six years, Minnie lived with the Andersons as daughter, but in 1933 a mysterious and painful malady struck her right leg. She spent an agonizing month in Bassano Hospital where a doctor diagnosed her erringly with tuberculosis of the bone. Her suffering deepened, and on

Brooks—capitol of the CPR's irrigation empire, Eastern Section.
NA 4389-33, GAA.

a treacherously icy Remembrance Day, 1933, the Andersons sped her to Calgary. There surgeons discovered cancer and amputated the leg in haste, at the hip.

In the children's hospital, Minnie recovered quickly, though doctors warned that the disease might have reached her lungs. Indeed, it had, and nothing could be done. The Andersons took her home, where her condition gradually worsened. Slipping quickly by March, she asked Carl one night to stay with her. That evening, he was to speak to the dubious district of his plan, but he promised Minnie to return if needed. When the call came, he cut his speech short, and hurried home. Next day, at age sixteen, Minnie died. Her death brought a flood of compassion from the community—and a deeper appreciation of her foster parents.

Shaken and vulnerable, Carl sought comfort in a higher source. "Religion, faith in God, was part of my life," he recalled, "but I admit I may not have been too sincere a Christian—until 1934."[5] After the second mass refusal, Anderson prayed. "I asked God to direct me," he wrote. "If I am doing right in trying to get the farmers to organize and take over the project, let me keep on trying. If I am doing wrong, please put obstacles in my path so I cannot succeed." It was a simple and earnest plea.

"I went to the next mass meeting with a renewed confidence," he said, "and strangely, the same group that had criticized me so before listened to me quietly, and many said I had a good idea, but they thought it was too large." Still hesitant, the farmers formed a large committee to deal with the matter.

In August 1934, the committee met with Sam Porter and George Walker in Calgary. Patiently, the railmen heard the ring of concession-seekers, and then told them they would consider Anderson's plan only. How did they know his plan? All the gawkers who resembled traveling salesmen, sitting at the back of meeting halls, it turned out, were CP spies who had breathed everything to Porter and Walker.

Thereafter, the committee adopted Anderson's stance that the farmers should assume the whole project. At another mass gathering in October, it delegated the duties of consummating a deal to a smaller circle, comprised of Anderson, Tait White, and Bill Sheldrake.[6]

The trio soon needed legal help, so with George Walker's knowledge, C.H.A. Powlett, a rail solicitor, approached them. Walker was bound for the head office in Montreal, and Powlett had not been named his replacement. Miffed, he determined to leave CP employ and to pursue private practice in Brooks. Powlett offered the farmers an intriguing proposal—he would work for free if the transfer of the district failed, but for twice the normal fee if it succeeded. The farmers agreed. The railway granted Powlett freedom to act in mid-November, and on December 1 it severed its *official* link with him.

To the delight of all, the small committee moved quickly. First it secured from Porter the operating costs, and Porter admitted a deficit—between $20,000 and $40,000 a year. Then on December 3, it hammered out a pact with Porter and his people. The agreement called for payment from the farmers of $500,000, $25,000 a year for two decades, interest free. The railway would give the district $150,000 to run the first year.[7] For a complex worth $20 million, it seemed the bargain of the epoch.[8]

A KICK IN THE STOMACH

Few were as exuberant as Bill Sheldrake, the strong-jawed farmer from Duchess who had been fighting CP men for years. A day after, Sheldrake wrote F.S. Grisdale, Alberta deputy minister of Agriculture: "The committee believing that should the present efforts result in the removal of the unbearable burden of the present contract from the occupants of these irrigated farms—they have labored in the greatest and most beneficial movement in the history of this province." He called the proposal "the most complete program of cooperation," the realization of the highest ideal of the United Farmers of Alberta. It meant "cooperative ownership and administration" of a huge block of 1.2 million acres, "cooperative distribution of water," "cooperative colonization" of unsold sectors, and "cooperative preservation of the permanent life of the project."[9]

Over Christmas and into the new year, the farmers chewed on the new deal. Some uneasiness appeared, particularly in Sheldrake's Duchess area where irrigation was more established, and some wondered aloud if the plan might be precipitous. The anxiety stemmed from several sources—the perception of some that Anderson's dynamism was impetuous, of others that the committee's understanding of vital issues was partial, of still more that half a million dollars in mid-depression could ransom King Midas. Naturally, too, local CPR minions feared for their jobs.

Hounded by dissident neighbors, Bill Sheldrake lost his verve and began to doubt. At January-end 1935, he filed a minority report which broke ranks with Anderson and White. After hard thoughts, Sheldrake now reckoned the terms of the take-over to be inconsistent with "the original intention which was to make such a bargain with the CPR that such unattractive things as 27 year contracts and 5% interest were things of the past." First priority was clear title in the hands of hurting settlers. Said he, "I am convinced that...should we sign on the dotted line with the CPR on the present basis, we have only swapped one millstone for another and in addition assumed the whole burden of responsibility."

"The Company can afford in return for taking off their hands this red ink proposition...to 1)—Make a clean gift of the project in its entirety, 2)—Make a clean gift of the $150,000 guarantee necessary to run for one year and in addition guarantee that certain large structures will not fail during the coming five years."[10]

Sheldrake's resignation shook Anderson and White, but they accepted it forthwith. "He is a radical of peculiar mentality," an irked Sam Porter informed a superior, "and some of those who seem to know him best do not appear to be greatly surprised at his reversal of

The key to irrigation in the Eastern Section—the Bassano Dam. A 10,527, PAA.

views."[11] It was too quick a judgement, and compassionless. Probably this was the great crisis in Sheldrake's life, and he was aware of the imputation of betrayal, the price, sometimes, of sensing the truth.

As for Porter, he occasionally ascribed to the railway a moral authority unwarranted—a virus that afflicted more than one CP man from time to time. Though a competent employee, he allowed Powlett to report to him and to Anderson simultaneously, and he paid Powlett for services after Powlett left the CP and while he represented the farmers.

Two days after the first deal, Porter wrote a confidential memo to secure the cooperation of William McLaws, solicitor in Bassano whom Powlett said would assist in promoting the deal. Porter authorized Powlett to make the contact, and he agreed to pay $400 (or the annual salary of some teachers that year) for McLaws's compliance. The lucre was to funnel through Powlett, who would, of course, delete his share.[12]

Porter was passably quick in offering L.C. Charlesworth of the UFA government Irrigation Council and Carl Anderson guarantees about the structural integrity of the Bassano Dam and the Brooks aqueduct. But then, as a little surreptitious post-Christmas cheer for the farmers, he told vice president W.M. Neal in Winnipeg—"I think the statement is drawn up in such a guarded way that we will never be called upon to bear any expenditures under its terms."[13]

And so it was—"I guarantee you," swore Porter to Anderson's committee, after legal advice, "that the Railway Company will be responsible for any extraordinary expenditures which may be incurred between 1st January 1935 and 31st December 1939, in remedying any defects affecting the safety of the irrigation works in the Eastern Section (and in particular the Bassano Dam) of which the Company, or its officials, *ought reasonably now to be aware....*" The last was the catch. The railway could hardly be aware in 1935 of a crack that might appear in the Bassano Dam in 1938. No one knew of any problems now, and that effectively eliminated any liability later. Of course, Anderson never knew of this little subterfuge, nor thus of all the reasons why he distrusted lawyers.

While Porter and counsel were crafting their weasel-worded warranty, Anderson and White faced opposition from a new quarter. A Contract Holders' Protective Association assembled that opposed the formation of an irrigation district on the grounds that the settlers had not been given "sufficient information of a true, definite and authoritative nature to enable them to pass judgement reasonably on the merits of the proposal." The group dreaded what Sheldrake now feared—financial bondage, not to the railway, but to the new district. Under the new arrangement, they calculated that fixed charges would be $4 an acre, an improvement of one plug nickel over the old deal.[14]

Sheldrake's replacement on the original committee was Harry Jones of Bassano who knew something about the perils of nonirrigated farming, having been tempered in the dry belt at Jenner. Led by Anderson, he and Tait White campaigned day and night. To satisfy their own doubts, they sought and secured a government audit of the CPR books, and an independent examination of the Bassano Dam. In an open letter to the *Brooks Bulletin*, they could not divulge all, they said, but they wished "to assure every contract holder that we are positive that all the figures furnished to us by the CP have been examined by competent accountants of the Government, that the larger structures of the project have also been examined and that the Government will be very sure that we and our brother farmers will be surely protected."[15] The statement caused the committee some anguish later. The truth was that the figures were *in process* of being examined, and that the examination was not nearly finished.

The government chose Hugh B. Muckleston as the "outside" assessor of the dam, who as its original designer, was scarcely free from conflict of interest. Fortunately, however, the dam was solid.

As for Powlett, he was in an interesting position. Working for Walker and instructed by Porter for years, he most likely knew the losses of the railway. If not, he certainly knew the railway wanted out. Working for Anderson's committee, he also knew most farmers wanted in. While it seemed he was taking a chance by offering to work for nothing if the deal faltered and demanding twice the fee if it succeeded, in reality, with both sides positive, the odds were long in his favor. He was, in fact, being employed by both sides, and as late as January-end 1935, he was still reporting to both groups. Anderson later said that Powlett never told the committee how much the railway wanted the deal, but if Powlett had spoken up, it would have revealed the small chance he was taking.

The railway anticipated considerable opposition from the Duke of Sutherland who had sunk perhaps a million dollars into irrigation lands. Porter felt that the Duke, who had been enticed into the area by CPR agents, would consider a farmer coup injurious to his already battered prospects. The Duke's solicitor in Calgary wanted redress and threatened to join the dissension, even to go to the legislature.

To quiet the Duke, Powlett, on behalf of Porter, connived with Sutherland's counsel to purchase the Duke's estate. Porter discussed the matter with Walker, and Walker spoke with the president of the railway. On January 30, the president approved a manoeuvre that called for payment of $54,000 through *a third party*, no doubt to disguise the railway's complicity.[16]

Meanwhile, the Contract Holders' Protective Association continued to urge caution. They believed, "that a lot of the figures advanced by the selling Committee are misleading, that complete and accurate detailed estimates of the annual cost of maintaining the system have not been advanced, that the scheme should not be rushed through with a 'hurrah'...."[17] Abetting the association were local CP loyalists, those misguided souls who pledged their fealty to a company that sought to orphan them.

On February 25, the audit reached Anderson's committee, and the triumvirate was horrified. Losses to the company, as owner of land and deliverer of water, totaled $2,123,828.21 for the past six years. Annually, they averaged between $300 thousand and $400 thousand, or ten times what Porter had stated.[18]

"I've had animals kick me in the stomach and sit me on my bottom, but I never got hurt, got the wind knocked out of me so bad as I did when I got that auditor's report," said Anderson.[19] The opposition was right, after all.

11 The Legacy

THE SUPREME MOMENT

DUMBFOUNDED AND HUMILIATED, Anderson and his committee dashed a letter to Porter, quashing the deal and demanding $400 thousand from the railway to take over the project.[1] Then, heads low, they went home.

With negotiations collapsing, George Walker, now in the Montreal head office, telegraphed Anderson's committee and requested a meeting in Calgary. The supreme moment at hand, he boarded a train heading west.

Electrified by the call, Anderson sped to Brooks and from there he and White drove a Dodge, courtesy of the CP, to Bassano to pick up Harry Jones. It was Monday morning, March 4. After Jones got in, they turned toward Calgary in a late winter deep freeze. Halfway there, Jones, almost a statue, grunted from the back seat of the limousine—"The back door of my barn closes tighter than the back door of this car."[2]

The showdown was set for afternoon.³

After the combatants were seated, Anderson opened with a tirade against Porter for concealing the horrendous losses. He was not interested where in the books, under capital charges or operating costs, the losses were placed; they were still losses. The downdressing done, Walker, now clearly in command, turned to his colleagues and said, "I guess he settled your hash!" He understood that Porter's admirable loyalty to the CPR had inclined him to less admirable obscurantism. Luckily, Anderson knew nothing of Walker's own hash in condoning the bogus Bassano Dam guarantee, or the tongue lashing would not have been as brief.

Anderson wanted $400 thousand. Walker balked.

The debate raged to and fro, Anderson against Walker, the others silent, almost mesmerized. Anderson, fiery, short fused, explosive; Walker, quieter, as most others were, but firm, intelligent.

Finally Walker offered $100 thousand. Anderson now balked. They broke for supper, replenished themselves and re-entered the fray at 8 PM. Before 9 o'clock Walker offered $200 thousand. Still Anderson refused.

The battle bore into the night, and near the witching hour, Walker offered $300 thousand. Though he had the advantage in that Anderson was not used to *sitting* that long, Walker was tiring. That, he said, was his final offer.

At this moment, Powlett, his eyes reflecting the gold ingots his fee represented (it would be $10,000!) and his stomach wound tighter than a propeller elastic, called his committee into the next room. "I know George Walker, and that's the last dollar you'll get from him," he blurted.

Anderson glared at the others. Both inclined to agree with Powlett, but Anderson wished to hold them to their demand in Brooks.

"Harry and I think we can make it," said Tait White, an honorable man, at length. "You've done a good job, but we aren't going in and outnumber you."

Anderson paced the room like a caged leopard, certain that Walker would capitulate. Then Harry spoke. "Carl, if we can't make it for $300 thousand, we can't make it for $400 thousand."

Anderson paced some more.

Finally, he said, "Okay."

He did not know that Porter, before that day, had obliquely recommended paying the whole shot.[4] So probably he was right—Walker would have given the rest. But the saving of $100 thousand did Walker some good, and the receipt of $300 thousand did the committee and the fledging irrigation district a world of good. They had acquired one of the largest irrigation projects on the continent for $300 thousand less than nothing.

More than any other single event in the history of the province, this settlement made life livable in the vast Eastern Irrigation Block. The old, insupportable contracts were trashed, and new ones were drawn up under terms more suitable to the times—$10 an acre, not $50. Operations and maintenance staff was slashed by half, and the farmers took up a lighter burden with renewed spirit.

During the takeover, Anderson had been a major actor in a long play in which all actors were necessary to the final resolution. At the time, he deemed himself in mortal conflict with a deadly enemy. Much later, he saw that without the "enemy" there would have been nothing to fight over, no Bassano Dam, no Brooks aqueduct, no canals, no reservoirs, no system. All this the railway had created and given, and hence it was a strange enemy, scarcely an enemy at all. Without Sheldrake, the hard early slogging would have been harder. Without the second thoughts of Sheldrake and of the Contract Protective Association, the truth might have been seen too late, and the farmers might have entered a new deal bitterly divided. Without Walker's selection of Anderson to lead, the settlers may never have found the necessary courage.

Every part in the drama was necessary to Anderson's gradually crystallizing and intensifying dominant motive—the creation of viable agriculture in the region. Slowly, this mission became clear. It began with a man naturally disposed as leader and with the simple petition to his Maker that he do the right thing and that obstacles appear when he was mistaken. Elbert Hubbard on his shelves professed that the obstacles *must* appear when he was mistaken. But it is one thing to err as to detail, another, as to purpose. Maybe it confused Anderson momentarily when his Maker showed him obstacles that his purpose might succeed.

The next step, every bit as important as the takeover, was to show that under the new arrangements the settlers might make a living. The transfer was an intensive labor of some twenty-four months; the next phase would take twenty years, or more.

By degrees, Anderson learned perhaps the greatest value of irrigation farming—growing feed for livestock, then marketing the livestock. The maxim was—if you don't feed, you don't farm. Under the old system, marketing was inefficient. A hog farmer, for example, hauled his hogs to Brooks, then sold to the resident drover at whatever his price, usually a dollar a hundredweight under Calgary quotes.

Convinced of the benefits of cooperative marketing, the Scandia and Rainier farmers formed the Bow Slope Shipping Association in August 1934, and Anderson was appointed manager. He selected fat lambs, cattle and hogs and sold them to the highest bidder, sight unseen by the bidder. The sale was by telephone after proper description of the stock to all prospective buyers. The animals went to Montreal, Toronto, St. Paul, Winnipeg, New Westminster and elsewhere, at Scandia and Rainier weights, less 3 percent shrink, and at prices equal to or better than Calgary prices.

Doubtless, the key in this novel adaptation was *trust*. For the plan to work, the packers had to trust Anderson as the locals did. So they tested him, and when he insisted on rigid quality and guaranteed it, they were pleased. Then they pressed him further. "One of the packers told me that if I would ship all our lambs to his firm—instead of phoning several others for bids—he would pay me a nice bonus on each car shipped, and no one would ever know it," Anderson disclosed. "It was tempting."[5]

He remembered his exuberance in spring 1930 after he borrowed $2,000 from the Royal Bank to buy sheep. The sheep cost $8, but the lambs would sell for $12 and the wool for $2. He was sure the flock would pay for itself in a year. Just then an old man turned to him and said, "You know I saw sheep like that sell in Michigan in 1905 for a dollar a piece."

"Oh, that time will never come again," Anderson retorted.

It came that fall.[6]

It took him six years to repay the debt, and he was still paying when the cozy offer from the packer appeared. He discussed the proposal with Lee.

"I don't like it," he said.

"You better not take it," she answered. "We'll get along."

So he refused.

"That was the best thing I did," he wrote years later. "The packers knew about it. I never told the farmers. But I got more business than I could handle alone, and it came from many packers." Protected by Anderson's integrity, the meat men were anxious to deal.

The problem now was how to supply the packers—how to get money to buy the livestock to eat the feed. Already gored by massive losses in the dry areas, the banks saw no wisdom in feeding, and would loan nothing for it.[7] So Anderson's association acted as a credit union with few deposits, a helper in emergencies.

"Advances were requested constantly, as soon as and often before, livestock was shipped," he said. One time a rancher flagged him down and requested a $50 deposit, a goodly sum then.

"When are you going to pay this back?" asked Anderson.

"As soon as I ship my hogs," he answered.

"When are you going to ship your hogs?"

"I don't know," the man said, "the pigs aren't born yet."

Sizing up the rancher's nature and need, like few bankers, Anderson advanced the money. In time, the loan was repaid.

All loans and advances in the dim interlude from 1934 to 1940 were repaid. Without the temporary cash help, many may not have made it. Until 1947 the Bow Slope Shipping Association worked out of Scandia and Rainier—often managing 2,500 cattle, 13,000 lambs and 15,000 hogs a year.[8]

As operations expanded, the greater resources of the banks were needed more and more, so Anderson and others pressed the province for help. Thus the Feeder Association Act was passed in 1938 enabling farmers with extra grain and hay to form associations to feed the surplus to livestock. Each association could borrow up to $100,000, and the government guaranteed up to 25 percent of any loss to the banks.

Anderson in his first year as manager of the Eastern Irrigation District, 1947. Photo courtesy of C.J. Anderson.

Hastily, the Bow Valley Feeder Association was formed, and in 1939 Anderson became supervisor. Soon, he was running four such organizations. He scoured the countryside north to Wardlow, Cessford and Hanna, and east to Hutton, Maple Creek and Tompkins, Saskatchewan, for feeder lambs to fill the orders. In the dry areas, now almost abandoned, the remaining diehards had gone into sheep to save themselves. Every two weeks, Anderson inspected the feedlots, selected fat lambs by the carload, received bids, and shipped the cargo. He and his helpers Wilson Trotter, D.K. Douglas, Bob Wigmore and Jock Sewall drove over 23,000 miles annually, often on the worst of roads.

Gradually, the funds available through the feeder agencies increased, and by the time he was done, Anderson had loaned $23 million to more than six hundred farmers.[9] In twenty-four hundred individual loans in forty years, there were just six defaulters.[10]

In 1947 Anderson was appointed manager of the Eastern Irrigation District, on the understanding that he could continue his many feed and marketing duties. On his first day in office, he learned from George Robertson, an old CP employee, that 87 percent of the ratepayers had title to their lands. As manager, he visited farmers in arrears, saw how they were farming, and encouraged them to follow the path of the feeders. At his retirement from the EID in 1964, the proportion of contractors owning their land outright was a phenomenal 99 percent.

Said Anderson, "That's what we strove for."[11]

"HERESY" AGAIN

Virtually the entire generation Anderson helped, plus half their sons and daughters, passed into spirit during his lifetime. In his eighties and nineties, his power of recollection never diminished, and his grip on a thousand transactions and many processes never slackened. Nearing one hundred years of age, he still spoke with astonishing animation and emphasis, instinctively stressing significance, moral, economic, or humorous. Nary an aspect of the livelihood of his region escaped him, down to the subtlest detail.

When pressed to reveal his inner self in these advanced years, he was self-critical sometimes, but never self-condemning. "In working with men, almost the first thing I learned was to be patient," he said. "When I became arrogant, impatient, or in a nasty hurry, I could rarely get cooperation. I had to remember to treat the others as if I were the others."[12]

He was aware of shortcomings and the struggle to limit fairly his own self-assertion. Once when he did not restrain himself, he censured the wrong person for failing to aid a farmer in purchasing some land. Learning of his error, he suffered remorse for acting "without patience or investigation." Admitted he, "I was not man enough to apologize until a long time afterward. I learned that the man I wrongly scolded was a greater gentleman than I was."[13]

It would have surprised many who saw him as a strapper of such force to know his willingness to bow to the wishes of his Maker. This disposition checked his ego and gave him humility, assurance, and balance. The prayer during the crisis with the railway he prayed the rest of his life. To this pillar of faith he added another, less a conscious request than an inner knowing and a deep joy that leapt from the knowing. It was the "happiness and contentment" he felt wherever he went, knowing he was protected "from accident, sickness or any sort of peril."[14]

These two dominating, emotion-charged thoughts—to do the right thing and to feel secure—defined his spiritual self-awareness. Guided and cared for, he needed no other help, and he achieved that enlightened self-sufficiency that has ever reached beyond the narrow, isolated ego.

True, Anderson showed his fellow settlers how agriculture might survive in a near desert, but his deeper purpose was to cultivate self-reliance in a circumstance demanding cooperation. It is no easy chore to turn people to the resources within and at the same time to cherish what they can do for others. But creating a balanced form of self-reliance soon passes beyond selfishness. In some ways, Anderson demonstrated the persistence of the central notion of Albert Truax, Nelson Burns and Elbert Hubbard, for it was likely that those who lived by the doctrine of the worthlessness of humans and their eternal separation from God might attempt less than ones who were certain of divine inspiration. It makes a difference what humanity thinks it is, what relationship it has with its Creator, and what therefore it feels it can accomplish.

For those blind to this potential, glum adversity sometimes shows the way. Anderson was aware how destitution could teach compassion, how a sense of impotence could nuture cooperation. He knew how hardship could steel the soul, help it to find itself.

When he was ninety, he asked four respected friends, all now elderly leaders in their various churches at Rolling Hills, what the Great Depression meant for people. A few became eternally embittered, they remembered, and denounced a God that had brought such loss. But they themselves, Anderson said, felt that "when circumstances make things appear that everything and everyone is against you, there is only one place to go." All asserted that "the only help they received was from God, who regardless of their different religions, gave them peace of mind and comfort and solace and confidence."

How exactly did God provide these qualities in the Depression? By drawing attention to divine laws concerning human action, or so Elbert Hubbard would have said. Spoke Anderson, not much differently, "Simply put, the Depression taught me the lesson of pleasure and value received in helping others, and that the rewards of right living are much greater than one realizes at first."[15]

DIFFERENT SPECIES OF ONE FLOCK

What Donald Albright was to the Peace in the northwest, Carl Anderson was to the EID in the southeast. Both addressed the problems of productivity and profitability, Albright more theoretically, Anderson more practically. Albright grew what could be grown in a country where many things could be grown. Anderson sold what could be grown in a country crippled without water. Albright taught how to farm in a new area, Anderson in a sector that had failed as dryland.

Both helped beyond normal measure and traveled off the ends of their respective universes to make their contribution. Both fought for better rail and road transportation and championed the farmer. Both were exhorters, indefatigable. Both valued integrity over mammon and were imbued with the high ideal of human service. Spiritually, they were of the same flock, believing that they were guided by a higher source, Albright as a maverick Burnsite and Anderson as a progressive Swedish Lutheran.

But there were differences too. Albright, like Willet Trego, was a good speaker, but the fiery dynamism of Anderson was not in him. Anderson regularly vented his emotions, Albright often held them within, the one exploding, the other imploding. And there was a thwarting element in Albright's temperament—his obsession with controlling the settlement process. Anderson directed too, but with a healthy respect for the dangers of a controlling personality. If Anderson became for a few what he disliked in the railway—too much the all-in-all for settlers—he was still more at peace with his mate and community than Albright. Strangely enough, he paid less attention to opposition, opposed it less, almost as if he were detached from it. He spent less time talking about optimism, and more being optimistic.

Albright discovered that a man at odds with the natural and multiple consequences of human choice cannot be happy, for denying that choice devalues the chooser. Albright fretted more. His focus: partly what others must do; Anderson's, mostly what *he* must do. Albright's load of responsibility was gargantuan; Anderson's, what he could assume.

In another way, Albright's interpretation of his work troubled him. If Anderson usually thought of the happiness that comes from service, Albright more frequently dwelt on the exhaustion. Even in service, consequently, he beheld a misfortune of sorts, a perception that was self-gnawing, because it underscored the price of the service, not the gift of it.

In selecting environment, do not pick one too propitious, otherwise you will plant your roses in muck, when what they demand for exercise is a little difficulty in way of a few rocks to afford anchor for roots. Genius grows only in an environment that does not fully satisfy, and the effort to better the environment and bring about better conditions is exactly the one thing that evolves genius.[16]

Fra Elbertus

He: "Gimme a box of Union matches."

She: "Whatd'ya mean, Union matches."

He: "The kind that will strike anywhere."

The Office Cat, January 15, 1927

The 11 Colliers

12 Unconscious of Their Nobility

A GROWLING MONSTER

IN THE SMALL HOURS OF JUNE 19, 1914, William Adlam inspected the mine of the Hillcrest Collieries in the Crowsnest Pass. Plodding through dark caverns, he detected gas at seven sites and fenced them off so that ventilators might clear them before the morning shift. At 6:20 AM Adlam emerged, forty minutes before 235 miners went in.[1]

As the first sun lit the Pass, the workers trudged in straggling rows uphill to the collieries. They could clearly see Bellevue, north, across the valley, where an explosion had killed twenty-nine of their kind in 1911. Or, they might view the Turtle Mountain slide, nor'west, that had flattened Frank in 1903. Both scenes lay before them in a vista of deceptive beauty.

Probably not many thought of these tragedies as they wound their way to the pits. The road in front, the night before, two wives

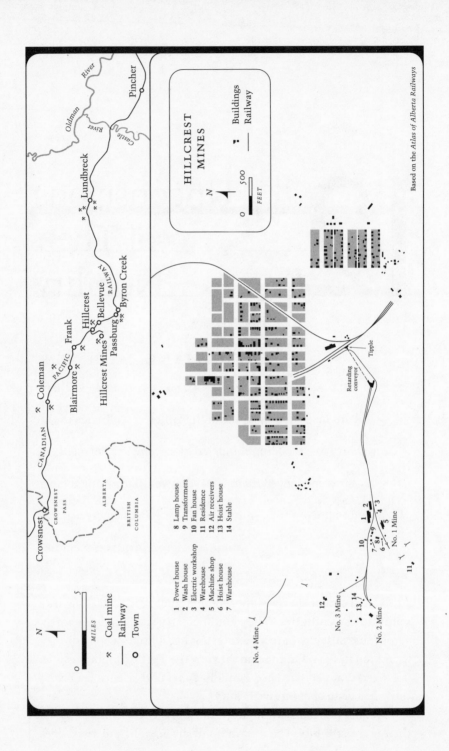

Based on the *Atlas of Alberta Railways*

HILLCREST
MINES

N

500
FEET
0

Buildings
Railway

N

0   5
MILES

⚒ Coal mine
— Railway
○ Town

Crowsnest
Coleman
Blairmore
Frank
Hillcrest
Hillcrest Mines
Passburg
Bellevue
Byron Creek
Lundbreck
Pincher

CANADIAN PACIFIC RAILWAY

BELLEVUE RAILWAY

Oldman River
Castle River

CROWSNEST PASS

ALBERTA
BRITISH COLUMBIA

1 Power house
2 Wash house
3 Electric workshop
4 Warehouse
5 Machine shop
6 Hoist house
7 Warehouse

8 Lamp house
9 Transformers
10 Fan house
11 Residence
12 Air receivers
13 Hoist house
14 Stable

Tipple
Retarding conveyor

No. 1 Mine
No. 2 Mine
No. 3 Mine
No. 4 Mine

about to give birth today or tomorrow, or maybe their workplace caught attention. The last was really two mines in one, with two separate, downward sloping drifts or shafts some six hundred feet apart, linked internally. Into the Number 2, or South level, some one hundred seventy-five men filed, while sixty more disappeared into the Number 1, North portal.[2]

At 9:30 AM a tremendous explosion perhaps sixteen hundred feet inside the South level shook the mine. The blast roared through the tunnels at typhoon speed, lifting rocks, coal, timbers, and cable cars, flinging them against walls and down corridors. Spewing from the mouth of Number 2, it projected a miner like a bullet into the cement engine-house, killing him on impact.[3] It blew another clean out of the mine, but landed him safely. Simultaneously, it ripped the roof off the engine-house. Then the violent expulsion abating, black smoke and lighter debris belched from the portal as if it were a chimney to a furnace.

Inside, men were cut down by ricocheting rocks, pelting fragments and searing heat. "It came upon us like a huge breath of coal dust, flying chunks and gas," said a survivor. "There was no report I heard. Just a dull rumble and a horrible, black, blinding, choking hurricane, the intensity of which seemed to grow every second like a huge growling monster of destruction."[4]

George Wild, A. Crawther and A. Stella were first to scramble out. Pete Dujay, working near the face of Entry 2, staggered through black soot, fell over obstacles, scrambled past two horses and three men, all finished, and got to the entry, gagging, on his last legs.[5] William Guthrie was running up toward the entrance when his foot caught in the frog of the railway tracks. Men poured past him, some seeking to help, but his foot lodged ever tighter in the grip. Mad with fear and acting on instinct, he grasped his pocketknife, slashed the boot off, and hobbled out half-shod.[6]

Outside, news flashed to Coleman, and Dr. Ross and Chief of Police Ford sped to the scene. They got there as the first miners stumbled into the air and shocked bystanders were set to rush into the mine to free the entombed. An ex-miner and survivor of the Bellevue explosion, Chief Ford prevented this folly, knowing full well the cloud of death swirling inside.[7]

Hillcrest during the disaster. A 1784, PAA.

The main gases in a coal mine were known as firedamp, in essence, methane, or swamp gas. It was odorless, colorless, tasteless and *suffocating*, a chief menace of miners and well diggers as they penetrated into the antediluvian origins of the earth.

When swamp gas exploded, it produced carbon dioxide, water and nitrogen, a trinity called afterdamp, which killed primarily by the vast, oceanic generation of CO_2, known aptly as blackdamp. Engulfed in blackdamp, a man simply lost consciousness, and the shades came down.[8] It was the afterdamp and the blackdamp that now wafted around the bewildered and disoriented miners and threatened their extinction.

Meanwhile, the government rescue car rushed from Blairmore with respirators, oxygen and other appliances.[9] A special train left Lethbridge with six doctors, five firemen and several nurses. Another special churned south from Calgary, and a third, east from Fernie. Within fifteen minutes of the explosion, the Blairmore car reached Hillcrest.

At first, rescue squads were driven back by the gases, and had to rescue themselves. One medic reached a crippled miner, and half overcome, had to return.[10] Another rescuer saw a heap of fifteen or twenty bodies, in a *mélange* with horses, rail cars, and rails. Two miners were brought out apparently alive, but gave up the ghost after an hour of resuscitation by four doctors.[11]

None of the sea of reporters converging on the stricken village ever forgot what now unfolded. Said the awed *Calgary Herald* scribe: "Stories of heroic attempts to stop and carry out friends who had been overcome only to be baffled by weakness, struck down by the suffocating gases and carried out later by rescuers are told with the simple directness and modesty of men quite unconscious of their nobility."

"Two men shall be working side by side: the one shall be taken and the other left," said the Scriptures. And so it was—one escaped and the other was "carried out a blackened lifeless form, twisted into some grotesque attitude...."[12]

Scarcely a man who made it out could have lasted another five minutes. Joe Atchison never heard the detonation, but the pain he felt. "It was just as if I had suddenly gone deaf or as if two four inch nails had been driven in my ears," he stated. "I was almost overcome by the shock and the smoke but started to run towards the mouth of No. 2. There were several working with me and they did the same as I did. A short distance ahead we came on Billie Neal; he was lying on the ground overcome. We tried to lift him and carry him along with us but by this time we were too weak with the gases. We carried him for a short distance, dragging him over a dead horse that had been killed in his tracks and then we had to drop him."

At that moment, mine Manager John Brown reversed the fans, driving air back into the mine. "The downward change of air swept the gases into our faces and despite our many struggles to get to the top we were swept backward," exclaimed Atchison. Down they went to duck the afterdamp which was lighter than air, and over and over they rolled downslope, back into the abyss. Finally they flopped into a pool of water, soaked their sleeves and sucked air through them, their nostrils at water level.

Said Atchison, "Gus Franz, a German, was about overcome and we tried to get him down near the water but he had no strength left and at last he became unconscious and we had to let him go. He was finally drowned by falling face down in the water. While we were lying at the water we could see one man not far away who had been almost cut in two."

The body count rises, Hillcrest Collieries, 1914. A 1776, PAA.

As the fan began to drive good air to them, they again attempted to escape. After a few steps, enervated and nearly gone, they slumped unconscious.

Seconds later, helping hands grasped Atchison and friends, loaded them into a mine car, and rolled them to the light. There doctors with pulmators worked on Atchison for three hours.

Finally, he stirred. "When I awoke from the horrible nightmare...I did not know what my companions were trying to do with me. I had been struggling fiercely for life up to the very second that I felt beaten and senseless in the big black death cell..." he said. His first impulse was to resume the struggle. "Not knowing what I was doing...I fought like a tiger against the friends who had saved my life...."[13]

By degrees, Atchison calmed. The life force re-entered him, and by afternoon he was helping with the bodies in the washhouse.[14]

Only four were recovered alive in the first two hours. By noon all forty-four survivors were out.[15] The rescuers, of course, continued their grim work, but now they brought out only corpses, two at a time, dressed in rough blankets. On and on they went, wrote one numbed witness, "toiling manfully back and forward to the mine like Charon's ferry boat into the dark waters of Styx."[16]

They found dead miners in every repose, some smiling, some gritting, some seemingly asleep, others in parts. The strangest was Tom Barnsley kneeling as if a sculpture, his pick upraised in his arms. "So set in the stiffness of death were the arms holding the pick," wrote one aghast reporter, "that they had to be broken before they could be crossed in the customary manner."[17]

Someone asked Manager Brown who was superintending the operation, and whose brother had been hauled out lifeless, if anyone were still alive.

"We have hopes," he replied.[18]

In town, all business halted, except for the telegraph office which had more than it could handle and where four operators coded out the disaster, received condolences and plaintive requests for information until their ears ticked and their wrists ached.

The whole town, now mostly women and children, crowded round the caregivers at the entry, surrounded by news hawks, officials, doctors, clergymen, and undertakers. If these witnesses had never seen anything to make them weep, the time had come. Eighty-six bodies were carted from the pit in the first twelve hours. Offloaded into the washhouse some yards away, they were stripped, washed with towels (so black and grimy were they), and identified. Most were known by the brass numbered checks each miner carried, but where the checks were gone, some were so disfigured and burnt that they defied identification. Wrote the *Calgary Herald* correspondent, "Wives and mothers at last found the body of a dear one among the almost unrecognizable corpses by means of signs that only love could decipher."[19]

"Women were helped out of the morgue dumb and powerless with grief with tears streaming down cheeks that were red and swollen with long weeping. The look in their eyes was one not to be forgotten by those who saw it."

Wrapped in white winding sheets, the bodies were loaded by twos into drays and carried 150 feet downhill to the miners' hall, now a gigantic morgue.[20]

Outside, the women stood or sat on the grass, their heads buried in aprons.[21] Some numb with sorrow slipped back down to the village to be alone. Said A.C. Yokome of the *Morning Albertan*, "Overcome... they sit on the verandahs of their humble cottages swaying to and fro in silent pain or moaning and sobbing in hysterical grief. For the most part the mourners are subdued in their expressions of sorrow, their agony too deep for superficial manifestation."[22]

In short order, five or six thousand spectators arrived from all points to take in the calamity.

There was no sleep that Saturday night. About 3 AM a seven-year-old approached the Coleman reporter.

"Do you think my daddy will be home by morning?"

"I hope so, my little man," the scribe replied. "But you should go home and wait till then."

"No, I'm going to the mine to find mamma."[23]

UNFATHOMABLE ANGUISH

The loss was incomprehensible. There were thirteen widows on one street in Peaceful Valley, a section of Hillcrest.[24] In the end, there would be ten times that many in the whole town. One had been married a month, two others, a week. There were four hundred fatherless children, over 90 percent under the age of eight. Two were born within hours of the calamity. Houses where young men "bached" were vacated of every occupant.[25]

Mrs. Petrie, a storekeeper, lost three sons. John B. McKinnon, reputed to be the biggest and most powerful miner in the West, was dead. At 6 foot 4 inches and 215 pounds, he was known as the Samson of the Pass. Just last Saturday at Frank he had lifted a thirty-foot piece of railway track in a demonstration.[26]

David Murray had dug his way out, found his three sons were still underground, and tore back after them, to join them in death. Almost the whole management of the mine shared in the tragedy. Super-intendent Quigley was gone, Fire Boss Tom Charles, Pit Boss Tom Taylor, too.[27]

In the miners' hall, mortician T.W. Davies of Coleman and a platoon of assistant undertakers from up and down the line faced a decade of work in seventy or eighty hours. Davies ordered caskets and coffins from Winnipeg and Calgary by the carload. Smaller shipments came from Macleod, Pincher Creek and Lethbridge. Still weak from a recent attack of pneumonia, Davies worked round the clock. In the five and a half days from Friday morning till Wednesday night, he got

The burial of eight score begins. NA 3965–70, GAA.

perhaps twenty hours of sleep. Between Sunday and Wednesday, they buried 164 victims in Hillcrest alone. Other corpses were freighted to their home towns.[28] Sunday was perhaps the largest funeral in the history of the Canadian West.

That day the Pass weather turned bad, blowing sleet and snow for the summer solstice. Hours before interment, the dead were taken in coffins down the long flight of stairs behind the miners' hall and laid out on the commons. There they were grouped by religious and fraternal designations—Roman Catholics, Presbyterians, Anglicans, Masons, Oddfellows, and Orangemen. After services in the forenoon, the coffins re-embarked aboard drays to the final resting place atop a low hill at town edge.

On that sleety, wind-swept prominence of wreaths and sobs, gravediggers had been excavating two long trenches since the day before and were still shoveling as the vanguard of the procession approached—to the somber tune and muffled drums of the "Dead March in Saul."

One woman flung herself on a coffin, a lass tugging at her skirts, a faithful dog curled round the loaded box. A man bent down before the top of another box was screwed tight and kissed a brother.[29]

It was a scene of unfathomable anguish, of magnified pain: every participant, every observer, save the children who could not quite grasp the meaning, took on the hurt of the distraught and dispossessed and impregnated everything animate and inanimate on that spot with the pangs of the deepest sorrow.

"When Grief is great enough it cuts down until it finds the very soul, and this is Agony," said Fra Elbertus. "And he who has it does not seek to share it with another, for he knows that no other human being can comprehend it—it belongs to him alone, and he is dumb. There is a dignity and sanctity and grace in suffering; it holds a chastening and purifying quality that makes a king or queen of him who has it. Only the silence of night dare look upon it, and no sympathy save God's can mitigate it."[30]

13   The Coal Spy

THAT DAMNED WORD

GRIEF ALWAYS SUMMONS SYMPATHY, and sympathy, Elbertus said, was the composite of all virtues.[1] But at first, grief may elicit only partial sympathy—impure because it selects for its love some, not all.

Almost every time a man died in a mine, someone pointed to the disproportionate sacrifice made by the salt of the earth. Fed by the sense of loss, such sentiments were among the trickles that dripped into the numerous tributaries of harsh doctrines about the relations among people and classes. The great river that flowed into the bleakness of eternal class chaos was Marxism.

There were many varieties of Marxist socialism—some sought compromise with the present system, others with different left wing brothers, and still more with no one. Amongst the myriad of conflicting, fiercely antagonistic theories, there were but two things in common—all damned material misfortune, and all claimed to be the purest descendant of their master Marx.

Some focused on economic action; others claimed only political solutions could help. Some worked through trade unions; others condemned them as the coils of the very python that held them. Some said capitalism could be reformed, others were sure it could not. A few worried about how much violence would be necessary to overthrow the bosses, most did not. One cohort thought an ethical humanitarianism would suffice; several sought revolution.

One band that turned to the latter was the Industrial Workers of the World. Launched in Chicago in 1905, the IWW presented a platform prefaced as follows: "The working class and the employing class have nothing in common. Between these two classes a struggle must go on until all the toilers come together, take possession of the earth and the machinery of production and abolish the wage system."[2]

The dominant Canadian Marxist socialist of the first decade of the century was an American, E.T. Kingsley. In Nanaimo, British Columbia, he tooled the cradle of the nation's socialism. Kingsley probably did not hate the capitalists any more than did a spate of other revolutionaries, but he expressed his anger better. So punishing a jawsmith was he, that his diatribes almost seemed beautiful, were they not so awful.

No conception of life that sets the world against itself, classes at each other's throats, first one dominating then the other, is possible without comparison with the circumstances of others, and without internalizing the loss that comparisons sooner or later yield. Kingsley had his own loss to mull over—the amputation of both legs in an industrial accident in California. As he lay in hospital, he fell to reading Marx's monumental conception of deprivation, into which his own case seemed so well to fit.

To the Socialist Party of Canada which Kingsley helped found, Marxist principles were immutable and "as absolute in their operation as the laws of gravitation or the laws which govern the growth of trees or icebergs."[3] It is one thing to believe in deprivation, quite another, to deem it law that decrees it. Most certainly, one of life's many forlorn little hopes, to Kingsley, was tinkering with capitalism so as to remove its abuses. It was impossible for trade unions to assist workers, impossible for economic tactics like strikes to better things. For these reasons, Kingsley was known as an "impossiblist," and doubtless those who confronted him thought him that.[4]

So how might the revolution come, if so much were not possible? Workers would sooner or later see the hobbles on their feet and the chains to their brutal overseers, and then they would dispossess the possessors. Kingsley's eyes rolled as he contemplated Armageddon: "the earth will tremble from the shock as slaves and masters meet in the death grapple in that supreme hour.... There will be a smell of blood in the air and the torch will light the heavens with the glare of destruction."[5]

By the time of the post-war upheavals, Kingsley's influence was waning. As if reanimated by whiffs of cordite on the wind, he beheld a world coming apart at the seams and came as close to gratitude as can men who see the world amiss. In 1917 the workers in Russia helped topple the Romanoff dynasty; then they lent their hands to the Bolsheviks who expelled the moderates. In 1918 German workers hoofed out the Kaiser. Bolshevik power rose across Europe and over the waters, and unions stopped the cogs of industry from Britain to Argentina.

On June 1, 1919, Kingsley summarized the meaning of these events in his life-long learning: "No living thing works unless it is enslaved. But just as soon as men were enslaved by Capitalism, it became necessary to invent some word to express their misery and their agony—and that damned word was W-O-R-K."[6] No man of foggy words, Kingsley got to the point, and quickly.

Now with his eyes on the homeland of the long sought Revolution, and deeply distrusting the Allied intervention, Kingsley told a Calgary gathering: "If the great Allies would only take their dirty noses out of Russia the peasants would clean up that country in a short time."[7]

With allowances for variations between how Kingsley thought the revolution should proceed and how it actually was unfolding (the "Old Man" of the party was a very doctrinaire fellow), Kingsley may actually have sensed bliss. Ere long, however, disappointment would have shrouded him again, and he would have insisted on revolution his own way. Had he sped to the palace of his longing—Russia—he would surely have been shot as a Marxist heretic by Stalin, later, though he may have starved along with twenty million peasants.

Underground at Wayne—lovelier than parts above, 1914 c.
NA 4804–5, GAA.

A ROOKERY OF MINERS

Pre-war estimates set Alberta coal reserves at over a million million tons, 87 percent of the Canadian total and 14 percent of the world's.[8] These figures were high, but reserves were still prodigious. From 1886 to 1924 almost 82 million tons of coal were mined, worth $270 million.[9] By 1918 workers and capitalists alike concurred that the industry was a centrepiece of provincial endeavor.

It was the operation of the industry they could not agree on. Led by miners, in the thirty months to July 1919, over six hundred thousand working days were lost due to strikes.[10] Squabbling mounted, violence broke out, and the province dampened the fury by establishing a Coal Commission to investigate and regulate the troubled industry.

With all their lacks, coal camps bred many who thought like E.T. Kingsley—who were certain that the solution to life's mishaps lay not within but without, not in reordering their interpretation of the world, but in reordering the world itself.

Discontent brewed everywhere, in all the major fields—the Crowsnest Pass, the Coal Branch south of Edson, Lethbridge, and

Drumheller. In Wayne, Alberta, a community including a thousand miners, not far from Drumheller, fuming slag heaps burned forever, flaring blue and purple from dusk on, poisoning the air by night and day.[11] Rows and rows of tumble-down flophouses and shacks, stood askew, chicken coops, as the men themselves called them, each coop perhaps fourteen feet square, enfencing five or six colliers. In this rookery forty men excreted into a single toilet, the rim of which crawled with pubic crabs.[12]

Water from the creek near the West Commercial Mines was bad. "If you drink a cupful you lose a day's work or two...," said W. Clapham, local union president. "I took a drink about a month ago, and it took the doctor two months to fix me up." If that suggested he was still sick, it had made him "as weak as a chicken." Dogs and horses dying in the creek had something to do with it.[13]

Frank Wheatley, a level-headed leader of the Alberta Federation of Labor, estimated it would take $2 million to sanitize the Drumheller valley.[14] Neither was he happy with his own amenities at Bankhead, near Banff. The nakedness of "fathers and sons together with their privacy exposed" he thought repulsive. Tiny lockers installed near the turn of the century were three feet high, one foot deep, and 14 inches wide. "[A man] pulls his mine clothes out, black as the ace of spades and shoves in his clean white shirt, which becomes in a day or so as black as his mine clothes," said Wheatley. The showers made the place a sauna.[15]

After the Spanish Influenza killed sixteen people at Lovett on the Coal Branch, the coal manager released two men and two teams to clean up the slum. "There was 64 wagonloads of tins alone, hauled out of the rows of houses, and from the bunkhouses," said W. Hutchinson, secretary of the Lovett local, who suspected the camp had never been cleaned since it opened. Another sweeping in August harvested ten more wagon loads.[16]

At the Cadomin Mile 22 Mine, thirty-two men were in one bunkhouse about twenty-two feet square—dirty, dusty, and unventilated, with windows nailed shut. There were just two wash basins and one water pail. A smaller bunkhouse, said J. Carberry, a miner, "has never been washed in the memory of any person there." In one two-storied bunkhouse, they could not scrub the upper story because the water would pour down through the floor onto the men below.[17]

Drumheller, scene of labor eruptions, 1916 c. A 2198, PAA.

One toilet twelve feet long, for 107 men, was used for a year. Said Carberry, "Refuse is thrown out of doors on the street, a collection of empty cans, potato peelings, ashes and slime and greasy and dirty water being the result." The well had to be abandoned, so they made do with the river, where they hacked holes in the ice in winter.

Up to one hundred fifty men lived in the boarding house. "The food is very, very bad," said Carberry. They had no potatoes for a fortnight, no sugar for a month. "We get eggs sometimes, but they're always boiled, boiled, boiled. There's no limit of time given to them. They're as hard as eggs can be boiled." The flour was polluted with coal oil, and the one cake they had was black as molasses. Carberry reckoned he had also tasted fruit in a pie once. "I couldn't swear it was fruit," he said. "I know it's yellow."[18] At least he did not have bed bugs in the hotcakes, a specialty of the Western Commercial Mines in Wayne.[19]

To complete Carberry's culinary delight there was a hole in the floor of the cookhouse where the *maître d'* slopped the swill down. "About a month or so ago in the warm weather," said Carberry, "it fairly stank there, and flies everywhere."[20]

Little wonder epidemics ran the rounds regularly—especially typhoid. A. Bryant, recording secretary of the Commerce local near

Diamond City, reported, "we get one every year, one in the spring and one in the fall." In his ten years there, he said, "I have seen as many as 80 cases of typhoid in the spring."[21]

"It's not exactly the money that counts so much, but if a man gets bad food and lodgings, there's trouble going to follow," said one miner.[22] For these and a host of other reasons, from cost of living hikes to safety and spotty, seasonal labor demands, dissatisfaction stalked the camps.

In the Drumheller valley alone, there were twenty-eight miners' strikes in 1918. When the 1919 Coal Commission asked W. Clapham of Wayne about these stoppages, he shook his head: "She was fierce. That's the worst place I ever struck for strikes, and you've got to stay with it. I've been there one year and nine months to my sorrow."[23]

THE SECRET SERVICE

By the last year of war, the United Mine Workers of America, District 18, perhaps ten thousand strong, had unionized practically every colliery in Alberta and southeastern B.C. A closed shop had eluded them, though, and in one annoying camp they were persistently denied more than a tenuous toehold. East of Wayne and south of Drumheller, the camp was J.F. (Frank) Moodie's.

Moodie was manager of the Rosedale mine, owned by the Canadian Northern Railway syndicate. To a socialist, he represented the master class and to an impossiblist, he was a master deceiver, for he had erected a model colliery of listerine spotlessness designed to maintain his bondservants by bribing them with tidy bunks and pleasant scenery.

Turning a blind eye to these facilities, the United Mine Workers resolved to bring Moodie to heel. So they seeded his operations with agitators, some visiting from union strongholds nearby, others infiltrating his workforce. At January-end 1918, plotters at the Club Cafe in Drumheller dispatched a Pole named Lien to convert Moodie's men. Moodie, however, pinioned the missionary, bound him, trundled him to the Red Deer River bridge and warned him off. Return, Lien heard, and take a horsewhipping.

Emile Usibella, head of the Star local, then resolved to complete Lien's work. As he canvassed the camp with the details of employer

Frank Moodie's pristine coal camp, Rosedale, 1914 c.
NA 2389–69, GAA.

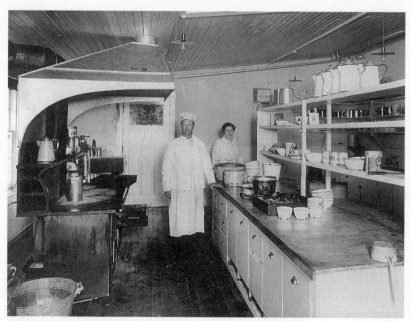

Moodie's model kitchen, Rosedale. NA 2389–51, GAA.

abuse, he stepped into the wrong house, whence a track layer and a bookkeeper loyal to Moodie took him in tow to the chief.

Moodie roped him tight for six hours, and, Usibella claimed, terrorized him and pressed a gun to his face. One provocation led to another, and in short order arsonists burnt Moodie's boiler house down and tried to incinerate his bunkhouse. A mob of three hundred pistol-packing insurgents, singing "The Red Flag," descended on Rosedale, hurling dire threats and demanding that nonunion miners quit.

Mounties hurried down and dispersed the uprising. Then Major Fitz Horrigan, commanding E Division of the Royal North West Mounted Police, wheeled a machine gun into position to defend the property.

Patience, never long in collieries, expired, and the whole United Mine Workers sub-district went out. In the interim, all interest focused on the Drumheller Opera House, jammed to the doors, where Frank Moodie was brought to trial for assaulting Emile Usibella with a deadly weapon. Through six hours of testimony the city sat agog. At the climax, Moodie was found guilty and fined $50.[24]

Chastened by what he later said was his first strike in twenty-four years of managing, Moodie wondered how it had happened. He concluded he did not know well enough his men's minds—but the remedy was at hand.[25]

At 10:20 PM, April 22, 1918, Moodie placed a clandestine telephone call to a room at the Palliser Hotel, Calgary. Answering was "Operative 3," a secret agent for the Pinkerton Detectives. Joining Moodie as a miner in disguise, the agent was instructed to find the origins of the recent strike, and to relay the temper of the colliers to Moodie.[26]

Next day, Operative 3 arrived at Rosedale. Apparently an experienced coal miner, he melted into the realm and began his diary. Almost his first informant blabbed out his every secret to date, then, in low voice, warned Operative 3 to eye his listeners carefully, because the place was crawling with Moodie snitches.[27]

A stableman said the previous strike had been caused by "jealousy" because Rosedale paid more than union scale.[28] During the disturbance, Moodie was nearly shot.[29] For some, that would have been the *pièce de résistance*, and many jubilated in Moodie's comedown. Speaking in the hall Moodie granted for the occasion, P.M.

*Frank Moodie, geologist, posing,
1919 c. NA 2389–58, GAA.*

Christophers, District Vice President of the UMWA, chortled at the "good lesson" Moodie had learned when he dropped $70 thousand during the shutdown.[30]

Ere long, Operative 3 encountered Harry Smith, the check-weighman, destined to be the principal thorn in Moodie's side for over a year. An Englishman about fifty years old, Smith despised Moodie with a passion, and Moodie knew it, though he could scarcely have divined the single-mindedness with which Smith plotted his ruin. Moodie hesitated to fire Smith because a checkweighman (who measured each man's output) normally commanded the confidence of the miners and because Smith had strong support among the many Russians and Austrians in camp. One estimate said the Anglo element at work there comprised no more than 5–6 percent.[31]

Moodie's foremen had little choice but to take on mostly union men, for miners were mostly that. A local union ruled by Smith existed, though Moodie was loathed to recognize in it even a stitch of authority, and he met its delegates as he always met his workmen, as *individuals*.

Moodie's continued resistance called up more opposition, oft at the behest of the UMWA. Hotheads, some strangers, some not, appeared at

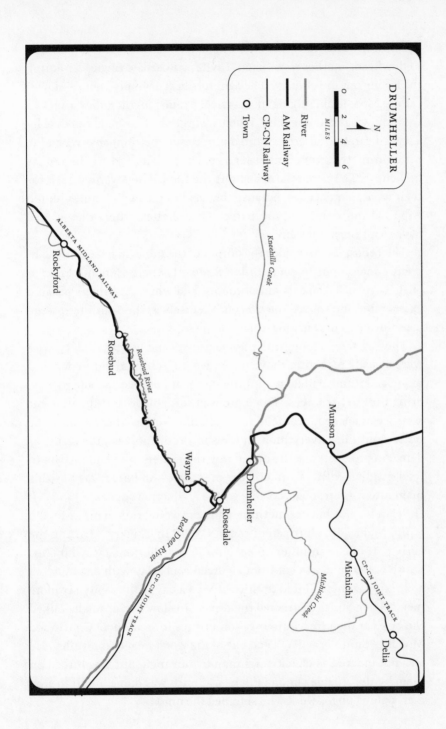

DRUMHELLER

N

MILES

0 2 4 6

River

AM Railway

CP-CN Railway

○ Town

ALBERTA MIDLAND RAILWAY

Rockyford

Rosebud

Rosebud River

Knee hills Creek

Munson

Wayne

Drumheller

Rosedale

Red Deer River

CP-CN JOINT TRACK

Michichi Creek

Michichi

CP-CN JOINT TRACK

Delia

the mine, wanting work. One had called miners out on strike at Yellowhead; another was Robert Taylor, a Rosedale ringleader during the falling out in February. The agitators began simply enough, down-calling Moodie and urging his physical expulsion, then they attacked well-known anti-union men. When a worker had his hand run over by a loaded car, the agitators wanted him to sue the company. When the pit committee proved unassertive, they clamored to change its makeup.[32] They complained about the food. They wanted cash for their work, not cheques, because they had to travel nine miles round-trip to Drumheller to find a bank—Drumheller, where they would have spent the money anyway.

They conspired to reduce the output of the mine, to force Moodie to grant concessions of every order. Suddenly there were not enough pushers to push the cars out of rooms, and when the miners became exasperated and shoved the cars out themselves, the Smithites passed a resolution to fine anyone caught doing so.[33]

They agitated amongst the horse drivers and boxcar loaders, who were already receiving above union wages, telling them to demand more, and if they failed, to quit, tie up the mine, cost Moodie money, bring him to his knees. The logic was serpentine, but it called for sacrifice of job and income in return for the workers' heaven once the union controlled everything. In the short term, at least, the plan was damaging to everyone. It rubbed raw the miners who had no cars to load, it idled colliers and box car men, but—and here was Smith's main intent—it frothed Moodie, whose production slipped.

"Can we not have something done regarding this man?" Moodie wrote Major Fitz Horrigan of the RNWMP in Calgary. "During the early part of the summer on account of instructions issued by Mr. Smith our output was cut from eighteen cars a day with one hundred and sixty-six men all told to thirteen cars a day with twenty-six more men." Then Smith instructed the drivers to slow down, and he talked the box car men into quitting, sometimes four at once. Continued Moodie, "Smith is an IWW and one of the worst men in the Valley. He was not elected as checkweighman by our men, but was forced on them by the outside Union Officials." Smith was doing his all to stop men signing up for work who shunned the union.[34]

The Operative, an American, took this trouble-mongering equably enough. After all, most of it seemed more pertinent to Moodie than to him—until one of the crabsticks mentioned the United States.

Fred Beinert, a German miner, asserted that if the United States were not "so handy," the Germans and Austrians would instigate a revolution and "clean up Canada" smartly. In this blessing, Frank Moodie would be shot, or failing that, the Moodies would be run out of camp, and along with them all English-speaking scum, especially *Yankees*. The "shooting" remark galled Frank Moodie; the Yankee remark, the spy.[35]

Beinert was probably shocked by the agent's umbrage; after all, he did not know he was speaking to a spy, and an American to boot. Operative 3 was unsympathetic—and thrashed the German thoroughly. Beinert took him to court, but succeeded only in fouling his own nest and in fingering himself for sedition.[36]

By the dog days of summer, the spy was worried. An insurrection of the workforce, so largely disloyal to Moodie, he expected "any time."[37] Smith and Taylor were seething with new epithets about Frank Moodie and his brother Kenneth, and obscenities in the several tongues of the colliers crisscrossed the airways of the mine like electrical arcs.[38]

For his part, Moodie did little to ground the disturbance. Radicals he considered beyond suffrance. And Austrians or Russians who pondered slowdowns or stoppages, he threatened with permanent unemployment, or worse, internment, in an Alberta detention camp.[39] Smith he barred from the bunkhouses.[40] When grumblers spoke up, he met them with withering flare-backs of anger, and from these tongue-lashings Smith and friends would stagger out, refocus their shell-shocked minds and return to the cold comfort of hating Moodie all the more. The next time he received a downdressing, Smith swore he would shut the mine down until Moodie apologized.[41]

At the Coal Commission hearings that year, miners' representative John Loughran told Moodie that men with grievances shrank from him, for fear of being branded Bolsheviks.

Said Loughran, "It's a matter of temperament, I think. You seem to be in a bad humour generally when those men call."

Moodie's reply minced no words. Said he, it was not always easy to keep one's equanimity when greeted as a "cocksucker," or even the fractionally more decorous "son of a bitch."[42]

THE PUTSCH

From before Armistice, a counter movement against the radicals brewed. Disgusted with Smith, a minority of miners now orchestrated his demise and that of his alien allies. Mike Scholz, friend of Fred Beinert's and a German national, no sooner stepped off the train in Calgary after quitting Rosedale than he was arrested for leaving without a permit and fined $24.50. He suspected the hand of Moodie, "that dirty skunk."[43] Tom O'Donald, the underground manager, fired a foreign driver who was loafing and cursing the miners, then Operative 3 reported another for booking off sick and going to Drumheller on a drunk.[44]

But it was Harry Smith, the kingfish, they wanted most. The charge might well be sedition, the favorite means of removing dissidents of the time. Especially in Alberta, authorities were paranoid about the "enemy within," and their fear led to more prosecutions for sedition from 1917–1919 than there had been in the previous *century* in Britain.[45]

Lo, there was evidence for yet another prosecution. Smith was holding meetings across the river in a modest $40 cabin he had erected. He read a *communiqué* from Alex Susnar of Brûlé that offered pamphlets on the Socialist revolution and Bolshevik movement in Russia for ten cents each, the contact to be Smith. This literature was banned, and its circulation, punishable by imprisonment.[46]

Smith's treachery was conveyed through channels from the spy, to Moodie, to the police. The last bided its time, then struck—but the cagey Smith was equal to the challenge. Friends in Edmonton informed him beforehand, and he speedily torched the offending heap. The officer arrived as Smith sat down to supper, looking like the cat that had swallowed the canary.[47]

But Smith had neither the time nor inclination to smile much that season. Someone else began spying on him—John Hillary, president of the local and a Moodie loyalist.[48] Several Anglos were certain Smith was overstating his work hours and allocating union funds for personal use.[49] Emboldened, the counter-revolutionaries prepared to oust him as checkweighman at the December 2nd meeting. A motion would come, and Smith would go.

On guillotine day, only half the membership showed up, mostly Smith's gang. "So," said the spy, "it was useless to try to get rid of [him]...."[50]

A week later, the contras tried again, now with a pack of twenty or more howling for Smith's skin. When the question of dumping Smith as checkweighman and financial secretary arose, the Austrians and Russians, numbering 75 percent of the total, backed Smith to a man. To complete the rout, the foreigners elected a featherhead as president. Kept by a hussy in Edmonton, the new placeman was "nothing but a pimp," grumbled the operative. "[He] has got no more idea about how to handle a meeting than some two year old boy...."[51]

Frustrated, the Moodie forces fired one of Smith's men. A delegation waited on Moodie and demanded the miner's reinstatement, upon pain of a strike. In seconds the appellants were scattered by verbal grapeshot. Yelping, they fled to Smith, who called the men out. Thus the brothers' war escalated.

Faced with a hard choice, the English-speaking members of the union withdrew, and all fifteen went to work as "scabs."[52] When Smith and company stomped back to work a day or so later, Smith was summarily deposed as checkweighman. In a fit, he ordered his lieutenant John Neuwirth into the drift to evacuate all miners at once. Out they came again, met and re-coronated Smith as checkweighman.[53]

Now the district office of the UMWA stepped in. It fancied neither internal schisms, nor the naming of ninnies as local presidents, and, influenced by the swelling ranks of returning soldiers, it resented the preponderance of foreigners among the Smithites.

Robert Levitt of the UMWA, a rescuer at the Hillcrest disaster, set matters right. The foreigners apologized for calling the Anglos scabs, the pimp president was deposed, John Hillary was reinstated, and John Neuwirth paid for his fealty to Smith with his job.[54]

Smith, however, was still in place.

One of many disagreements that autumn concerned medical care. The Smithites called for a doctor and a hospital, an agitation that struck Moodie twice—it would divest him of control of the hospital funds, and it besmirched his role as camp "physician." Though no professional medico, he had the knack of an army doctor and was instinctively comforting to the hurt. He tended to all injuries personally, even stitching men's heads and hands, and by all accounts, was an excellent first aid man.[55] Moodie told the men he could not justify a doctor at $400 a month sitting on his haunches most of the time, so none was procured.[56]

Perhaps it was too late anyway, for the Spanish Influenza was already in the valley, having arrived in Canada aboard troop ships as an afterclap of war. The flu killed more than twenty million world wide, savaging especially young adults aged twenty to forty, the same cohort the war had decimated. In Alberta, it struck 38,000, finishing 4,000.[57] At Drumheller, with a population of perhaps 2,000, there were 1,200 cases by October 17, and 59 were in graves by early November.[58]

The disease hit victims like a chop in the neck: first shivers, back throbs, and blinding headaches, then collapse. Fever tore through the body like an inferno, fanned by a barking cough. In two or three days, a turn came—either the illness subsided, or it overswept the patient's defenses, and pneumonia and other infections set in, submerging the life force. Cyanosis developed, a bluish purple discoloration of the skin, verging on black. No wonder some thought it the Black Death, again.[59]

In Drumheller, Mayor Fulton directed the defense until he fell ill, then Drs. Graham and Gibson were run off their feet. Probably Gibson had a mild dose of the disease earlier, giving him immunity for the heavy work. One druggist went down early, and the other was blasted by *The Drumheller Mail* for profiteering. A petition was couriered to Edmonton to cancel his drug dispensing privileges.

In the last week of October, the stricken died like flies. On the 28th, Moodie sent six men with tools to dig graves in Drumheller, and they buried twenty-five.[60] Train crews laid off sick, and miners fled upon hearing the toll up and down that valley of squalid hovels and hutches.

Operative 3 expected Rosedale to be spared, given its "first class sanitary condition," but Harry Smith was one of the first to fall ill.[61]

Five days later, there were twenty-eight cases in the bunkhouse, enough to keep the informer out most of the time, despite daily fumigations.[62] On November 2, only fourteen miners were able to work, of perhaps one hundred thirty, and three or four of the afflicted were very low with pneumonia. The first died two days on. By then, there were ninety cases in camp.

As of November 7, three were dead, including John McLain whom Operative 3 called "one of the company's best and most trusted employees," a man married just six weeks. Frank Moodie, along with Tom O'Donald, his inside foreman, accompanied the corpse to a Calgary cemetery.[63]

Throughout, the only caregivers at Rosedale were the Moodies who entered their ghastly ward alone and who looked after the men as their own children. It was living proof of Frank Moodie's declaration to the Coal Commission—"There's only one reason that I am at Rosedale, and that's my interest in the men there....You could not keep me there five minutes, if I was not interested in my boys there. Those boys are part of my family."[64] Whatever be said of Moodie, this act of human compassion endeared him to some forever.

In the Christmas season, a group of grateful survivors gave Moodie an Edison phonograph. "We feel that in Rosedale we were fortunate in having in our midst one who was not only able to cope with the situation but whose sympathetic nature instilled confidence where all seemed hopeless," said the gift-bringers. "We appreciate more than we can tell you your self-forgetfulness and painstaking care tendered to the many who were so mercilessly attacked by the recent dreadful plague."[65]

On December 22, the informer turned in the bootlegger from Drumheller for bringing a suitcase of hooch. The distinct lack of cheer in this pre-Christmas snitching and in his log of tales for the year finally felled the spy. On Boxing Day, the influenza pressed its hand on him, and the very next morn, Moodie, the camp medic, was staying that hand.[66]

Thus ended 1918, the final year of war in Europe.

14 The Brothers' War

DRUMHELLER CELEBRATES THE PEACE

OVER 45,000 ALBERTANS SERVED IN THE GREAT WAR,
and more than 6,100 were killed. During the bloodletting
in Europe, ethnic tensions in Canada ran high as Canadians of
German and Austrian descent were regularly hounded and
harassed, and the persecution did not end with Armistice.

By midday November 11, 1918, telegraph wires hummed with the
news of victory in Flanders. In Drumheller whistles blew, the
mayor declared a half holiday, and celebrations began. Citizens
sang hosannas and shouted hurrahs, running through the streets,
free at last from all the suffering and slaughter. They piled
flammables at the end of Main Street and strung the Kaiser in
effigy above. As dark struck, they lit torches and kindled the
makeshift faggots, and in the swirls of the Kaiser's misery, the
band trumpeted patriotic airs.

Drumheller just before Armistice festivities, 1918. P833, PAA.

But delight was soon overrun by dementia, and the masses by degrees became a mob. The mob then turned toward two Germans in town rumored to have refused to contribute to the Red Cross and the Victory Loans. Led by Tip Blaine, a burley barber, thirty-nine-year-old father of three, and E.G. Hagglund, powerful proprietor of the Reno Pool hall, one hundred jingoes rounded up aging John Teschler and Henry Cook and drove them to the Club Cafe. Cook they rode in, none too gently, on a car radiator.

That night the outcasts were forced to buy Victory Bonds. At the Club, their tormentors draped them in the Union Jack and ordered them to ascend a table and swear their deep love for the colors. They were able to stand down only after expressing their sincerest apologies for being born German.

Gangs then leapt into cars and raced out to humiliate every German in the surrounding countryside. Five carloads drove to Old Man Horner's. They knocked on the door about 9 PM. Sick with the Spanish flu, the elderly gentleman shuffled to meet the patriots. Blaine asked him to buy a Victory Bond, but Horner said he had only $68.15 in the bank. That would cover a $50 bond, replied the assailants, at least one of whom had no bond himself. Someone suggested a radiator ride for the tottering old man to loosen him up, but Blaine refused. "British fair play, boys," he said. "The old man is sick."

Half spared, the shaken Horner subscribed to a bond. Touching the flag to his lips and waving it, he revealed the whereabouts of his son.

Thirty minutes later, the humiliators arrived at a darkened door. Blaine and Hagglund roused the sleeper and marched to his bed.

"What the hell do you want?" young Horner asked.

"We're selling Victory Bonds," a patriot answered.

Horner no sooner declined than someone tore the covers off his bed and told him to get his bank book. At bedside he subscribed.

Next stop was Albert Arnold's. Arnold had been a lieutenant in the German Army before coming to Canada seven years before. The flotilla landed at his place about 11 PM. As the jackals surrounded the house, smashing windows with boulders, a whisky bottle, and even a whiffletree from a horse harness, Blaine approached the front door wrapped ceremoniously in the Union Jack. Inside, Arnold was terrified, fearing he was about to be torn to pieces. He asked what they wanted, but got no response. Blaine walked in the front door. Arnold again asked, and now heard—"We've got you now, you son-of-a-bitch!"

Bedecked in his flag, Blaine stepped across the room and opened the inner door to Arnold's refuge. He was met with a sounding, stupefying shock—a bullet square in the chest. Down he went with a groan, dying.

Outside, the jackals scattered like foul. Arnold slipped out the back door, minutes later, and fled across fields to a neighbor who drove him to Delia where he surrendered to police.

Thus Drumheller celebrated the peace in Europe.

In saner moments, both Blaine and Arnold were praised, Blaine as "a general favorite for all his rough, western manner [and] always ready with an open hand when a friend needed help"; Arnold as "a quiet, gentlemanly fellow, a good neighbor and generous friend."[1]

On January 20, 1919, Albert Arnold was tried in Calgary for murder. His attorney was A.A. McGillivray, one of the best courtroom lawyers in the nation. McGillivray heard the prosecution witnesses, cross-examined them scornfully, then startlingly allowed the jury to decide before any of his own twenty-one witnesses were called.

The jury deliberated less than a minute, and found Arnold—not guilty. "Self respect and love of one's country are good things to have," said Mr. Justice Stuart in summation, "but exaggerated self-respect may turn into insufferable egotism."[2]

A FEARFUL WORLD

There was enough egotism that year on both sides of the labor front to last a decade. In the first three months, three labor conventions, too much for unstable minds of any political persuasion, brought the working class to a fever pitch.

Operative 3 recovered from the flu in time to accompany Harry Smith to Medicine Hat for the Alberta Federation of Labor annual convention in January. En route, he encountered Alex Susnar, firebrand from Brûlé, full of bluff and bluster. Susnar told the Drumhellerites that the next time there was trouble with Moodie, they were to inform him at Brûlé, and not a stitch of work would be done until Moodie was "whipped into line." Many on that trainload of radicals equated liberty with Moodie's expulsion.

At the Hat, the convention toured local industries and discovered slight boys under the ages of fourteen or fifteen years working nine and ten hours a day for $1.50.[3] At Redcliff they saw lads eleven to sixteen toiling, also a small girl aged thirteen, daughter of a returned man. These scenes so exercised their indignation that several clamored to rush over in a body and pull the child slaves out. The whole afternoon of the second day, they plotted punishment for the errant capitalists. A committee of three was struck, all Edmonton radicals, who promptly filed a complaint against the offending glass company.[4]

Next day, a sorry superintendent of the company hurried to the tribunal, genuflected, and admitted his guilt. Many wanted his skin, especially when he implicated several union men, but Susnar took the floor and delivered, said Operative 3, an overlong address that bled the mob of its best bad blood. In the ensuing fatigue, someone mumbled that the courts might do something.[5]

A trial was forthwith set for Redcliff on January 10. At 4 PM that day, with the convention in mid-session, two envoys whisked in from Redcliff to announce that the manager of the Dominion Glass Company had pled guilty to the exploitation of child labor and was fined $5 and costs. The matter settled, the committee received the accolades of the convention.[6]

The gathering then demanded a stop to the suppression of free speech and free press instituted during the wartime fury over sedition. To back their demands, they threatened a General Strike. In this debate, Harry Smith took the podium and laid bare the sins of that "long whiskered gink," Frank Moodie. He reported the recent kindling of his revolutionary literature and the tricking of the gink and his lawman lackey. But the priceless Bolshevik tracts he could not replace due to the suppression still in force.[7]

On the last day of the convention, the delegates authorized a committee to draw up the constitution of a new political party. Its tenor, the spy could only guess, given "the rankest kind of agitators" gripping the drafting tools.[8]

Next month, the annual meeting of The United Mine Workers, even Harry Smith ranked one of the hottest in memory.[9] In March came the climax—the Western Labour Conference in Calgary—among the most cantankerous the spy ever saw, for the place swarmed with IWWs and Bolsheviks.[10] At the UMWA get-together, Harry Smith spoke briefly; at the Western Labor Convention, not at all. In fact, he missed two sessions of the latter entirely.[11]

His brief word to the mine workers revealed more of his fearful and distrusting nature. In the past decade, he had twice attended international conventions of The United Mine Workers of America. There he discovered the same discards that littered Alberta, more Moodies— except these were the international president of the union and his organizers! Said Smith in disgust, everything was railroaded through by "a machine run clique from beginning to end."[12]

One might reasonably ask what would have pleased Smith and his ilk? The specific concessions they clangored for, from six hour days to release of political prisoners, were pieces of a larger want. Their Marxism held the beginnings of wisdom, for it sought to address one of the greatest problems facing struggling humanity—how one may be bound and thus not free. To this great spiritual question, their answer was largely material. The yoke of oppression bound them, and the economic system was the oppression. Hence the simple, but terrible cure was to overturn the system.

Cashioni of Wayne professed their hope when he said the seizure and nationalization of industries would bring them "all that is in the best of life."[13] A theft would usher in happiness and peace. Oh, it was not theft, most of them averred, for workers naturally owned everything anyway, and it was not class domination they desired, but its end. Such claims were scarcely convincing. How might class domination vanish by forcefully ejecting managers and operators and by systematically dispossessing capitalists, including small time investors, some poorer than they were? How might another's distress ever purchase peace?

Harry Smith was a demonstration of why radical socialism often ends in dictatorship. What it cannot trust in those it overthrows, it often finds in the replacements, and what it finds in the new leaders is the same vast disrespect for the rank and file it said so animated the capitalists. Yet the new leaders are every bit as determined to maintain control as the old were—thus one reigning class merely supplants another. But the little man who carries them to power, despite their tiny opinion of him, should labor under no illusions. A society based on class dominance will be found in the end to be based on dominance alone. Little wonder Arthur C. von Stein called communism "the opiate of the asses."[14]

Smith was one in a school of small fry reformers who grossly misunderstood freedom. A bondservant of his own anger, a hostage to his flights of vindictiveness, he was hopelessly bound by his own emotional states, by his tortured ego. Where was freedom in disdaining the international labor bosses, the Moodie brothers, the Moodie loyalists, indeed, anyone who disagreed with him? Hatred consumes. It is a dark master that completely absorbs one who unleashes it. It grants freedom for nothing else and imprisons its creator as suffocatingly as an iron mask. Smith could never see the inevitable—that those who are filled with hatred see a fearful world, and that those who see such a world can never be free.

Revolutions never eliminate fearful minds, for even if the old order is dispersed, there is always fear it might not stay dispersed. The forceful ejection of Moodie and like operators could not bring freedom, for it must enslave the revolutionist to the perpetual overthrow of the dispossessed.

That winter, Cassioni, the fury from Wayne, paid a grudging compliment to Moodie. Hate Moodie—yes, but he liked him "better than any of the other Operators because Moodie is a fighter and a good one, and once we get [people] like that whipped into submission they make the best men to do business with."[15] How the slave would cow the master! But how far Moodie was to be broken, or how a cringing captain left without a will might respect himself and still please his overseers, the investors and now the workers, Cassioni did not explain.

It was all a pipedream. Moodie could never be defeated, nor whipped into submission; nor could he become what he was not, except voluntarily. And when he changed, if ever he did, and became more like the compassionate doctor, all the time, only the falsest of interpretations would count that as defeat.

Between Cassioni and Moodie, or Smith and Moodie, it was a case of strong men learning what it is to encounter themselves in others. Their savage exchanges were means of determining the limits of their own insistence.

MISFORTUNES MYTHICAL AND NOT

Now was the hour of these exchanges, of workers in hope that the offices of power would be divested of obstreperous operators, that investors would lay down their claims and hand over their comforts, that profiteers would cease to profit. Few groups ever feasted so ravenously on so mythical a misfortune; none ever sat at so nutritionless a repast. It is one thing to feed on a genuine personal sorrow and another to feed on someone else's sorrow that is sought after but never comes.

In a mysterious way, the pursuit of ruin for others strikes at the self of the ill-wisher, leaving him joyless and empty. "Any man who plots another's undoing is digging his own grave," said Elbert Hubbard, who took no sides in this dispute. "The hate we sow finds lodgment in our hearts, and the crop is nettles that Fate unrelentingly demands we gather."[16]

The longed-for displacement of owners, investors and managers was ill-conceived otherwise too. The radicals had no conception of the sacrifice they demanded, or of the fruits they expected, and they knew exceedingly little of investment costs or the profitability of coal mining.

By 1925 a thousand coal mines in Alberta had been opened, and two-thirds were already abandoned, at losses in the millions. Between just 1913 and 1918, 352 mines were given up.[17] Total investment by

1925 was $12 million, and a single venture, the Western Canada Coal Company, forked out $570 thousand developing its mine and another $540 thousand on a branch line to the CPR. The tipple alone of the Crow's Nest Pass Coal and Coke Company at Coal Creek, across in British Columbia, cost $196 thousand. Safe to say, the average coal digger did not appreciate such sums, and to any who did, they were astronomical.[18]

Nor did many owners appreciate these sums, or they would never have been in the business. And neither owners nor workers fully respected their dangerous vocation.

Going into an underground coal mine was like entering a volcano just cooled. If ever there was a demonstration that the earth was still moving, mountains still upthrusting, plates colliding with inconceivable pressure, a coal mine was it. It was as if a leviathan had taken a mountain in paw and crushed it, then coal magnates and miners, fools all, burrowed holes in the steaming compaction with its gas entrapments ready to burst at the slightest perforation.

This terror was the feral child of the technology of the time. Coal was needed, and it was supplied, often at cost and risk vaster by far than the coal pioneers ever anticipated.

Alberta and British Columbia coal mines, especially those of the Crowsnest Pass, were extremely dangerous. Gas levels in some were twenty times greater than in the notoriously gassy Pittsburgh mines of Pennsylvania. In others, explosive dust lay in the tunnels thirty inches deep, and rocks on the roofs hung by a thread. Responding to tremendous pressures and to human fiddling, conditions changed constantly and varied even in the same range of mines. At Hillcrest, for example, gas problems did not appear until well after the mine was developed. Dust there was finer far than in most other mines, and it held high percentages of combustibles.

After the Hillcrest disaster, the coroner's inquest criticized everyone—inspectors, companymen and miners, but not until twelve years later did George S. Rice discover the probable cause. Hillcrest had a special spark-inducing roof rock found nowhere else in North America or Europe. Most likely, a fall of that rock ignited the gas, then the coal dust.

So what was to blame for the endless train of injury and death? Very often conditions were; conditions that could never be completely corrected. The gas could be cleared, but it would reappear; dust could be controlled, but never eliminated; rockfalls could be decreased but never wholly prevented.[19]

Sometimes the miners themselves brought their own sorrow. In the hundreds of strikes in the coal fields, there were very few walk-outs over safety issues. In fact, two months after the Hillcrest disaster, when an inspector there forbade shot firing, fearing the explosion would trigger another catastrophe, *then* the men struck. Some actually preferred dangerous mines, with gas pushing behind the face—because the coal came free more easily, as if the nether regions were handing it over gladly.

You were only as safe as the stupidest man in the mine, some said. Several miners were caught with matches, and some even smoked in the drifts. Gas was so common that colliers forgot what it might do. In one case, men drove a pipe into the coal to tap escaping gas which they lit to heat their coffee.

For every thoughtless capitalist, there was a careless miner. Both stemmed from a common ancestry, as Elbertus said, though not always did it seem divine. There was little point in arguing that one and not the other was to blame for the suffering that went on underground, or that one and not the other could manage the mine more considerately. Compassion is a very individual thing, scarcely the preserve of a single class.

Still, among the workers, there were many who did care. Joe Knight, the Edmonton Hotspur, told the United Mine Workers that Bolsheviks fought to curb excesses, and whether organized labor was Bolshevik or not, it did the same—particularly in its fierce opposition to the misuse of children.[20] Unions encouraged better conditions, better security, and they dispensed the milk of human kindness to their own destitute and crippled as regularly as did the churches. Between 1906 and 1924, there were 608 fatalities in Alberta coal mines and 827 serious accidents. From 1920 to 1924, an astounding 16,477 accidents occurred of every sort.[21] Without the unions' constant succor for the fallen, there may never have been moral force enough to institute a Workman's Compensation Act. Every union had plenty to do besides strike.

In one local, at Blairmore, in 1919, four hundred men each paid 25 cents into a pot. The local then gave $40 a month to five hard-up cases—or, double its income for the purpose.[22]

In this bailiwick was a man with a wife and four children, a Briton in his forties, who had scabbed in the 1911 strike and who in a subsequent mishap was struck blind. The man had nothing to feed his family, and his doctor who had never seen them eat, appealed to the union secretary for help. Now the appeal set off a crisis of conscience among unionists. Hard by the bitter 1911 walkout, their sense of loyalty overwhelmed their pity, and they refused to help.

Later, something touched them, and relenting, they took a collection. Whence the change? Perhaps they saw more in the man than a traitor. Perhaps a higher value sprang from their already elevated notion of loyalty, or maybe loyalty itself overran the narrow confines they first placed on it. Surely there was more to goodness than the hard and fast allegiance to the order, and likely the order itself, the union at its best, summoned these higher impulses. This human affection fostered the beginnings of escape from the curse of separateness—the separateness of race, sex, age, or class, of worthies from unworthies, loved from unloved, clean from unclean. All separation, Elbertus said, was false—anyone who had been at Hillcrest knew that. Unionists called each other brother, and that was a quantum leap beyond calling no one brother. It was also a stride toward seeing brothers everywhere, even oneness.

The union movement had not quite reached this point when the Western Canada Labor Conference in Calgary extolled left wing revolutions, then proposed one itself—secession from the American Federation of Labor and The Trades and Labor Congress of Canada. Time had come for the One Big Union to set matters aright. It was this concept of oneness the workers would essay first in their attempt to secure their deepest wants.

At March-end, the district executive of the United Mine Workers voted to "fall in line" with the One Big Union. Alex Susnar made the motion and John Kent of Drumheller seconded it.[23] Newly crowned president of the UMWA was P.M. Christophers—a man of many suspicions, thought Operative 3, one forever preaching about the "Master Class" and the "Wage Slaves," one with plans for reversing the roles, making the latter slavemasters. In the red spring of 1919, the spy's earlier forecast seemed about to materialize: with the election of Christophers as president, he said, "there will be trouble all the time and lots of it as he is one of the most over-bearing and radical agitators I have seen...."[24]

No sooner did Christophers begin piping the United Mine Workers across the Great Divide to the One Big Union than he had an interesting encounter with Steve Baggelli, a district organizer. Bagelli told him that the OBU had no head, no plans, no money, no organization, that the miners would be made the goat, and Christophers, Susnar and others would ride it in the end. The comment naturally angered Christophers. But Baggelli said if it all blew up in their faces, he himself could always return to flailing a pick—which was more than Christophers could do.[25] Perhaps he was right—Christophers eventually became a member of the provincial legislature.

Meanwhile, propagandists for the OBU spread out over the coal workings of the province. At April-end, Operative 3 journeyed four miles to Wayne to attend an important meeting. Here was a great moment for coal miners, a climax in the history of labor radicalism in a town with its fill of radicals. The meeting was scheduled for 2 PM, but no one told the main inciters present, including Mrs. Knight, John Kent, Fred Beinert, and Harry Scholz about the baseball game. They tried to hold the meeting anyway, but managed an audience of just seven—the junta plus two Italians who had probably seen better games than baseball. The revolution would await the final out. Then, just twenty-five filed in.[26]

"THEM BLOODY BOLSHEVIKS"

Meanwhile, opposition to labor extremism mounted from another source—the returned soldiery. It was fed by their great dissatisfaction that Austrians and Germans were working and not Anglos, not themselves, that is. At Rosedale near January-end, there was fury over the firing of English-speaking waiters in the cookhouse and their replacement with Austrians. Rumors flew in early February that three thousand newly arrived veterans in Calgary were set to rampage through southern Alberta, tossing foreigners from jobs rightfully belonging to the preservers of the proper empire. Drumheller valley was targeted for the clean up.[27]

The motive for the purging became clear in April and May when the UMWA voted over 90 percent to join the OBU. In the Crowsnest Pass the majorities were even more sweeping, while at Rosedale, the vote was thirty-four to six in favor.[28]

On May 8, four days after the Rosedale vote, a man named Frazier was run out of Drumheller. Jack Beatty, the station agent and a veteran, informed Operative 3 that there were a couple more they were going to make "walk the plank," and Smith was one.[29]

When Smith's ally, John Neuwirth (reinstated following his dismissal) heard of the banishment, he said they would get Frazier back soon enough, and it would not be long before "us workers" turned the tables on the "dirty low down parasites." No one was ever going to run him out of camp (lest it be the union, for being five months behind in his dues).[30]

On May 24, District 18 miners struck. A handful of Anglos remained loyal to Moodie while almost all the foreigners followed Smith from the workings. The boarding house was closed to the foreign speaking element, as was the company store. Why the latter action should have surprised the Smithites is unclear, but it did, and their anger festered more.[31]

At a union meeting on June 2, Smith and Neuwirth were ordered off the property by Kenneth Moodie and a provincial policeman. Amid confusion, the radicals changed the meeting place, and fifty of them hiked out, leaving seventeen loyalists. One loyalist abused the few foreigners left, calling them "Bohunk bastards" and blaming them for all the trouble.[32]

Moving across the river to sparser accommodations, the dissidents elected Smith financial secretary and Neuwirth president of the local. There were now two unions and two sets of officers—but the loyalists held the books and the bank deposits.[33] Loyalist President Hillary refused to hand them over, and dissident President Neuwirth threatened force.[34]

The Smith-Neuwirth faction raced to the Standard Bank in Drumheller and demanded the union money, but the bank manager refused. They then directed the police to arrest Hillary, but again were refused.[35] A week later, there was another confrontation at the bank, the loyalists arriving just twenty minutes ahead of the rebels and withdrawing the funds. Smith and Neuwirth stormed in, and learning of the withdrawal, Smith, the spy said, "went up in the air like a mad bull."[36]

The empty account vexed the rebels all the way to the grocery store where they were running a bill on the strength of union funds they never had. Still spitting, they ordered two hundred pounds of potatoes, fifty pounds of sugar, a dozen boxes of macaroni, a case of canned cream, and a crate of eggs, and told the storeowner to deliver them to Neuwirth's hostel down river.[37]

Four days later, on June 20, Moodie ordered many single men and some with families to work or leave. Paralyzed, these hesitators feared the label "scab" and the retribution of Smith.[38] Before the week was out, replacements were pouring into camp, veterans. The surface gang filled rapidly and the underground crew more slowly, given its specialized nature. Under the new dispensation, no aliens would be employed, and several of them, living in company quarters, were told to vacate.[39]

As the loyalist crowd swelled, Jack Nazeroff of the rebels trod into camp and denounced the whole scabbing bunch. The Operative warned him to go easy on the word "scab" as the veterans in camp had not forgotten throttling the Bosch. Realizing he was in a den of wildcats, Nazeroff "left camp about as fast as he could walk," some judging it a run. Meanwhile, the Bolsheviks across the river were meeting all trains and intimidating all potential workers.[40]

The soldiers answered with a counter-purge. This would be, they yawked, a "clean white man's camp"—a term intended to degrade without the advantage of color. No marking distinguished this dumping ground of the despised, except on their tongues. You could not see them as different; but when they spoke in accents foul, you knew they were not white.

Two or three ex-servicemen detrained to the caterwauling of Smith, Nazeroff and others who called them scabs and sons of bitches. The servicemen hightailed it to camp and relayed the slander to their brethren. Word spread like a windstorm, and soon a horde of fifty came howling over the top and struck across the river in search of the foul-mouths who hastily departed for the ridges.

To all others on strike, the soldiers offered an ultimatum—work, or get out, in fact, be put out. In the darkening, they scoured the shacks and hoodoos for Smith, but he was too well hidden. They fanned out toward the station where they suspected he would board the midnight local, and they combed the coaches while the conductor held the train.

As the engine rolled out, Smith appeared from nowhere and raced to board. But the vigilantes saw him and swooped down.

Surcharged with visions of his own dismemberment, Smith ran for it, a stampede at his heels. Down to the river, he sprinted, dove into the brush, and disappeared.

Stifling his gasps, he lay still as the veterans pounded by, then back, criss-crossing the tangle, shouting his name with the very profanities he reserved for Moodie. Thrashing in the gloom till 2 AM, the vigilantes finally wandered home, like a pack of hounds fallen off the scent.[41]

Next day, the soldiers ordered a Belgian family loyal to Smith to be out by noon. When it was not, Kenneth Moodie asked the troops if they might wait momentarily, as Mrs. Lamburt had gone to Drumheller for a horse to help the moving. Grudgingly, the vets agreed, but they told Moodie they meant business and intended a purging. It would be best if *they* did it, not the Moodies, for there would be no mistake: after their prejudice was honored, only "good" men would be left.[42]

Within hours, a deputation waited on Kenneth Moodie and requested the turfing of Nick Winychuck, a fireman and one of the few foreigners still about and still willing to work. Not a single alien would be tolerated, regardless of leanings. Moodie acquiesced, though perhaps he and his brother had another nightmare about who was running the company.

Next, a summons was issued for Smith, likely for inciting civil disorder. It required his appearance at, of all places, Rosedale. He appeared momentarily, was remanded, and run out of camp. On the newly set date of July 16, he wisely stayed away.

During all this, the vets raided Smith's camp again, found four Austrians and gave them till sundown next day to be gone. Sunup would be late enough, they replied.[43] On the 16th the warriors assembled to watch Smith's comeuppance, but when he did not show, they made ready to cross the river and vandalize the radical camp. Said the Operative, "I had hard work to keep them from going...."[44] Having helped sow the whirlwind, the operative now stood before its gales.

The spirit of the veterans rose steadily that hot July, and as they relinquished the struggle on the Marne for another on the Red Deer, they were thankful that they had lived, that they had jobs. By the time of the Peace Holiday in Rosedale on July 19, some were even euphoric. The aptly named Charles Giddy, outside foreman, enthused that this was "one of the best times" of his life; he could not believe the difference in men until the last few days. These new sorts were no shirkers, no malingerers; they did what they were asked to do. He no longer heard, "me no savvy, me no get in box car," as "them bloody Bolsheviks" would say. Giddy was through with Bolsheviks.[45]

A week later, Smith was hauled before the courts in Drumheller. The magistrate found against him, counseled his removal, and warned him away from the Rosedale miners.[46] The judgment marked well the mood of the veterans.

Almost in anticipation, Operative 3 no sooner turned in the boozers and bootleggers at the Peace Holiday than his hand went lame and the "summer complaint" gripped his innards.[47] Apt symbols these ailments were—it was as if the feeling were gone after so many secret blows rained on friends and foes, as if his insides were churning over offenses he sensed near, still to come. Just before the great labor conference in Calgary, his teeth ached, and his mouth was swollen and bleeding.[48] He suffered another intestinal attack on Wednesday, August 6, and could not work.[49] Almost certainly the next day he was badly hurt—likely from a fall of rock from the treacherous roof in the mine.

THE EXPULSION

Two days later, the offenses came. Vigilantes began the expulsion of the OBU men early Saturday evening, August 9.

About 7 o'clock, several men approached Robert Macdonald, a Scot and resident of Drumheller for two years and a half and a worker for the ABC and Newcastle mines.

"Here's another OBU guy," someone said. "Take him away." Two vigilantes grabbed Macdonald on each side and several others shoved him into a car driven by an employee of the Standard Bank. They drove him to the horse barn of the Manitoba Mine where John O. Sullivan, Irish nationalist, secretary of the miners' local, and later Communist militant, was under guard. Shortly, other radicals arrived under escort.

One goon showed the detainees a handful of loaded shells. Another pointed above and said, "We're going to hang you up to that beam." A third grunted, "I wish we had some bombs. We'd damn soon clean out the valley."

They squeezed Macdonald into a car owned and driven by J.H. Ecklin, manager of the Bank of Commerce in Drumheller and were accompanied by William Henderson, owner of the Jewel and the

Western Gem mines. Off they sped to Munson, twelve mines west, then eight miles past. The car stopped, and a vigilante ordered, "Unload and keep on going!"

Worried about his wife who was in "a delicate condition," Macdonald instead retraced the cartracks to Drumheller. He arrived early Sunday morning to find his wife "in a state of collapse." About noon, a neighbor woman said news was out about his return. Despite the Sabbath, a mob was en route to regurgitate him again. When the wife fell into another fearful fit, Macdonald hiked to the Calgary train.

John Kent, like many of the labor radicals, was a British subject, born in Yorkshire. At 2 AM Monday morning, there was a knock at his door in Wayne. "What do you want?" he asked. No answer.

"Snatch that screen door off," someone shouted. Off it came at the hinges, then a heavy boot burst the lock.

Kent grabbed an ax and called the violators in. When they halted, he went out on the step and saw revolvers. Back he edged into the house, followed by half a dozen of the raff. He put down the ax, and they marched him out, and they stuffed him into a car, which rushed to rendezvous with three other gangs at the Veterans' Club. One of the three escorted none other than President P.M. Christophers.

A kangaroo court convened at 3:30 AM and offered Christophers a chance to explain his antics. It had patience enough to listen, but not to be convinced. When he finished, the vigilantes forced him to sign: "Here on my bended knees before God, I swear I will have nothing more to do with this movement."[50]

Rejoin the International UMWA, and find work, the court demanded, turning to Kent.

"No," Kent reacted. "I'll be driven out first."

"Give him the full penalty!" someone cried.

After breakfast, courtesy of the Great War Veterans' Association, Kent and a few others were taken toward Munson, shown a hill, and told to disappear. Kent managed a wry smile and a guard snapped, "Take that smile off your face, you son of a bitch, or I'll shoot it off."

Somehow Kent got back to Wayne, very late. But a friend warned him that another mob was after him, so he slept in a box car before sneaking home at 5 AM, then shipping out for Calgary.

The vigilantes dumped Remy Steurbaut, a Belgian in Canada for nine years, down Rockyford way. He tramped home in ten hours and caught a train for Calgary. Thomas P. Thompson, a Scot in Canada since 1911 and in Drumheller for the past three years, was in the Drumheller Cleaning and Dye Works when a posse of two hundred descended on him. Before he could move, they shoved him into an auto.

"Have you got a rope?" someone hollered.

"Yes," a brute answered.

It was a roundup, they told Thompson, like a cattle drive, save that the steers were "Scotch renegades." The main street vigilantes included a grocer, a mechanic, Justice of the Peace Sibbald, and Gibson, the ex-bank manager who had stymied Smith over the union funds.

Mine owner Henderson shook his fist at Thompson: "Thompson, I told you what would happen to you; didn't I tell you we would get you?"

Henderson was ready to slam Thompson with his cane.

"Hanging is too good for you!" spat the owner.

When they got to the bridge, someone said Thompson ought to be tossed over. Somebody offered him a last drink, and a hooligan snarled, "We should spit in it!"

On they drove and finally took Thompson's blindfold off. W.W. Maddison, real estate agent, sat in the front seat. Possibly reckoning the redundancy of his calling after a miners' Bolshevik revolution, Maddison growled, "Never come back to Drumheller or the next time we will take you out in pieces."

Thompson walked till daylight, reaching Delia at 6 AM.[51]

During this night of the long knives, Moodie was on the prowl too. Perhaps the excitement kept him from wondering if things would ever be the same again. Or perhaps he was already ruminating on his fond hopes years before when he erected his model camp that was to end all worker squalor and discontent. As the night finished, he had the grim satisfaction of knowing that some "citizens'" squad or other had rounded up Harry Smith, his enemy, in the early hours, and thrown him out.[52]

There is nothing so savage,
cruel and blindly unjust
as class hatred.

We believe things first and
look for proof later; and when
the idea is once fixed in a
man's mind that someone is
his enemy, reasons light as air
are to him confirmation
strong as holy writ. The
individual who thinks he is
hated, will be hated, in fact,
very shortly.[53]

Fra Elbertus

"Uneasy lies the head that
wears a frown."

The Office Cat, October 4, 1926

15 The Cat's Antidote

A VERSE FOR ALL

ON WORD OF THE VIGILANTES IN THE DRUMHELLER VALLEY, perhaps most people felt the radicals had received their fairing. Work stoppages were so recurrent and high coal prices so vexing that there was little to do but laugh. The Office Cat discounted the experts' caution that the world's coal supply was limited—it would last much longer than thought—thanks to the millions of strikes in future.[1]

As for the other annoyance, penned the feline:

Mary had a ton of coal
She worked ten years to earn it.
She froze to death the other day,
She couldn't bear to burn it.[2]

In the interwar years, nothing escaped the sharp eye of The Office Cat. It seemed he had a special word for everyone:

For *Albert Truax, Nelson Burns and the Burnsites*—"Outside of the fact that we are bossed by tradition, enslaved by doctrine and ruled by habit, we are a free and glorious people."[3]

Of *Dr. Mary Percy Jackson*—"If you believe slavery is dead, ask some popular doctor."[4]

Of *the Sunset Prairie settlers*—"Poverty may be a blessing in disguise, but the disguise is perfect."[5]

For *Donald Albright*—"After one has done the best he can, he commits a crime against himself to worry over the future."[6]

For *wilting drybelters*—"Don't worry about the hot weather; you may not live through the whole summer."[7]

For *farmers everywhere*—"A mortgage isn't so bad. It's nice to have something on the premises the neighbors can't borrow."[8]

Of *Lois Valli*—"To be thrown upon one's own resources is to be cast in the very lap of fortune."[9]

Of *Willet Trego*—
  Let poets sing their lilting songs
  And gaily strum the lyre;
  Give me the man who whistles while
  He's putting on a tire.[10]

For *irrigationists and the CPR*—"Little drops of water on little grains of sand make a hellava difference in the price of land."[11]

Of *Carl Anderson*—"Character is not made in a crisis. It is only exhibited."[12]

Of Lee Anderson—"Happiness is a perfume which you cannot give to others without spilling a few drops on yourself."[13]

For those fighting a class war—"Many men who talk glibly of labor and capital never did the one nor had the other."[14]

For Bolsheviks in the 1930s—"If everybody loses interest in making money, there soon won't be anyone from whom to take the wherewithal to divide up among those who are depending on this source for their income."[15]

THE JESTER

"The Office Cat" was one of the longest running and best known humor columns in the history of the Canadian press—appearing almost daily in the *Medicine Hat News* from 1921 to 1951. No one knows who the Cat was; no more than a handful ever knew. Surely A.J.N. Terrill knew, for he was editor and manager of the paper almost the whole time the Cat appeared.

Some opined that the column was syndicated, but it never bore such acknowledgement. In its first few years, it actively solicited humor from subscribers and readers, and it credited local wits and wags, such as Tiny Ratliff, Bill Cousins, Doc Gershaw, Doc McEwen, Lorne Laidlaw, and M.A. Brown. Where these lights got their quips, who can tell? Perhaps they read as widely as Alf Terrill whose messy desk was heaped high with American news dispatches.

Almost certainly Terrill himself concocted hundreds of witticisms. He was a poet, and the Cat wrote limericks. He was an observer of life, and the Cat was a peeping Tom. He was a philosopher who reveled in the truths of familiar quotations, and the Cat was a contrarian who distorted old maxims and did not lie.

Born in 1869 at Hamilton, Ontario, Alf Terrill was descended from British Empire Loyalists. One grandfather was a pioneer educator for the deaf and dumb, and all his offspring instructed this disadvantaged group.

Terrill went to Ontario College, worked briefly for the Grand Trunk Railroad, and then journeyed to Maryland where he learned the news-

The Office Cat inimitable—
Alf Terrill. Photo courtesy of
Patricia Jones.

paper trade from an uncle. Over the next years, he worked for the
Baltimore Herald, the *Toronto World*, the *Peterborough Examiner*, the
Barrie Advance and the *St. Catharines Journal*. In 1904 he came to
Medicine Hat to work with Fred Forster of the *News*, and seven years
later he became editor.

Quiet and kindly, Terrill was little given to demeaning sentiments. [16]
He was a liberal seeking fulfilling freedom, but his column was a long-
standing comment on constraint. And constraint to him meant the
controllers and the dictators of his era—especially the forces of reaction to demon rum and damsel flapper.

GOMORRAH

Prohibition ran in Alberta from 1916 to 1923, and in the United States,
from 1920 to 1933. It swept through in a blaze of moral and social
reform, and for a time the zeal of the Purity Leaguers, the gospellers of
uplift, and the last of the Templars of Temperance fed on itself. It
demanded sacrifice, but during the Great War such demand was in
good company. As life after life was extinquished in France, the
surrender of social comfort in Canada, minute by minute, seemed both
appropriate and inconsequential. At least so the average person

deemed it a while, for it was an epoch when the Creator and Eternity occupied more time than usual.

A leader of the prohibition movement in Alberta was the Social Service League. Crammed with archdeacons and canons and reverends—all too anxious and unready for the Millenium—the League published *The Searchlight*, a purity probe for the times. Secretary H.H. Hull worked hand in glove with the Alberta Provincial Police. He would unload complaints, the police would act, and Hull would forward felicitations to police bigwigs to cite in reports.[17] Liberal Attorney General Mitchell even issued a grant to the League for "special detective work," and with a few more shekels and the slightest urging, the organization would have conducted liquor prosecutions and public scourgings itself.[18]

Immediately after the dry victory, teetotalers and anti-topers rushed to the service of the new state, like a White Guard bent on enforcing the new morality. Stool pigeons and stooges materialized over night, informing the provincial police of any and all infractions. Invariably they combined great virtues with deadly faults—sincerity with intolerance and fortitude with foolishness—combinations all too common in the moral history of the culture. In the end, the essence of their exuberance was excess.

Typical of temperance zealots who cooperated with the attorney-general's department was the aptly named Inspector W.F. Gold. Shunting from point to point, he reported booze infractions here, misdemeanors there, and indiscretions everywhere. Once he implicated a Calgary detective who allegedly procured grog under the name of Fluke McLuke, dranks quarts of it, and bootlegged the rest. Another time he reported the intoxication of firefighters in the mountains near Coleman. No one escaped his gaze—there were two brothers in a gang of youthful inebriates at High River "reputed to never see a sober day," sluts who detrained regularly at the Lloydminster Alberta Hotel, a Crowsnest Pass blacksmith who kept a drink in his closet, a shoemaker who swore a lot.[19]

Gold had just identified the Gomorrah of Alberta—Alderson, in the southeast. There a lowlife named Brown ran a "vile restaurant" packed with booze, gamesters and whores. "On Saturday last," Gold disclosed in July 1917, "for my personal honor as I happened to be in

town, they celebrated by having five men drunk. It was a manifestation of their bravado." Brown answered a recent fine by extending his
hours—and the good citizens of the burg were now losing sleep.

The shenanigans were too much for the Reeve and councillors who
petitioned Gold to unleash the Liquor Department on the libertines.
But no one could stop Brown and his supporting cast which included a
fake waitress and a fake coiffeur who showed their real skills in the
backroom. In the end, Brown, like everyone else in town, was a victim
of drought. With complete crop failure that year after the bonanzas of
1915–16, money vaporized and the "sporting" element was first to
vacate. Obviously no geographer, Brown left for Lomond where money
and crops were just as short.[20]

Fixated on moral conditions, Gold, meantime, raced to Retlaw—
and rumors of new and worse depravity.

But where lay The Office Cat's sympathies in all this? Frankly, a
chocolate hue dulled his lustre; a part of him damned rules, regula-
tions and restraint. A little license, he pleaded, even a single caper:

I've often been told that to dance is a sin;
That I'd have to eschew it if heaven I'd win;
That smoking is wicked and drinking is worse;
That the Devil himself owns the man who will curse;
Now in view of these warnings I've led a good life;
Only one girl I've kissed and she is my wife.
Things sinful and wicked, I never have done—
Let me warn you right now
I ain't had much fun.[21]

Even saints fancied fun. Had not Saint Augustine himself prayed—
"Oh Lord, give me chastity and continence—but not yet"?

So the Cat began his romp with a recipe for home brew:

Chase a bull frog three miles and gather up the hops. To the hops
add the following: Ten gallons bedbug poison, one quart of axle
grease, one bar homemade soap. Boil mixture thirty-six hours, then
strain through an IWW sock to keep it from working, and add one
grasshopper to each pint to give it the kick.[22]

Soon bootlegging and boozing became a national pastime:

Helen's in the kitchen
Washing out the bottles;
Paul's in the pantry
Taking off the labels;
Ruben's in the cellar
Mixing up the hops;
Johnny's on the front porch
Watching for the cops.[23]

Four and twenty Yankees
Very very dry,
Journeyed up to Canada
To get a case of rye.
When the rye was opened
They all began to sing,
"Who the hell is Harding,
God save the King!"[24]

Enforcement of prohibition was futile, despite the pains police took. In 1920 three or four men in the Alberta Liquor Branch were badly doped and nearly killed. Next year, two officers were made wretchedly ill by the poisonous brew they drank for evidence. Once, the force was alerted to a shipment along Calgary Trail and had to patrol for five days to effect a capture. Near a deserted farm, constables waited in a comfortless ravine for two weeks, hoping to capture a moonshiner and his illicit still. They were sucked nearly dry by mosquitoes, and after the arrest, one officer was laid up another fortnight with puff ball welts for a face. Near Gainford, men watched a vacant mine for a week before the offender was nabbed. At Onoway, five constables surrounding a suspect's farm nearly froze to death as the temperature dipped out of sight four nights straight. Near Lethbridge, another officer on duty contracted double pneumonia.[25]

The main problem was massive and growing opposition. "My experience," wrote the Lethbridge Alberta Police inspector in 1918, "is that people who never turned a crooked hair in their lives are bootleggers, gamblers, wife beaters and even worse things today."[26] The mayor of Coleman was found handling liquor and convicted. The Chief of Police at St. Albert was fined for having booze in his hotel, and his counterpart at Wetaskiwin was debited for being drunk and pummelling a respectable citizen at the railway station.[27] Both kept their jobs.

Half the populace subverted the Liquor Act: it seemed the women favored prohibition, the men opposed it.[28] "We have had complaints from people about the 'terrible conditions' that exist in their town, and when we have investigated the complaint and caught the offenders, the whole town was up in arms, wanting to hang, draw and quarter the detectives who were responsible," moaned Sergeant Stott, chief of the Liquor Branch.[29] Local magistrates had taken to censuring constables before the courts. In one place, opposition was so great, a crooked Justice of the Peace actually helped frame two operatives, laid charges and arrested one. At Chauvin, after securing evidence regarding the sale of hooch, agents were bombarded with stones and other missiles.[30]

Moral anarchy now held the field, and like moral autocracy, it ended badly, soon enough:

Mary had a little jug
She corked it up too soon;
The stuff inside began to work
And started toward the moon.[31]

"Remember the days when we used to worry about the boys being blown up in the trenches?" asked the Cat. "Now we worry about them being blown up in the cellars."[32]

Prohibition epitaphs grew common:

Under this bank
Lies Harry Stiff.
He swallowed a tank
Of homemade quiff.[33]

Under the sod
Lies Deacon Hale.

He winked and drank
Some "Ginger Ale."[34]

There was a young rounder named Lou
Who made up a batch of home brew.
He took a wee nip,
Just a moderate sip,
Funeral—Tuesday at two.[35]

Meanwhile, prescriptologists, called doctors, dished out alcoholic prescriptions for every ailment under the skies, from leprosy to liver flukes. Just two physicians, one from British Columbia, another from Manitoba, racked up an unbelievable ten thousand orders for booze in a single month![36] In Alberta some doctors sold prescriptions in bulk to druggists who simply filled in the name of anyone who wanted a bottle. Petty clerks no sooner opened a drug store than they were rich enough to retire.[37]

But not all profited, the Cat saw:

Here lies the body of Frederick LeFarge,
His death is too sad for description.
He was killed by a mob in a terrible charge
When he carelessly dropped his prescription.[38]

The limerick was in fun, but by 1922 the Liquor Branch was in shambles. Three of the seventeen men were fined for disobeying instructions, and another five were discharged for disorderly conduct.[39] That fall a policeman was shot in Coleman, and in spring, Emil Picariello, bootlegger, and Florence Lassandro, a passenger in the death car, were hanged at Fort Saskatchewan. Almost any defence would have saved Lassandro, but then almost any legislative sanity in the beginning would have saved her, and others, too. With prohibition ending that year in Alberta, the sanity arrived, late.

"Prohibition is now working smoothly," the Cat concluded, peering now at the American fiasco. "The only thing left is to stop the sale of liquor."[40]

REFORMERS AND FLAPPERS

In these years, the Cat maintained a running battle with moral reformers bent on restraining libertarians and everyone else.

Many reformers, not all, are such because they need to grapple with their own intolerance. Their minds are darkened with absolutism, their own authority is over-extended, their sense of responsibility, over-stretched. The inevitable result of accepting too much responsibility is martyrdom. Completely unable to be responsible for everyone else, these renewers seek to impose their morality for the good of all, and when they fail, as fail they must over time, they deem themselves martyrs to a cause renounced by an unthinking and insensitive rabble.

Many reformers evince a disdain for individual choice—*their* choice is all right, even God-inspired, but that of others is so error-ridden that it ought to be abrogated entirely.

"Hell is full of professional reformers," a minister declared. "We regret to hear this," lamented the Cat, "for we were hoping there was room for many more."[41]

All reformers were "tyrants in false whiskers," and most "wore rubber boots and stood on glass when God sent a current of Commonsense through the Universe," affirmed Hubbard.[42]

Of course, Elbertus and the Cat were reformers too—but with a difference. Neither *insisted* on reform, nor believed that human law would cinch it. "*Natural* law" would, said Hubbard, and he meant that we naturally discover the fruits of our action, and green fruits beget stomach cramps, and cramps beget different diets.

Natural law would take care of the flapper revolution too. Women of the 1890s were cosseted and corseted, covered from neck to ankle, voiceless politically, reserved socially. The new generation shortened their skirts over a foot, donned silk hose, bared their backs and bobbed their hair. From old confines they broke out, like captives of some dark cave.

Both Elbertus and the Cat instinctively opposed any form of caste. Alf Terrill's attitude toward women was best seen in August 1922 when he noted a Belgian beauty contest in which an eighty-year-old white-haired mother of five was crowned. Opposing the common view that beauty was the preserve of the young, Terrill boldly asserted, "There is nothing strange, nothing unusual, in eighty-year-old beauty.

The glory of whitened hair, the strength of gentle lines, the serenity of kindly eyes, the benediction of a happy countenance—there is beauty, for true beauty must have character."[43]

The strength grew from facing adversity; the kindness, from seeing sorrow; the benediction, from surmounting disappointment; the character, from standing against the current.

Now, the Cat, somewhat waywardly, did notice more than character in a flapper.

"I'd just as soon see a girl dress in public as powder her face," grunted a reformer.

"So would I," said the Cat.[44]

A yard of silk, a yard of lace,
A wisp of tulle, to give it grace;
A flower placed where flowers go;
The skirt knee-high, the back waist-low;
One shoulder strap, no sign of sleeve,
If she should cough—good morning, Eve.[45]

"A woman dancing the Charleston broke her leg," the Cat announced, "but probably nobody noticed any difference in her dancing."[46]

Poor girl, "she was pure as snow—but she drifted." [47]

There had been some bad drifting in earlier winters, too, the Cat had heard. Still, it seemed that "Members of the younger generation [were] all alike in many disrespects."[48]

CATNIP

But every notion of disrespect was by no means bad. There was in the Cat's heart a curious opposition to moral dictation even by time-honored precept, or long-lived maxim. Like Nelson Burns, he wished to overstep dogma, and like Elbert Hubbard, he wanted people to think for themselves. It was not that the old saws were false, but that they were so cut and dried, solidified in stone, that they were as limiting as the moral reformers. The maxims were like creeds—mind closing, fossilized truth. They were pre-shaped and inflexible, and it was always easy to mistake them for the end of truth rather than the beginning.

When left with fewer and fewer local submissions, and more and more to his own devices, Terrill invented the term "Cat-grams" which were like Robert Quillen's "paragrams," published in the *Edmonton Journal* in the early twenties. "Cat-grams" or "paragrams" were paragraphs compressed into a single salty sentence. Alternatively, they could be epigrams turned upon themselves, rather like reversed maxims, or old saws with new edges.

Some examples:

Absence makes the heart grow fonder—of more absence.[49]

Beauty skins deep.[50]

A thing of duty is a bore forever.[51]

When spinsterhood is bliss 'tis folly to be wives.[52]

Hell hath no fury like a woman's corns.[53]

To the lady who wears short skirts: As she shows, so shall we peep.[54]

Whatsoever a man sews that also shall he rip.[55]

He who hesitates is bossed![56]

All work and no pay makes Jack a school teacher.[57]

Where there's a still, there's a sway.[58]

Jug not that ye be not jugged.[59]

You can lead an ass to college, but you can't keep him from drinking.[60]

New edges on old saws: many were novel formulations created by the interplay of the new experience with the old wisdom. Habit, the Cat knew, was not necessarily sacred. Some conventions were inane, some observances of custom, retarding, some traditions, insipid.

The Office Cat began a thirty-year run in mid-March 1921 when worry and despair sought the balm of laughter.

For the city of Medicine Hat, the previous decade had fallen flat. At the peak of the 1912–13 boom, Mayor Nelson Spencer predicted a population of twenty-five to forty thousand in a year. The June 1915 census lacked some—at eight-plus thousand. By then the city had utilities for four times its population. With three hundred vacant buildings, perhaps four hundred men unemployed, and at year-end, $400 thousand in tax arrears and a whopping $3.7 million debt, a movement began to stop paying taxes and let the city go bankrupt.

Mayor Archie Hawthorne agonized as he surveyed the industrial core in late 1915—a dozen major industries, including the Potteries, the Crayon plant, the Tent and Mattress Company, the Sanitary Fountain Company—were all dead. The Woolen Mills lay in ruins, and the glass bottle plant was now a stable.[61]

Surrounding the city, the dryland empire agonized too, as brute nature wrested the fields from farmers.

Throughout, the Cat and the strong resisted defeat.

A stranger drove up to a hot and dusty farmer and his young son.

"Looks as though we might have rain," he said.

"Well, I hope so," said the farmer, "not so much for myself as for my boy here. I've seen rain."[62]

One day Lois Valli met a rancher from the parchment north of the Red Deer River.

"Did you get any rain, Louis?" she asked.

"Yes, we had a four inch rain," he answered. "One drop here, and another four inches away."[63]

A gale was blowing out Alderson way when a farmer went for a loan on his property. The banker said, "I'd kinda' like to see your land."

Just then a big gust hit the bank, and the farmer answered, "Well, open up your window, 'cuz here she comes!"[64]

Neil Rutherford of Bowell remembered a commission, possibly in 1919, sent from Ottawa to value the dry land. It asked his Uncle Bob who said—"Twenty cents an acre."

The commissioners laughed and left. Twenty years later, in the thirties, the chairman returned, hunted up Uncle Bob, and declared, "You were just twenty cents too high on that land!"

About 1980, a woman from Medicine Hat interviewed Neil and asked about seeding.

"I put a crop in in '41," he answered, "and it hasn't come up yet—and I'm not putting another one in until it does come up!"[65]

Moaned the Cat:

His horse went dead and his mule went lame;
He lost his cows in a poker game;
Then a cyclone came on a summer's day
And blew his house and barn away.
An earthquake came when they were gone,
And swallowed the ground the house was on;
The tax collector then came 'round;
And charged him for the hole in the ground.[66]

Mumbled the feline: "It's some consolation to find yourself at the bottom of the ladder when it breaks."[67]

A sense of humor is a measure of human resilience. Those who can laugh at themselves are armor-plated, protected from the folly of taking themselves too seriously. Anxiety and despair are soluble in laughter. Humor is attracted to the poles of human experience—from delusions of grandeur to delusions of insignificance. And it has the power to destroy either.

The general downswing of the Great Depression brought more calamity to Saskatchewan and Alberta where the slide in per capita income was the worst in the country.[68] Between 1931 and 1941, a quarter of a million people left the Prairies for good.[69]

The politics of agriculture world-wide boggled the mind. To prop up prices, nation after nation reduced acreage and output and butchered oversupplies of livestock in a killing frenzy. Americans plowed under ten million acres of cotton in August 1933 alone; the next month they slaughtered six million little pigs. By year-end 1933, Brazilians had destroyed twenty-two million bags of coffee. Danes burnt five thousand cattle carcasses a week, and in one span New Zealanders drove fifty thousand lambs into the sea.[70]

"The first essential in doctoring a depression," the Tom proclaimed in 1933, "is to overcome the patient's conviction that he is going to die."[71] "The secret of success," he snorted, "is a secret to many people."[72]

But in the end, not to him. The key was *self-possession*—in the face of woe. And the struggle for this sublime control of self and ultimately respect for self involved bouts of pessimism verging on despair. Mostly in the depths of the Great Depression, the Cat penciled the following:

> "Colleges now prepare youngsters for everything except the obscurity and poverty that most of them will get."[73]

> "Most of the people who keep on expecting the worst fail utterly to grasp the significance of the present."[74]

> "The fewer ambitions you have the fewer disappointments you'll have over failure to realize them."[75]

> "Maybe a laugh is good for what ails us, but alas! What ails us isn't good for a laugh."[76]

By steps, these spiritless lines were warmed by a realization that there was something comical in ruin itself, or perhaps better, in the *appearance* of ruin. The world might be rotten, and the rotten might survive, but so much rottenness births a smile. So much thwarting does too.

> "There's nothing perfect in this world, unless it be some nuisances."[77]

> "Another potent aid to longevity seems to be worthlessness."[78]

> "The reason why we believe in the bromide, 'The Good Die Young,' is because the only chance any of us have to die good is to die young."[79]

> "Observance of all the health rules would probably cause us to live longer than we could afford."[80]

The Cat represented both sides of the post-war conflict about the meaning of life, but in the end he sided with an old, old position. He was not narcissistic, not nihilistic, infrequently cynical, occasionally disillusioned, but most often hopeful and certain of the power within.

After twenty years of thought, the Cat ranked as no futilitarian. For him, humanity was not imprisoned on some dim and dank planet careening chaotically through a meaningless and disordered universe. It was free, and the full flowering of *true* freedom was its purpose, freedom guided by service, acceptance and love. Spoke the Cat inspired, "The freest of all human beings is he who gives most, loves most, forgives most, endures most, thinks most, and scatters his influence as the farmer does his seed, in good soil. A man is very free when he makes others feel free about him."[81] It was forever true: "the person who has complete control of his own conduct doesn't try to control that of others."[82]

So minded and braced with saving humor, sons or daughters of the Depression might face poverty and adversity with confidence.

One other element to self-possession existed: the Cat was refreshingly self-depreciatory. Very early on, he defined an editor as "one whose business it is to separate the wheat from the chaff and then print the chaff."[83]

Every period of socioeconomic turmoil requires a psychological stabilizer, like a mind-gyro, to maintain the emotional equilibrium of the strained and the suffering. It is said that humor is the divine antidote for the exaltation of the ego, but it is every bit as much the divine antidote for the destitution of the self.

To Elbertus, the real self could never be made destitute; only an absurdly false and flimsy self could, one molded of littleness and fear.

Cold circumstance, he knew, had the power to brutalize only one uncertain of himself—and that was as true of the common run of humanity as it was of its saints.

Why is there laughter in an existence that none of us laughs at? Why is there mirth in a world of struggle and precarious chances? Prosperpina is the goddess of death, and no one has been found stronger than she— except Momus, the god of laughter, whom Proserpina cannot slay. Laughter is no accident. It is something rooted in the depths of our being. Pain is deeper than all thought; laughter is higher than all pain.[84]

Fra Elbertus

"A joke a day will keep
the alienist away."

The Office Cat, November 26, 1925

The Saint

16 Father Louis

ANOTHER MOSES

IN THE SOUTH OF FRANCE, the old priest was regaling
young Louis Culerier and another with tales of his days with the
renowned Bishop Vital-Justin Grandin in the wilderness of the
North-West Territories of far off Canada.

"Who knows, said Léger, "maybe one of you will be a
missionary."

Forthwith, an answer shot into Culerier's ear, and he alone
heard—"Yes."[1]

Born in Soulitre, France, on September 22, 1873, Louis Culerier
was won to the order of the Oblates of Mary Immaculate by the
same Grandin, touring France, enlisting support for his missions.

At Lachine, Quebec, Culerier entered the novitiate in 1893 and
was ordained in Ottawa four years on. He first served at St. Albert,
North-West Territories, in 1898, and by century-end, he had
pastored at Leduc, Calgary, Cochrane, Canmore, Pincher Creek
and Fort Macleod. Then his great patron, Grandin, entrusted him

with the administration of the new seminary in St. Albert from 1900 to 1905.

Later, Culerier was vicar at Calgary and Edmonton, before accepting the Mission of Edson in 1914.[2] From Edson he strode into the wilds, taking the Word to a parish a hundred times the size of most today. From Duffield, 90 miles east, to Willow River, 440 miles west, and perhaps 100 miles north and south, his flock ranged. In this expanse, he tended the scatterings of perhaps a hundred Catholic families, mostly coalesced in thirty-odd hamlets and sub-hamlets.

Twice a month, he forayed into British Columbia, and though he entrained when he could, mostly he walked. It seemed that he walked off the ends of the earth in those days. In April 1915, he headed 300 kilometers northward to Ronan, Peavine, Greencourt, and Whitecourt, and in two weeks he "liberated" some 250 souls.[3] At Wildwood he anticipated a wagon to take him 50 kilometers to Greencourt, but the way was impassable, so he waded out on foot. Over 30 kilometers he slogged through the mud that day, another ten the next, plus a river he forded. "Fatigue, poor roads, mishaps, bad luck, vexations, murmurs against the unfolding of events," he wrote—"oh, that hike of a mile and a half over deadfall. It's damnable!"[4]

Near Christmas 1919, he was at Pocahontas, 50 kilometers east of Jasper. The return train to Edson no longer passed through Pocahontas but through Bedson, across the Athabasca River. The river had frozen once, and now water ran over the ice, wearing it away. Culerier took a ten-foot pole and prodded the bottom as he waded into the freezing current, but in places the ice was down deep. Fearing to cross, he had almost given up when he saw three tree trunks sprawled athwart the current downstream. By this time, another wayfarer had joined him.

Below ten centimeters of flood was the ice, solid ice, and on this unseen platform the friend shuffled along, his leaky boots quickly seeping with freeze. It was like watching a man walk on water.

"I thought of Moses who had crossed the Red Sea with dry feet!" said Culerier. "I took off my boots and socks and rolled up my pants and underwear." Then he strode across what seemed a tepid "footbath," then out, over a hundred meters of sand, to a tree trunk, down, high and dry. He dusted his feet off with an old newspaper in his bag, wiped them with a handkerchief, and donned socks and shoes. The ensuing walk kept his feet warm, and he suffered no ill effects.[5]

Everywhere, Culerier lugged a seventy-five pound leather backpack, a converted suitcase, containing the portable essence of the Church— chalice, cassock, candles, wine, wafers, pennants, and hymnals in French, German and English. He also carried a flute. "For 19 years of vagabond life," he wrote, "this simple instrument that cost 20 francs helped make my catechisms more appealing, helped reduce the pain of some demoralized miners, and filled up many solitary hours for me."[6]

In 1916 Father Louis bade adieu to McBride and the torturing thousand kilometer round trip. Now, more and more, his work centred on the Coal Branch.

HALFWAY BETWEEN HEAVEN AND EARTH

The Coal Branch began its half century of life in the high settlement period of the Canadian West, as the Grand Trunk Pacific Railroad laid track south of Edson, Alberta. Tunnelling before the appearance of steel, the mines were producing by year-end 1913. Townsites mushroomed in 1912 and 1913, but the great influx occurred in the five years after 1916. In 1916, the total population in the Branch was 315; by 1921 it was 1,527; by 1926 2,758.[7]

The Coal Branch sold its fuel mostly to the railways. From 1922 to 1926, it produced 2.5 million tons of bituminous coal, and 1.9 million tons of sub-bituminous coal, the former 27 percent, the latter 84 percent of the provincial sum.[8]

The total payroll for the Coal Branch in 1923 was $2.4 million. Most colliers were neither wealthy nor poor, but could save enough for periodic voyages to the old country, to England or Italy, for example, or a trip to the coast.[9] Mining paid well when there was work. By the early 1940s, Mrs. E.A. Brown, desk clerk at the Imperial Hotel in Edson recalled Coal Branchers sauntering up and down main street. Said she, impressed, "Many of them had diamond stick pins, diamond and gold cufflinks."[10]

In the years of Culerier's ministry, the towns of the Branch, though never incorporated, grew to maturity. Of the three largest, Mountain Park burgeoned soonest, with a modest 141 souls by 1916 and 336 five years on.[11]

Rarely has a town been more magnificently placed. The setting for this highest village in Canada was an alpine wonderland, a perfect postcard, evoking the spirits of the mountain, sprites and gnomes

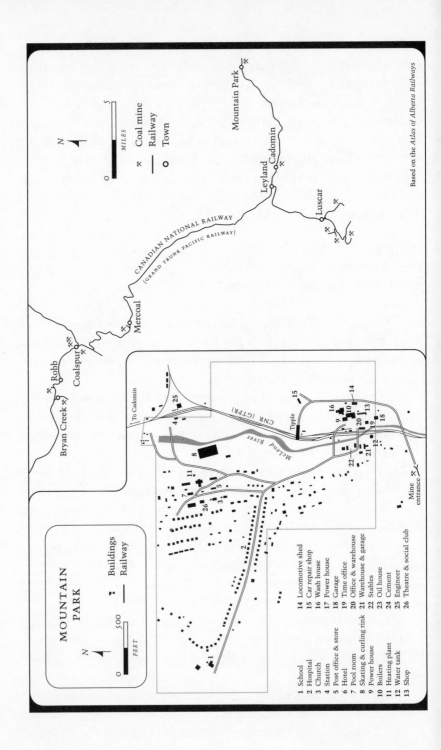

MOUNTAIN PARK

- Buildings
- Railway

FEET
0   500

1 School
2 Hospital
3 Church
4 Station
5 Post office & store
6 Hotel
7 Pool room
8 Skating & curling rink
9 Power house
10 Boilers
11 Heating plant
12 Water tank
13 Shop
14 Locomotive shed
15 Car repair shop
16 Wash house
17 Power house
18 Garage
19 Time office
20 Office & warehouse
21 Warehouse & garage
22 Stables
23 Oil house
24 Cement
25 Engineer
26 Theatre & social club

To Cadomin

CNR (GTPR)

Tipple

McLeod River

Mine entrance

N

MILES
0   5

✕ Coal mine
— Railway
○ Town

Bryan Creek ✕
Robb
Coalspur
Mercoal
CANADIAN NATIONAL RAILWAY
(GRAND TRUNK PACIFIC RAILWAY)
Leyland
Cadomin
Mountain Park
Luscar

Based on the *Atlas of Alberta Railways*

A winter wonderland—Mountain Park, 1920s. A19404, PAA.

cavorting 6,200 feet above sea level. *The Edson Herald* once said that "the thriving...Mountain Park lies, as some of its inhabitants think, halfway between heaven and earth."[12] Nestled in a glacial valley fronting Mount Cheviot and Mount Tripoli, the camp was breathtaking with its sunlit "towering peaks and vistas of drop-curtain scenery." Proper description, said another Edson paper, would "challenge the novelist...to an exercise of his best genius"; it would "bankrupt the English language."[13]

The high meadows were awash with mountain flowers, hummingbirds, bluebirds and swallows. In the crisp mornings, deer, elk and moose grazed with horses and cattle.[14] Fur bearers abounded, and trappers took them in spades—one in a single winter bagging 137 coyotes, 34 weasels, 19 lynx, 3 mink, 2 foxes, and 10 skunks.[15]

It was a berry picker's paradise, with huckleberries, blueberries, raspberries, wild strawberries, and red and black currants at every step round the coal camps. A single foray at the height of season could yield a hundred pounds of huckleberries.[16]

In Mountain Park, as elsewhere, life was regulated by the mine whistle—one long blast meant work tomorrow; three shorts, no work. At 9 PM another whistle ushered in eventide.

By 1926 Cadomin and Luscar were both larger than Mountain Park, Cadomin, with 806 inhabitants, almost twice the size.[17] Four years on, Cadomin had three hotels, three churches and a spacious community hall where tipple boss Fred Falkner ran movies twice a week.[18] There were two department stores, a butcher shop, drug store, dairy, bank, and a new recreational complex, fixed with bowling alley, curling rink, and billiard tables, courtesy of the Cadomin Coal Company.[19]

The wild beauty near Cadomin. ND 3–3250 (a), GAA.

The town boasted a symphony orchestra, the only one between Edmonton and Vancouver.[20]

Despite these amenities, the streets and alleys were sometimes a refuse heap of cans, rot, and muck. As in most communities on the lee of the Rockies, it was ever windy, and the gales contributed to the human-made disarray. Once, Mina Gourlay saw a woman's nightie darting aloft, followed by a horse trough! Coal and stones sometimes hurled through the air, and one time several box cars blew off the railway track.[21]

More dangerous were the mines—less so in the hard coal areas like Bryan, Lakeside and Mercoal, more so in the soft coal centres of Cadomin, Luscar and Mountain Park. "At Mountain Park," Vic Riendeau recalled, "you could count on at least one [death] a year."[22] From 1920 to 1929 forty-two men were killed in the Coal Branch and eighty-seven, seriously injured.[23]

Individually, the miners were courageous, even heroic. On the last shift of the last working day of 1939, workers were just drawing the pillars inside the Cadomin mine when a deadly exhalation of methane gas released without warning. Hugh Docherty went down first and was dragged by fire boss Pete Nicholson to the chute. Just as Nicholson arrived, he fell into the chute, and with Docherty in tow, cascaded one-hundred-fifty feet down, damaging his back, slamming

Cadomin Coal Company—the heartbeat of a community.
ND-3-3245 (b), GAA.

his body and landing at the bottom on his face. Alex Woods pulled out Joseph Nickjoy. But Jimmy Maddams, like David Murray at Hillcrest a generation before, clambered to safety, realized two comrades were still entombed, and ran back into the cloud of death to save them. At age 29, he died with them.

Like Maddams, many in the Branch were extraordinary one way or another. John Kapteyn ran the Mercoal Hotel. If ruffians wrecked the property, he laid complaints promptly, took the culprits to court, then paid their fines. He valued his clientele, however rough, and the guilty usually repaid him when they could.[24]

Then there was Jack the Frog, officially Jack L'Heureux, the premier moonshiner in the province. For some of the time, at least, when he was not operating a restaurant in Mercoal or Coalspur, he lived hidden in the bush with a blind, black woman, secreted away from meddling gendarmes. The police finally discovered his alpine distillery by cutting loose his horse, tethered in camp, and Dobbin went straight to

Jack's still. The Frog rehabilitated in prison for a time, but when released, he suffered a relapse and shipped parts of a new still to the Branch in the names of several sectionmen. Then he shipped himself, detrained, and meanspiritedly stomped through the underbrush to his betrayer, Dobbin—whom he shot.[25]

Taken collectively, Coal Branchers balked at nothing and were fiercely competitive. For three straight years in the late 1920s, the Luscar Collieries Silver Band swept the prizes at the Edmonton Exhibition.[26] In the 1930s, the Cadomin Maroons were repeat champions in Northern Alberta senior baseball. And in a thrilling three-game showdown in Calgary, in March 1936, the Luscar Indians beat the Coleman Canadians for the Alberta senior hockey crown. Before four thousand fans in Calgary, they lost 2–1, then won 3–2 and 4–3.[27] For years, some of the best amateur hockey on the prairies was played in the Branch.

BOOTLEGGER ON A MERCY ERRAND

These were the communities Father Louis Culerier served for fifteen years. At first, his outreach was not always fondly received, and for a moment, he may have felt Fra Hubbard's rather hard judgment on missionaries—as "sincere, self-deceived persons suffering from meddler's itch."[28]

"The Journal of Tonton Meric," was about that itch. It was a children's story that Culerier likely composed and that captured his painful first encounters.

Visiting coal miners at Lovett, the padre of the tale knocked at a door.

"Come in," said a rough voice from one of half a dozen men quaffing down beer. "What do you want?"

"It's the priest come to visit. Are there any Catholics here?"

"What priest?" said the rough voice. "We have enough of our mules to bother us. No need for a priest."

And no welcome either. The only recourse—"retreat in the midst of wild laughter."[29]

In time, the scorn became affection. The people of the Branch Culerier baptized, married, and buried, and in all their trials, he consoled and comforted them, taking on their misfortunes, dispelling their gloom, spreading hope and the majesty of his selflessness. For

Men of the mines whom Father Louis served. Mountain Park,
mid-1920s. Photo courtesy of Ed Waritsky.

these gifts Coal Branchers might have canonized him, if they could
have.

Three vignettes characterize his legend. On March 1, 1918, a
husband and wife went chopping wood a stretch from their home
where they left three children, the eldest four and a half. Returning,
they found the shack in ashes, the children burnt to death. Father
Louis's reaction caught what people of the Branch loved in him—his
acceptance of them, their ways, their choices. "What good would it do
to philosophize and moralize?" he wrote. "I would have done things
differently. Accidents happen despite all precautions. The poor are
limited in their choice of methods."[30]

In shepherding coalbranchers, no favor did Culerier withhold, no
service, however unconventional. Never a stickler for outward form,
he willingly adapted to customs around him.

In November 1918, amid prohibition, he was visiting workers down
with the Spanish Influenza when he stopped at Jack the Frog's restaurant in Coalspur for supper. The hostess anxiously whispered to him,

asking if he might deliver a message to Bill Simmonds's camp, three miles off, near the minehead. Always amenable, he took from her a package that looked like a wrapped Bible, though he guessed aright the contents. An hour later, he knocked at a door, was invited in, and beheld four feverish miners abed. He had brought the remedy, a Jack the Frog special, and it saved the quartet, or so they were sure. Two weeks later, Simmonds accosted Louis, shook his hand and told him that no finer "Bible pedlar" ever walked these parts. The tale Louis titled, "Bootlegger on a Mercy Errand," and the locals passed it round the Branch in awe.[31]

Perhaps that Christmas Harry King, proprietor of the Mountain Park Hotel, prepared a gift for Father Louis—a Christmas cake, iced and decorated.

"Now Father Louis, this cake is for you," said King. "If you give it away to anybody, I'll never let you come inside this hotel again."

King jested, but Father Louis missed his tone. A blend of goodness and meekness, Louis in practice was kindly, patient, and accommodating, if by nature unpolished and unsure socially. His marriage to the church so absorbed him that the joys of banter largely escaped him. Nonetheless, as a light-bearer he had passed one test of a beautiful soul, for he was attractive across denominational lines.

Hours later, Louis slowly retraced his steps to the hotel.

"Well, Father Louis, how did you like the cake?" King asked.

"Mr. King, I have a confession to make," said the priest ashamed. "Mrs. Snovitch, whose husband is in the hospital, needed that cake far more than I did. She has five children to feed. Those children are hungry, and this is Christmas Eve."

So taken was King by the sincerity of the apology that tears welled in his eyes. He wrapped his arm around the padre's shoulder and said— "Father Louis, I'm not a Catholic and I don't believe in saints, but if there is such a thing, you're it." Before the night was out, the story reached many ears, and the family of the sick miner received many gifts.[32]

Over the years, a dozen such incidents added to the legacy of Louis Culerier. But there was more to him than this, much more, for like many other saints, he bore a heavy burden, so heavy that in his darkest hours it was quite insupportable.

17 A Church Rat

THE VISION

CULERIER'S TROUBLES DATED FROM BEFORE THE

TURN OF THE CENTURY when health concerns first arose. In

1889 he had large glands on his neck, and the next year, another

swelling appeared above his left ear, which physicians seared with

silver nitrate. Excruciating toothaches wracked him in 1894.

Later, a tumor erupted on his upper thigh, which was surgically

removed, though the incision leaked for years.[1]

During his service at the seminary of St. Albert, the physical manifestations of a deeper spiritual malaise multiplied as a yoke was fitted on his broad but inexperienced shoulders. First, he had to learn English in twenty months—from May 1898 to January 1900—though as he said, "I learned in quantity, but nothing in quality."[2] Then he was charged with all English sections of

The sanctuary at St. Albert where Father Culerier worshipped.
ND3–4686 (g), GAA.

teaching. "That's a little *much*," he groaned, "...without knowing the language or the subject matter."[3] Theology, Latin, English, Math and Geography, he taught, for twenty-two to twenty-six hours a week. He rose at 4:30 AM, logged half a day of preparation for classes, was exhausted by 7:30 PM, insensate by 10:30, then he fell into bed.[4] Sometimes he rose at 3 AM, and one presentation to the convent took fifteen hours to ready.

"Such a situation quickly wears a person out," he confided to his diary; "the body becomes ill and the soul suffers. There is a limit at which point the person no longer gives anything. The result is a series of disappointments...."[5] Compounding his labors, six weeks later, he was named chaplain of Gray Sisters Convent.

There were just too many teaching duties, priestly duties, and managing duties. Every day he had "instructions to give to the nuns, and fifty details of household economics" to tend to. "I am at once teacher, economist, vicar and chaplain," he moaned. "My first duty today was to light the stoves....I chopped wood, and before supper I went around to light the lamps. I was also asked twice about the laundry."[6] Every moment between classes went to material matters. "It is impossible to open a 'spiritual' book," he complained. "Everything is money, bread, butter, sugar, meat. To my great regret the theology books sit and gather dust, and I can't do anything about it."[7]

Bishop Grandin had told him to be a teacher, and he had agreed.[8] But this, this was not teaching; it was everything else. So, on May 30, 1903, Culerier chose to resign as bursar at the junior seminary. "It is necessary that a professor possess a deep knowledge of what he is teaching; that he may transmit his knowledge; that he be clear, interesting, methodological, appropriate...," he wrote. Desperate to shake off his cumbrances, he cried, "I long to be amongst the rankings of simple men."[9]

The resignation was not accepted. "I hesitated, I objected, finally I accepted and succumbed," he said.[10] Sick in July 1904, he again begged dismissal as bursar, and was again refused.[11] So overworked from September 1 to October 20, 1904, was he, that he suffered headaches every single day, sometimes all day long. Casting a jaundiced eye on two other colleagues also broken in health and spirit, he wrote, "I cannot continue...."[12]

In the deep of winter 1905, he broke. Beset with chronic insomnia, gastro-intestinal and urinary malfunctions, he found his eyes glued shut with a pustulation known as granulosis, and he slumped into deep depression. On the night of February 17, he fell asleep immediately, which was unusual. At 2:10 AM, a vision came: "I was... 'strangely' wakened, softly and suddenly, due to the pressure...of two hands placed on my blankets, one at my elbow, the other on my right hip. The two hands deliberately shook me...and I felt a complete sense of well-being throughout my whole body." He looked up and saw in an orange aura Bishop Grandin, the soul who had won him to the cloth, the Grandin dead since June 1902. The specter healed him, then retreated toward the door.

Father Louis sat bolt upright, and thought, "a dream, a nightmare, an illusion, a hallucination? What does he mean 'healed'? I feel so weak."[13] Louis reached for water for his burning, crusted eyes, then rising, he walked into the night, saying his rosary. On the way, he retched.

Bishop Grandin's tomb and behind, right, Father Louis' "merci" for the healing. ND–3 4686 (b), GAA.

Back in bed, he tried vainly to sleep, then to read, but he could do neither. Doubt gripped him, and he wondered if the vision were real, if anything that evening were real. After breakfast, he retraced his steps and found grim confirmation in the pool of his own vomit.[14]

The healing seemed imperfect, however, because the pustulation stayed. Seeking aid from a fellow priest, he was pointed to nuns who gave him some eye drops.

"Bishop Grandin is much nicer than you," he said, attempting humor. "The old Bishop is a smart doctor."

Upon informing colleagues of Grandin's intervention, he told his diary, "I look useful making this declaration." But an associate asserted, "You pretended that Monsignor Grandin came to your room Feb. 18, 1905 around 2 AM, but this was a dream, an illusion, a lie that your sick mind told you, and your claim of 'cured' doesn't stand." When Culerier told Father Lacombe of the miracle, that priest shook his head and declared, "Oh my, the lunacy is starting."[15]

Monsignor Legal disbelieved the healing entirely and instructed Lacombe to escort Culerier to Gamelin, Quebec, near Montreal, where

Father Louis with nephews, Mountain Park, 1925c. OB 1413, PAA.

a "very good doctor" would see him.[16] There, at St. Thérèse asylum, Lacombe left Culerier with the strange parting—"O.K. little Father, play the fool."[17]

For six months, dizzy spells and depression beset the patient which alienists met with tests, tranquilizers, and hot baths. As Culerier recorded, "I found myself overdosing of 'cure'"[18]

GALLONS OF TOXINS

Returning to Alberta, Father Louis became vicar at Calgary, then Edmonton, before his exemplary career in the Coal Branch. There he was at peace most of the time. There he conducted the mission of an isolate beyond the constant control of superiors, beyond, in some senses, even the church, for the hierarchy virtually never visited. From 1918 to 1924, he heard birds singing, saw flowers blooming, and felt harmony brimming. "Things are normal!" he exulted. "I'm busy enough! Happy!"[19]

The climax of these halcyon days occurred as his chapels were established in the Branch. In the footsteps of Grandin, he went back to France, appealing for help for these bethels, and it came, some from his sister Berthe. At Cadomin in spring 1924, a shortfall threatened the chapel, and at the height of crisis, a "good man," F.L. Hammond, president of the Cadomin Coal Company, handed Louis a cheque for $1,000. The grateful priest wept.[20]

That fall, Louis Culerier began another decline. It was his long-standing nexus with the church that troubled him again. "We start with nothing!" he wrote Father Lacombe, his superior. "We live like rats in our small churches. No one seems to care. When the nest is made, we get sent to start all over again under the same conditions One has to ask himself if it's worth it to continue. To jot things down? What's that good for? Who will see clearly in twenty or thirty years?... We're setting ourselves up for a fall. The system lacks support, sanction, and direction."

"Every diocese presents the sad spectacle of promising, active young men who are suddenly incapacitated from work and condemned to long periods of rest in order to rebuild their shattered nervous forces," he quoted a pastoral source. "In some cases the cause of the prostration may be overwork, plain and simple. Of course, the only remedy then is to reduce the volume of work to more reasonable proportions. There is no use to attempt the impossible. If it's done, a heavy penalty will have to be paid."[21]

"I've been told, as others also have: 'we count on you, little Father, to look after all the missions,'" Culerier continued. "But how can I do that? No help what-so-ever....In 1916 I thought I was going to get a modest dwelling in Edson, at the center of all my posts, that which I alone deserved, since the departure of Father Beaudry for Lac St. Anne. I lodged in a corner of the church: this lasted eighteen months. I was like a church rat in a church."

Scrimping and scraping, he bought a mean 12 x 24 foot shack and some worn furniture for $325. "The diocese didn't furnish anything for that," he wrote, "nor the congregation OMI, nor Edson's parish." Then in January 1920, he had to resettle in Coalspur. Again he secured a hovel, but luckily this time paid for by parishioners, through raffles.[22]

It was an old, old story relegated to his diaries all too often. Isolation was the bane of missionaries, of drybelters, of 'most anyone else— "few relations with civilized people, few books, little taste for studies," Culerier wept, "no chance to cultivate the letters or the sciences...." It all made for an "intellectual laziness, a deadening of the faculties."[23] Brother and sister missioners, north, along the

Mountain Park after Father Louis left, 1935. A 6830, PAA.

MacKenzie River, were even worse off, for they lived in misery, malnourished, deprived, scattered, poorly lodged.[24]

By fall 1925, nearing age fifty, Culerier wrote, "I was sick and tired, or was it that I was just tired!"[25] His last years in the Branch were fortunately uplifted by the company of two nephews and by the contraction of his personal parish. After 1926, every three weeks he stayed 10 days at Mountain Park, 5–6 days at Cadomin and 3–4 at Luscar.[26] In 1930, he left these places forever.

The next three years, he spent in St. Albert and North Battleford, Saskatchewan, where his spirit slowly ebbed. Extended priestly cares now crowded in again, and as his revulsion mounted, he hid in the chapel at St. Albert. When Father Langlois admonished him, Louis replied: "Don't you understand that I am threatened by general paralysis?"[27]

While at North Battleford, he begged Langlois to allow him to return to teaching, to light instruction—a nice transition to retirement, he thought, for he was nearly sixty. It would allow younger priests to do the pastoring.[28]

But Langlois responded: "What we lack at the junior seminary is men of experience; experienced in life, experienced with children, experienced with souls more than with books."[29] Three more attempts in February, April and June 1933, Culerier made to shed the killing work.[30] By now his body had taken on the gross disharmony, and he was besieged by bladder and urinary tract ailments, constipation, rheumatism in his left arm and shoulder, and insomnia, always insomnia. Beginning the year with six hours of sleep a night, he had by August just two.[31]

Desperately, he sought attention and release. While in Hobbema, Alberta, he rang the church bells for no reason, he jettisoned furniture from a window, and he called a nun an idiot.[32] Tranquilizers became his solace, and he ate them like candy. On September 5, they ran out, and two days later, he was still awake.[33] He staggered to the Gray Sisters Convent in St. Albert for help, and in the parlor, his dazed eyes caught a portrait of Monsignor Legal which, he said in delirium, *smiled* at him.[34] Two weeks later, he was again en route to Gamelin, Quebec, and the asylum.

There he met more control, more constraint. "I was...treated like a prisoner in the asylum," he wrote, "and I protested with all my conscience."[35] With one overseer, he argued in several languages, and finally he tossed a glass of milk into a reverend father's face.[36] So they cast him into maximum security where he braced his iron bed against the cell door and refused confession.[37] All the while, he had no ink, no diaries, no flute, no books, not even a dictionary.[38] The books he wanted in order to live "intelligently and nobly."[39] Failing that, he kept busy doing what he had learned so well—"praying and suffering."[40] Said he, "I live in a desert like John the Baptist."[41]

Gradually, he gave in, became a child again, compliant and obedient, and slowly caring hands began whatever recovery a surrender of one's will allows. "I had gallons of toxins in my anatomy," he wrote. They gave him prostarin to urinate, another drug to defecate, sedol to do something else, and veronal to sleep. And in November, the nuns gave him a new flute.

After a certain calm held him, his resistance surfaced again, alive but unwell, transmuted into an old form. At Gamelin, a generation earlier, Lacombe had left him with the odd parting, "O.K., little Father, play the fool." Now the meaning became clear. Once again Culerier played the fool—seeking the freedom that eccentricity, even insanity allows to one sworn to obey an institution strangely as compassionate as it was confining.

Alas, the disadvantage of his game lay in the degraded reputation of the fool. That reputation was a cross. "I carried it poorly, with some reluctance," he said sadly, "although not altogether without some love."[42]

He thought a long while about his profession, his order, his career, himself, then concluded: "I will not place myself back into regular, mandatory work. I doubt ever being faithful to a regulated life in a community (no pleasure in owning up to that)."[43] The molehill of his self-esteem the charge of insanity had blasted to atoms.

Shaking, he wrote, "I can't live anywhere in Alberta or Saskatchewan without being an embarrassment."[44]

18 The Cross Bearing

HOW HAD THE SAINT COME TO THIS? How could one so loved for his compassion and so lionized for his steadfastness feel so uncomforted and unsupported? The explanations of his misfortune thusfar given—his overwork, his distaste for certain tasks, his resistance to clerical direction—were symptoms of a deeper hurt.

As his lectures to the brides of Christ at the convent of St. Albert attested, Culerier was conflicted within. The conflict was really between two diametrically opposed conceptions of human and divine nature. When one conception dominated, his life overflowed with love and self-fulfillment; when the other usurped, he was wracked by guilt and self-loathing. One belief system generated harmony, the other suffering, one a sense of self-worth, the other, of self-destruction. One gave gifts, the other demanded sacrifice.

The oscillation between these two conceptions explained better than all else Father Louis's state of mind and ultimately his state of health. He was quite right—he could not serve two masters.[1]

THE DUST OF THE ROAD

What conception caused Culerier's suffering? Asian spiritual adepts have repeatedly said that *wants* produce trouble, worries, and suffering. If so, Culerier was more direct—he *desired* suffering.

"The followers of Christ must pass through an austere school of suffering and renunciation," said he. "The cross is their lot. They must carry the cross—as Christ has done, cheerfully, patiently, may its burden be ever so crushing!"[2] And he warned, "the cross is heavy—the cup is bitter, but it is nevertheless most salutary. Our intentions must be purified. Never forget that the closer you stand by your crucified Lord, the greater the share you shall have in his sufferings."[3]

So fervidly did Culerier pine for the agony of his Master that he imputed motives to Christ, asserting that Christ's every wish, every obsession, from the moment of his birth, was to hang on the cross: "No doubt our Blessed Savior loved the cross."[4]

Culerier told the nuns about Saint Teresa of Avila who beseeched the Lord to withhold even the slightest of consolations and to not forget too speedily her past indiscretions. Practise penance and humiliation constantly, Culerier urged. Pray the "true humble prayer":

O my God, behold in thy presence a poor, insignificant, helpless creature. Plunged in my nothingness, I prostrate myself before Thee. I wish I had an offering to make Thee, but I am naught but misery, and Thou art my all, my riches. My God, I thank Thee for having willed that I should be nothing in thy sight. I love my humiliation, my nothingness. I thank Thee for having deprived me of certain satisfactions of self love, of certain consolations of affection. I thank Thee for the deceptions, ingratitude and humiliations that have befallen me. They were necessary to keep me from straying away from Thee. O my God, be Thou blessed, when Thou sendest me trials. I love to be consumed, broken, destroyed by Thee. Reduce me more and more to nothingness. May I be in the edifice not the polished stone but the grain of sand picked up in the dust of the road.[5]

The prayer was a profound judgement on God Himself, a god who willed the prostration of his children, who purified them but brutalized them in the process. The saving sense of humor of Saint Teresa of Avila might have helped Father Louis.

Near the end of her life, Teresa undertook a hard journey from Avila to Burgos, Spain, to found another monastery. Crippled with arthritis and down with fever, she huddled in an oxcart which plied its way through sheets of rain and ruts of mud. As the cart slipped precariously sideways, she leapt off, splatting in the mire. Her patience ended, and she looked wet-faced to the skies and dared complain to her Maker: "Father, amidst so many ills this comes on top of all the rest!"

A voice answered, "Teresa, this is how I treat my friends."

To which the muddied saint replied: "Alas, Lord, that is why you have so few!"[6]

Culerier did not find his own pain amusing. He sported a species of hunchbacked humility, an affliction, very visible and wretched, with a sole pseudo-redeeming quality—it was one item he owned that God did not. "The only thing we may truly attribute to ourselves—the only thing whereof we may claim to be the author," he pronounced, "—is our faultiness and sinfulness."[7] That people might almost be proud of this depravity could have struck some as faintly ironic.

But the business-like Culerier chortled not a whit. The problem was how to acquire humility, and the strategy was tried and true. Said Culerier, "Evidently, there is no other means except *acts of humility*, otherwise called humiliations."[8] Though he carried no quirt, as did others, his mind was a more-than-able substitute for physical flagellation, and it readily found the humiliations he sought.

That may have given pleasure, but it did not please, for what he willed happened, yet he despised his will. "Self will," he told the sisters, "is like a worm which will spoil the best fruit," so he set out not to discipline his will, his creative power, but to obliterate it.[9]

Fra Elbertus mused sadly, "Punishment remains as long as the sinner hates himself."[10]

Elbertus knew the consequences of Louis's thinking, and though he might not have argued with the reverend Father, he saw humanity so very differently. We were God's people, His radiance lived in all, and we realized our potential through that radiance, through love. So we ourselves, he said, were "gods in the chrysallis."[11]

No wonder Fra Hubbard called no church in Christendom home, though matters of spirit, heart and ethics were dear to him, and his counsel was cherished by tens of thousands. Theologians who preached the depravity of humans, he labeled "inkfish" who spewed murk and melancholy at everything that swam. "The old...view that regarded man as a sinful, lost, fallen, despised, despicable and damned thing has very naturally tended to kill in him enthusiasm, health, and self-reliance," he judged. "Probably it has shortened the average length of life more than a score of years. When man comes to realize that he is part and particle of the Divine Energy that lives in all he sees and feels and hears, he will, indeed, be in a position to claim and receive his birthright. And this birthright is to be healthy and happy."[12]

Happiness, alas, was leagues from Louis. Never seemed he to sense that humility might come sooner through love than humiliation. Humiliation is the scion of scorn, humility, the child of human respect, the state of mind that inevitably follows the recognition of sanctity in others.

This is not to say that Culerier's route to self-understanding was invalid, not at all, for it did involve the eradication of the ego, and with that sense of separateness from God and others gone, one might more easily experience the unity of the universe and the bliss of its Creator.

Humility can be accomplished by dismemberment and disfigurement of self, but it sometimes occurs over prolonged periods that dismemberment and disfigurement alone are realized. If practised obsessively, as an end in itself, humiliation can keep one from discovering one's true identity. It is valuable only as a *means* by which sooner or later the miserable are flung into the lap of God.

SCRUPULOSITY

Every honest attempt to find God yields its own fruit—and its own specific dangers to the harvest. Excessive attention to humiliation can lead the soul down side excursions of fetid backwaters and swampy bayous, shoals and dead-ends, where spiritual diseases breed and delays occur. It was fitting that Father Louis lectured to the nuns of St. Albert on the spiritual disease of scrupulosity, sometimes contracted in these backwaters.

"A scruple," Culerier said, "is a fear of having sinned grievously where the fault is plainly slight...." Scrupulosity entailed an endless and senseless reiteration of every tiny circumstance concerning an action or omission. It was a paralysis of the decision-making process, characterized by a mind that changed every moment, fearing it was wrong, fearing it was transgressing. It was a fixation on every stitch and nuance of the paltriest peccadillo—an insistence that it be upgraded to the vilest of mortal sins. Convinced of his worthlessness, the penitent felt driven more and more to the confessional but found less and less relief. Advice was sought and given, but never did it quiet the turbulence in his mind. There was nothing but wrongdoing and error, not even the perverse delight of temptation, for as soon as temptation arose, the penitent was certain he had yielded.[13]

"Are scruples dangerous?" asked Culerier. "Yes and they are very harmful. Above all they disturb the peace of the soul....Without this peace, we lack the courage to do anything, we lack initiative, we are easily discouraged...." Often sufferers were "gloomy, despondent, inconsistent, shy and hesitating." They endured "the most terrible agony, night and day, [with] every avenue of spiritual comfort ...closed." "No wonder such souls seek relief in a torrent of tears— abandon themselves to sadness, melancholy and despondency!" said Culerier. "No wonder that at last some land in asylums, others go to an early grave, and even some put a violent end to their suffering."

Culerier told the nuns of a priest-friend afflicted with scruples. Emasculated, the man huddled in his sanctuary, chapfallen and impotent, repeating phrases over and over, certain he had said them improperly. The single word "amen" he reiterated again and again, sure he had mispronounced it, so low was his opinion of himself.[14]

When Culerier pondered the cure for this abject wretchedness, this soul filled with self-contempt, he did not suggest a new conception of the self, one more self-respecting, more self-affirming. He did not regularly urge his rapt listeners to see themselves as part of the *light*. He did not say they had the power within to rise above affliction.

The cure, he told the sisters was "unconditional, absolute submission to the direction of the confessor, in other words, entire persistent obedience!"

OBEDIENCE

"Do you know what the religious life really is?" Culerier asked the nuns. "It is nothing else but a *house of corrections—a reformatory* where the *soul* has to consent to be *worked over*, to be smoothed and filed down...." "The convent," he emphasized, "is a *hospital* for sick souls."[15] These sick souls—and the seminaries were full of them too—required discipline.

Discipline could be instilled by submission to higher authority and exacted by a vow of obedience. For the Oblates of Mary Immaculate, this, above chastity and poverty, was the foremost of vows, and it was intimately related to Culerier's suffering.

What was the vow? "Obedience is a permanent disposition to comply with the orders of lawful superiors," Father Louis answered. Obedience was "the real teststone of our religious spirit...the only thing that counts. Whatever is not done in conformity with obedience is practically useless, a waste of time and energy."[16]

"The vow is to safeguard against the excesses and errors of our reason, often perverted and always deficient...against our natural weakness ever ready to recoil before a sacrifice and against our inconstancy...." The vow led to the "most perfect union with God and the closest likeness with Christ."[17]

"As a religious, I must obey superiors not merely because the material welfare of the community demands it, not merely because obedience is the absolute condition for order and discipline within the bounds of the community, but I must obey exclusively because I see in my Superior the representative of God."[18]

The sisters were to realize they were always under obedience. "Take no responsibility on your own shoulders," Culerier chimed. "Distrust yourselves."[19] "Your Superiors must carry the whole burden; you are merely at their disposal, you are merely a tool wherewith the Superiors...bring about whatever is best for the glory of God or the welfare of those under your care."[20]

These lines Culerier said as he felt the church wanted them said, but deep down, he was torn over the issue of obedience. This great rule he himself could not always honor.

He told the sisters of the conversation between Saint Dominique and the devil:

"What class of religious are most represented in hell?" asked Dominique.

"The Superiors!" the devil answered instantly.[21]

Then Culerier shared the recent utterance of the Holy See: "It is easier to find a good bishop than a good superior."[22]

Why? asked Culerier. "Because the qualifications demanded of a good superior are so manifold that there are very few people, if any, that possess them all, and therefore...there are very few superiors in whom there are no flaws."[23]

The perfect superior was a perfect enigma: "She ought to know everything, be perfectly acquainted with the ins and outs of every department, but...she must not show that she knows anything. She must see everything, yet at the same time she must be careful never to notice anything. [She]...ought...to have a heart as soft as wax for all, whilst in regard to herself she must be like a block of marble....Lack of respect, of obedience, even plain insults she must meet...with a smile."[24]

Patently, only a marvel could comply. So the superiors were very like their charges—"liable to all the frailties human nature has inherited from our first parents."[25]

Did these frailties entitle subordinates to disobey or to consent grudgingly? "By no means," snapped Culerier.

Did the bondage of blind obedience justify leaving the church? Again, no.

What did leaving mean? Little, perhaps, to those who had not professed their perpetual vows; much to those who had, for the latter had somehow had formed "their *own special* **conscience**." That conscience, Culerier informed the nuns, warped the mind, told it that God had never really called, that a holy vocation was not really lost, for it was never possessed.[26]

"A certain religious applied to the Holy See for a dispensation from his vows." said Culerier. "The reason he gave was that he was not fit for the common or community life. It took him thirteen years to make this strange discovery." All that time, he lived in the community without a peep of trouble, and suddenly it "dawned on him" that he was unsuited. The case was typical.

Not all who left were sons of villainy, Culerier allowed; some were worse. The example of Judas was instructive. "Shallow, inconstant and unreliable," Judas was ambitious, thankless and avaricious— riddled through and through with anti-qualities. "The same causes,"

Culerier declared, "are at work more or less in every apostasy, in every defection from a God-given vocation."[27]

The judgement was harsh, and though it was projected to sisters, it was also meant for himself. Here was Culerier's misfortune, his cross, the heaviest of all—to be in a holy profession that did not suit him, to want release, and to see in that desire base betrayal. Here was the most terrible of thoughts, human wretchedness at its meanest. And how horrifyingly logical it seemed, for if all apostasies were the same, if he were the true runt of the fallen Adam, corruption incarnate, his ghastly destiny was to disown his faith and Lord. The guilt would sink a zeppelin.

Thus Culerier poured his contempt on all apostates-in-the-making, all defaulters, all renegers, all leavers. Their lame excuses invariably ran: "Owing to uncontrollable circumstances, the life in the community has become unbearable to me. The religious life is henceforth for me no longer a means of Salvation but rather a means of damnation."

But whose fault was it? "Are you free from all responsibility?" Culerier asked. How will you ever "quiet your own conscience?" How will you stand the scorn of your former colleagues of the cross who must treat you as "a subject of disedification, of scandal?"[28]

"A dispensation," Culerier warned, "is very much like a surgical operation....A *diseased limb* is *removed*, cut away, in order to save the *whole body*." Leaving was far less a release than a disgrace, and the leaver was to remember that the endorsement by a superior of his request represented a demand that the community be freed from...a dangerous and henceforth useless member."[29] So much for accepting the choice of one who after much heartrending had changed his mind!

Perhaps Culerier himself contemplated a dispensation, because the vows troubled him. When he considered the vow of poverty, he commented snidely: "I always lived in true poverty, so well that I neglected to take care of myself."[30] What he thought of the vow of chastity, we do not know, but when he reconsidered the vow of obedience at age sixty-one, he condemned the notion of obedience entirely. Not only did his lectures criticize superiors in general, but he knew surely that superiors did not always represent God. When his mind broke again in the thirties, he attacked what he called "the administrative weaknesses in St. Albert."[31] "Father Binet is a success (in the order of imbecile missions)...," he told Father Provincial Langlois. "You make him a SUPERIOR, he is inferior. Get rid of him."[32] When he was summoned to silence regarding his apparition, he refused. "It's good to hide the king's secrets, but it is honorable to reveal and publish the works of God," he noted simply.[33]

"Obedience versus competence—perfect oppositions," he mused.[34] The former was a species of control that demanded permanent infantilization, perpetual servitude. And such demands were deeply disturbing; indeed, if the truth might set him free, the church had not.

BEHOLD IN EACH CHILD AND WOMAN NOTHING BUT GOD

Did Culerier find freedom? It is the function of the feeling of separation of humanity from God, and of each spirit from the rest, that it should result in suffering and that the suffering should lead in time to a cure.[35] The cure was the full realization of the truth—Fra Elbertus might have said—of the sacred worth and vast potential of all souls.

In the aspect of life closest to his heart, Culerier had already discovered this verity. Before leaving the Coal Branch, he delivered two remarkable lectures to the nuns of St. Albert on the subject of education. He reminded the sisters that their community had been created to care for children orphaned by a cholera epidemic. Focusing on the centrality of love, he declared: "Love begets love. If you want to win the love of a child, you must meet this child with unselfish, sincere, pure supernatural love. This love must not originate from the exterior appearance of a child, from its looks, its winsome behavior nor even from its talents, or a natural inborn goodness."[36] These forms of attraction were, in fact, dangerous, for they withheld love. "You must not forget that you exclude from your affection others to the same extent that you lavish it upon the special favorite."[37] The key to teaching mastery, Culerier affirmed sublimely, was to "behold in each child nothing but the living image of God."[38]

An old teacher once said, "The heart of a child is in many ways like ivy which needs support in order to climb upward...If it finds no support, it will creep on the ground. Soon it rots and decays." But lend it a trellis and "its leaves and tendrils will be the larger and fresher the higher it is able to climb. Blessed is the school where the teacher is like...an oak on which the joy of the children's souls can...climb heavenwards."[39]

Out of love would grow patience. "No other vocation makes such heavy and constant demands on patience as the work of education," said Father Louis. "Children's tears dry quickly, but they leave on the soul deep, lasting scars when an impatient hand wield[s] the rod."[40]

Culerier understood a deep truth about the province's public schools. Keeping religion out of them was impossible. "A neutral school," he intoned, "was nothing but a dream. It shall never be a reality." Why? Because sooner or later, teachers develop personal convictions and reveal them to students. "The school therefore will always be what the teacher is," and the system will always share what the teacher has become.[41]

Then, turning to the nuns, Culerier expressed his great adulation. Priests may be "hissed" and insulted, but never the sisters. Why? "Because in you the world admires the very incarnation of what is holy, noble and pure...the highest expression of charity, of devotedness to the interests of mankind."

"The human heart knows ills and wounds so deep and at the same time so secret—I almost felt like saying so sacred—that even the hands of the priest, the God-appointed physician, will [not] be allowed to touch them—but these very wounds will be laid bare before your eyes!" he exclaimed. "Why? Because the world expects of you love and sympathy, so deep, so tender that a woman's heart alone can be the soil where such a love will thrive...."

"Yes, in your lives the world expects to find combined what is greatest in Heaven and earth—a charity truly human and truly divine—truly human because it can sympathize and because it can stoop down to the very depths of human misery; truly divine through its healing and uplifting influence." Then Culerier smiled at the brides of Christ seated before him and whispered—"You are the image and likeness of God."[42]

Father Louis need not weep that he had not found love, for he had. That it was in the sisters and the children, he would discover soon enough, was but the beginning.

PEACE IN THE ASYLUM

The Reverend Father Langlois wondered how the old warrior was faring. It was now fall 1936, more than three years since Father Louis's latest commitment to Gamelin.

Father Louis, left, at Lac la Biche, Alberta, nearing his end, 1943.
OB 2829, PAA.

The news was only partly cheering. Culerier's mind was still confounded, still reeling, still flitting from one to another of those who had drained his lifeblood, dampened his spirit, stolen his dreams. "The good Father pretends to play the lunatic to illustrate his grand fatigue and to blame his superiors who refused to honor his demands for rest," reported Dr. Georges Ravenelle.

The Church did not allow the sane the liberty of disobedience, so Father Louis claimed it as a madman. The ploy did not free him, however, for he had long since bound himself to an endless catena of blame, incrimination, and judgement. And in these attacks he could not forgive and thereby release those he felt had imprisoned him. Thus he held his superiors to account, and they held him. Commented Dr. Ravenelle: "In our opinion, he wouldn't know how to exist clearmindedly without judgement...." And judgement brought anything but a clear mind.

Some days an uneasy calm crept over Culerier, and he almost accepted what he had been, but he could not stop judging. His voluminous diaries written and rewritten and rewritten again, in minuscule hand, were proof of that. Said he, still sorrowing, "Let us be content we have pleased God with our work, even though it wasn't crowned."[43]

From time to time, the other side of Culerier's tormented self appeared, the saintly teacher soul in him, and with it came the promise of eventual escape from his trammels. Added Dr. Ravenelle, he was studying and rendering service at various religious offices. And he was guiding a blind man on his walks.

> Only the souls that have suffered are well loved.[44]
>
> *Fra Elbertus*

"So live that when you come to die
your death notice won't appear among the
list of town improvements."

The Office Cat, Aug. 7, 1922

The Feast

Epilog

EXEUNT

On the day the Second World War ended in Europe, Father Louis, back West for some years, wrote a page in his diary entitled, "Toward Gamelin," as if it were "Toward Golgotha."[1] It was the old disturbance again.

As his mind neared its breaking, he lashed out, broke the silence imposed on him about Grandin's healing, broke protocols about criticism of his order, and attacked the faith, all before succumbing again, becoming once more an infant cooing at the caresses of his step-mother, the church.

Nearing his end that autumn, Louis requested his own commitment to the asylum at Gamelin. There, week by week, he lost weight, and on December 28 he reported that he was suffering from myocarditis. "You don't survive heart disease," he wrote. "You die."[2]

In the morning of January 24, 1946, at his usual hour, he prepared to celebrate mass. A sister asked how he was, but he said nothing. Wishing to don his vestments, he suddenly raised an arm, motioned, and tried to grasp something. Given a chair, he sat, then, pale and drawn, a cold sweat beading on his face, he was taken to bed. A priest anointed him, began prayers for the dying, and in moments he was gone.[3]

A complex misfortune Culerier's had been. All his life, he had sought his own identity, finding it in vileness, wondering why the villainy was not in women and children, and in the end, surrendering to a strange conception that separated him from most of human creation. Perhaps the source of his confusion stemmed from Jansenist teachings prevalent in France and Quebec, a dark, Calvinist strain of Catholicism that even the official church abhorred. These teachings stressed an inherent wickedness and worthlessness of humanity, and for Culerier they undermined the authority of the church and the discipline of its orders. Where was the wisdom, indeed, in obedience to a hierarchy as bespotted as Adam?

It seemed that obedience was necessary to the survival of the Oblate Order, but was obedience to the order necessary to the survival of the individual soul? This was the great question Culerier faced. And when does loyalty to the order, to its discipline, become harmful? The answer seems to be—when it loses its sense of higher purpose, and when the higher purpose itself is not love. But when does that happen? For the church, at its best, perhaps never; for Culerier it happened when the will of the institution replaced his, *without his full consent*. And that consent he could scarcely offer, given the difference in his mind between God and the church.

Why not leave? Even without the guilt he heaped on his shoulders, leaving was inconceivable, for where would he go? What else might a priest do those days? So he stayed, unhappy and conflicted.

The institutionalization of religion always entails a degree of constrained conformity, more in some times and cultures than others. But because the true self is controlled from within—self conquest is surely an internal affair—it often despairs awhile at what directs it from without. It is not that rigid adherence to a particular vision of a church yields nothing of value. Loyalty, even to a partial vision of truth, is one of the tests of sincerity and of courage. Martyrs have died for a cause only partly right, but they may also have risen to new heights of patience, perseverance, dauntlessness, and duty. No life is a waste.

The remains of Culerier's Coal Branch — Cadomin ghost town, 1953.
PA 3159/2, PAA.

The harvest of experience always has something to do with the discovery of self and its responsibility. One may learn what one is personally responsible for by taking responsibility for others, or by giving it to others. Either way, a cross is borne for a time. But among those who have humbled themselves into impotence and oblivion, even a tiny cross is cumbering.

It is a measure of the vastness of human potential and attainment that Culerier, a man of so petit an opinion of himself, could have touched so many that they later reckoned him a saint. When King Coal died in the 1950s, the towns of Culerier's Coal Branch lost their reason for being, and one by one, most were dismantled and abandoned. These surrendered sites, old-timers well knew, were the scene of Father Louis's greatest triumphs.

Near the end of the war, Gordon Albright, who had enlisted, received compassionate leave to help relocate his father and mother to Haney, British Columbia. Like a burnt-out bark, nearing the coast, its voyage done, Donald sank.

Sincerely, to the end, he embraced his own motto that it was a privilege as well as a duty to serve—though perhaps he took it overmuch as a *duty*. The Office Cat once chortled that a thing of duty was a *bore* forever, and he meant that sheer duty can fatigue. It fatigues to the degree to which it clashes with the wants of those to whom the duty is done. Service to others is made holy, and less wearing, by high regard for the others. What wore Albright thin was that he suffered fools neither gladly nor at all, and he saw rather more of them on the outskirts of the Peace than he could countenance. Many a day and night he spent in the persistent, but tiring overcare of those who could think for themselves, but think differently, whether wisely or ineptly. Thus did he trudge upstream much of his life, facing the stiff current of his own cynicism.

Perhaps, Gordon saw more of where his father had been, than where he was bound, for where he had been was clearly etched on his haggard face and marked on his tremoring frame. Parkinson's would soon have him—a sad spectacle that spoke to Gordon about his father's search for a higher spirituality, for immediate contact with God. "One's contact is in direct proportion to the joy that one feels, and joy cannot be hidden," said he. "It shows internally and externally. It shows in one's health. One cannot experience this bliss or joy and be sick—because it heals, it heals all human ills. And to me this is the simple proof that my father had not achieved this higher level."[4]

Yet Donald did have moments when the heights were scaled and the summit air was breathed. Noble *intent* is always honored, and nothing but nothing, not even disease, can prevent the well-doing for which one is born.

This, Gordon sensed. "There are mortals who listen to the music of the spheres, And each man marches to the drummer hears," he quoted the bard. Donald's proud drummer had led the advancing hosts into the North. "My father wanted to contribute to anything that could conceivably improve the quality of life for the pioneers of the Peace," said he. "I feel that he did everything a man could do to contribute to that main goal. He did have a true compassion for his fellow man, as obscured as it was at times, as darkened by bursts of temper. But I think it shows that he did have a very deep appreciation of the meaning of love in terms of human service."

Sometimes apostles may be forgiven their strength of personality, for without it, there would be no apostles at all.

As a Burnsite, Donald had cherished the saying, "God's word to me is...." Now in his last days he asked that the Bible be read to him, and he renewed an old quest.[5]

On May 1, 1946, three months after Culerier's passing, Donald Albright followed.

Willet Trego was never as wealthy again as he had been in 1917 when a quarter of a million dollars passed through his books. His wife Myrtle fell ill with breast cancer in 1933, and about then, perchance sensing her passing, Trego was badly burnt saving a man in a fire. That year Myrtle died, as did their daughter Lucille, of tuberculosis, in Arizona. During the Great Depression, Trego's economic fortunes so waned that by 1940 he had lost the farm and was nearly destitute. By then, just south of the Centre Street bridge in Calgary, he had a tool-shop that made tillage implements, harrows and rod weeders.

In the last year of his life, he went to Chilliwack, British Columbia, to visit son Les who had built a house for him and who remembered him with as much devotion as a son ever offers a father. On his final journey, however, Trego, left after a few days for Edmonton to see his daughter Ruth. When he arrived, a CNR stationman called Ruth, saying an elderly gentleman had her phone number and was disoriented. After a brief stay, Trego entrained for Calgary where on March 9, 1951, he trundled to his favorite boarding house. On the morrow, he arose, walked toward the bathroom, and fell dead in the hall.[6]

Thus passed one of the people's guardians. For sixteen years in the prime of life, he had done his all to exact for settlers fairness from the railway. It was only the kindness he bestowed on men and animals that he asked. And he suffered as all do in the difficult endeavor of changing other minds.

Trego's misfortune was to pay the toll that attacks on others take on oneself. Assaults on another's sense of equity usually stir animosity—witness the fruitless exchanges between Frank Moodie and Harry Smith, or those that so alienated Trego from Colonel Dennis. Animosity drains, depresses, degrades; it also detains. It binds its antagonists in a reverberation chamber of insult and incrimination—and it grips them in cold embrace until the conduct of one or the other is revised. Even when the storm abates, it can rage on in resentment. Possibly Trego regretted his reminder to the world in 1923 of the former sins of the Canadian Pacific, sins it had made good. But no one can remind another of past errors and have offered release.

Hubbard sometimes noted how we resemble those we criticize. Trego's near perfect replication in Bolivia of the CPR system he despised in Alberta was certainly ironic, and had he persisted, the irony would have grown by the minute. Yet in it were two good thoughts—one for settlers that they might know someone cared, the other for Trego that he might see how easy to do what one condemns.

Frank Moodie left Rosedale some months after the red scare and the expulsion of the "Bolsheviks." In the 1920s, he joined the search for oil, and in 1927 he became managing director of the Sentinel Oil Company of Black Diamond, Alberta. In 1936 he predicted that within three years the province would be "drowned in oil." So much would flow from the earth that it would be impossible to market until a pipeline were built to the Great Lakes.[7]

In the deep of winter 1938, Moodie's car skidded into a ditch near Midnapore and flipped over, badly injuring him. Half recovered, he entered the 1940 provincial election as an independent in the Calgary riding contested by Premier Aberhart: he finished with a third of one percent of the votes, dead last of fourteen runners.[8] A harder blow came in December 1942—news of the death overseas of Flying Officer Kenneth William Moodie, his son. A few weeks later, on January 22, 1943, Moodie himself passed on.[9]

Harry Smith, it seems, stayed several years in the Drumheller valley, for he represented the ABC local at the District 18 convention of the United Mine Workers' convention in 1933.[10] After that, he is lost sight of. From what can be learned, his nobility seems hidden. He was not one to die for his cause; in fact, few of his gang were. Men will normally give up their lives when their motives are more positive than negative. It is difficult to die for something you are against, and it is difficult in civilian life at least, to die for a cause when one's primary motivation is hate. One may want to kill for such a cause, but not die.

Rosedale, about the time the spy and Frank Moodie left.
A 6082, PAA.

The natural courage of coal miners was always best wedded to high principle, for courage is the consort of compassion, not calumny.

As for Moodie and the spy, Elbert Hubbard said, "There is one thing worse than to be deceived by men, and that is to distrust them."[11] Distrust creates the perception of deceit—distrust someone, and he will appear to act accordingly; he will be seen to be deceitful. Look for deception, be certain it is there—and it will "appear." "When you grow suspicious of a person and begin a system of espionage upon him, your punishment will be that you will find your suspicions true," said Elbertus.[12] He meant that people find what they want to find; their perception bows to their wishes. And mistrust is a punishment because it is frightening and calls forth inordinate energy in worry and forboding and the construction of defenses. Mistrust is fatal; it is faith in fear and kills by exhaustion.

In late September 1919, Operative 3 partially recovered from his shoulder injury and tried to work. Next morning, he was so stiff he couldn't rise.[13] Two months later, he was again sick, this time with a severe cold, and by year-end, his career at Rosedale finished. Away he slinked, likely southward, to report to the Pinkertons in Spokane and to steady himself for another assignment.

A misty figure he had been, though something of his nature appeared between the lines of his diary. Because he could be neither a

Elbertus in thought—
his epigrams, the lessons
of experience.
From The Selected Writings of
Elbert Hubbard.

nondescript nor a boss, there was quite a technique to his role. Setting himself in the second echelon, he was able to get bank managers, radicals and reactionaries to speak their minds. Bearing a certain authority, he was willing to take a stand, to confront the acid-tongues around him. He was a corrective to radical thought, and a balance wheel for the excesses of the ex-soldiers. Naturally attracted to good, he valued dedication, opposed hypocrisy and unwarranted criticism. Loyal to his dubious trust, he worked well.

Yet his occupation was dangerous to peace of mind. At his worst, Operative 3 was a talemonger and a gossip, paid to do what Smith did for free. Over time, spying is very hard on the psyche, because it is exceedingly judgmental, and judgmental without recourse. No response is possible to clandestine *communiqués*, and so they utterly disrespect the invigilated. They are a kind of trial where the accused is undefended and silent and cannot hear the verdict, and does not know he has been condemned. They are a violation of trust and resemble the cold work of a sniper. Great offense occurs in spying—the betrayal of everyone, even friends, and that betrayal inevitably begets intense, even insupportable disharmony in the mind of the betrayer. When once the magnitude of the offense is grasped, the road to recovery can be long.

"The worst about a double life is not its immorality—it is that the relationship makes a man a liar," said Elbertus. "The universe is not planned for duplicity—all the energy we have is needed in our business, and he who starts out on the pathway of untruth finds himself treading upon brambles and nettles which close behind him and make return impossible. The further he goes the worse the jungle of poison-oak and ivy, which at last circles him round in strangling embrace."[14]

Of course, Moodie was implicated in all this; moreover, what the spy told him could scarcely have been more disheartening.

By the time of Frank Moodie's death, Alf Terrill's career was ebbing. Nothing Terrill did in the 1940s matched the sparkle of his humorous musings during the two decades before. Late in winter 1947, one who had lightened misfortune by laughter, the venerable Office Cat, died in Medicine Hat.[15]

MISFORTUNE

Misfortune is like a fishnet. For Father Culerier, the net tightened until it became a noose. For the Burnsites, it held until it was leapt over; for The Office Cat, it sank to the bottom; for Anderson, it was as important and as inconsequential as the perimeter of the Eastern Irrigation District. If the Burnsites left the net, most others of this story stayed in the pool surrounded by the net until they made the pool a finer place to inhabit. One can find freedom in the pool or beyond it; one may have to leave or not. But it does not so much matter where one is as what one thinks about the net.

Escape from it, from all constraint and affliction, invariably requires an understanding of how misfortune can be transformed into something else. Misfortune must be taken in and digested; it must be feasted on, so that it strengthens rather than poisons. It must enter one's system as misery and pain and be changed into might and self-confidence. If not digested properly, if the feast be fictive, the alchemy may fail.

The starting point is the assimilation of some form of dissonance or discomfort. Thus Donald Albright feasted on the misadventures of the settlers of the Peace; Willet Trego, on the miscalculations of the Canadian Pacific Railway; Harry Smith and Frank Moodie, on the misconceptions about each other; the spy, on the misrepresentation of who he was; Anderson, on the confusion of fifteen years of irrigation practice; and Father Louis and Lois Valli, on even more years of self-doubt.

Some fed on their own mistakes, some on the mistakes of others. But the most advanced of them instinctively distanced what happened outside themselves from what they were within. Thus Carl Anderson understood better, or perhaps sooner than Donald Albright that one feasts on the *misfortune*, not the *Self*, that the Self, properly perceived, cannot be devoured, or diminished, or even gnawed at, because it is unassailable. Thus Albright thought he could be worn down and hurt; at some deeper level, Anderson knew he could not. The one grew sick and tired; the other hardly experienced these states and lived half a lifetime longer. One was overcome by calamity, in the disease that took him early; the other was virtually calamity-proof.

It is the achievement of this state that is the ultimate purpose of feasting on sorrow. Calamity-proofing is the product of fattening on disappointment and becoming more because of it.

One does not have to laugh at misery, as if it were a joke, as did The Office Cat, but one does have to realize that once it is overcome it cannot threaten anymore. Indeed, it never *could* threaten because of who we are and have always been, and in that sense, all misfortune is illusory. It is a burden the enlightened know they can bear. It has power to fatten when it leads the sufferer to a true self-appreciation, to awareness of self-mastery and infinite potential. To be able to stand firm amid the crash of breaking worlds is surely a remarkable achievement—but it is the grail of great spiritual seekers everywhere.

What purpose has suffering? The discovery of this grail no less, the discovery of the real Self, the Self imperturbable and priceless.

IT FORMED MY CHARACTER

Following her escape from the barrens south of Alderson, Lois Valli continued her poetry and began a career as an artist. Gifted, she drew notice in time, an attention that Buck took to poorly. He feared, it seemed, the flowering of her personality. Ignored and belittled, Lois spent, she said, "more than sixty years battling for position, never giving in...one Briton who never bent the knee to Caesar."[16]

Perhaps it took the birth of their third child, Angela, when Lois was forty-five, to evoke the best in Buck. Or maybe Angela saw something others did not. Angela, he really did love. As a child, she remembered his coming in from combining, covered in chaff and dust, picking her up and hugging her. One Christmas in the middle of the night, he turned on the tree lights and held her until she went to sleep. She went everywhere with him, even missed school to travel with him to sheep, wool and potato meetings across Alberta. As a pre-schooler, she visited the Boy Scout camps her father ran at Dinosaur Park and the Cypress Hills. Beginning in Alderson in 1926, Buck had a long record of scouting service, and his charter was signed by Byng of Vimy. He and Angela loved horses and rode in the Brooks parade together for years and south to Kinbrook Park on weekends from June to harvest.

Angela saw the great inner reserves of both her parents. Both were physically tough with terrific pain tolerance. One Sunday afternoon when her father was about sixty years old, he and a local lawyer decided to break a yearling colt for fun. Not knowing this business, the lawyer failed his part, and Buck was left heaving atop the bronk, without reins. Plunging down on the saddle horn, he cracked his pelvis in at least two spots. Tumbling from the colt, he yanked the lawyer off his horse, roped the colt, dragged him snorting to a hitching post and snubbed him down. The two then went to the house where booze dulled their pain.

Another time, Lois stepped out onto the crumbling wooden step at the front door to shake a rug. The step collapsed, and she plunged four feet onto a metal stake anchoring an antenna. Her hip was badly injured, turned black, and the hematoma swelled to the size of a grapefruit. Using a stock prod as cane, she hobbled around for some days in sheer misery, but said nothing.

"Dad stayed tough and feisty until his driver's license was taken away," said Angela. "He lost his independence then, and in a year in his own words he was 'the shell of the man I used to be.'"[17]

In the deep autumn of his life, stricken with Parkinson's, but refusing to be institutionalized, Buck became an incredible burden for Lois. She sustained gall bladder attacks before entering Brooks Hospital on December 3, 1978, with pancreatitis and double pneumonia. On January 2, she had gall bladder surgery.

In the 1980s, Lois suffered more with her gall bladder, stayed at Foothills Hospital in Calgary for a time, and had a brush with death. In "January 1988" she sensed "a shadow" looming:

The shadow came very close to me once.
I felt the cold gaze as it looked into me.
I was not afraid.
I looked back, unblinking, I would have gone
without a sigh.
I was held back by the ones who were always at my side.

They wore white, pierced me, poured life into me.
Always standing between me and it, forcing it to retreat.
One day it will come again and push all help aside.
That is according to the plan.[18]

"My creativeness is crushed," she wrote in "February 1988." "Shall I ever bloom again?"[19] She longed to sit on the Red Deer River in the sun and the breeze and paint away her weariness. Said Elbertus, "Misery comes from lack of full, free self-expression and from nothing else."[20]

At last, with Buck hospitalized, she visited son Ted, by then a noted veterinary at Guelph, Ontario. While she was away, on September 25, 1988, Buck aspirated and choked to death.

Lois still lives in the old place, out in the country, north of Brooks, where she writes poetry and paints. Her subject is the prairie which she studies with sensitivity: "People who spend their lives on the Prairie develop a 'hate love' feeling for it. We know all her moods. If that ever-lasting wind stops we look at the sky & try to judge from the clouds what is in store. Each wind has a voice. Well we know the whine, the moan, the shriek. Each strikes an accompanying chord within us— unspoken hope, fear, anger. We recognize the voice of THAT coyote giving vent to all the pent-up feelings we dare not express."[21]

Lois found that part of freedom that is given when one accepts what has been and what is. She looked to nature where despite its harshness, it is sometimes easier to accept the way things must be. One winter she fed pheasants, but the foxes ate them all. "Well, we can't have everything," she quipped. "I guess we'll have foxes."[22]

Pondering the hard times on the Nine Bar, she declared, "I treasure those years because now you could not starve me to death in any way. I could go out onto the prairie and survive. And that's what it did to a lot of people. It grew me up and formed my character. Probably made

Ruins at Alderson, north of the Nine Bar Ranch, 1990.
Photo by D.C. Jones

me harder and tougher than I otherwise would have been if I'd stayed in town. But given a sack of flour and a sack of oats, I could have survived like the sheepherders did."[23]

If some in this saga sought the power of God, Lois sought the power within—though I think now, because of their grandeur, they are the same.

———————

I first saw Lee Anderson in Brooks in June 1984. She was flitting around the rooms of her home like a frightened deer and had suffered two strokes. She was blind in one eye, the apparent result of a bungled cataract operation in Medicine Hat. A big red slash stretched across her vision, and the doctor blamed himself. After her second stroke, she was half blind in the other eye.

At night, Carl would read to her, for she loved literature to the end. On the morning of July 18, 1984, she was suddenly stricken as they sat for breakfast, and she died in his arms.

The next day, his birthday, Carl came home to an unbearable emptiness. He tried to find solace in television, radio, books, but nothing satisfied. Thinking of their lives together, he nearly broke. Finally he picked up the book he had been reading to Lee in the nights before her passing.

A slip fell out, a poem penned by Helen Steiner Rice:

After the storm the sunshine
After the winter the spring
After the shower the rainbow.
For life is a changeable thing
After the midnight the morning
Bidding its darkness cease
After earth's trials and trouble
The comforts and sweetness of peace.

With this message was another from Lee, written a day or two before her death:

May these few words of compassion
Give you help and comfort in your sorrow
And give you courage
To carry on today and tomorrow.

Carl was racked recalling their long lives together, remembering the pretty school marm he had courted more than half a century before, thinking of her gentle guidance for so daunting a man as he, thinking, always thinking, and ruminating. He wanted to drive to British Columbia, to go out on the railway track to end it all. Then he stopped and remembered a promise to Renie Gross, a writer, coming over next morning to interview him about the Eastern Irrigation District. So he stayed. She was gentle, considerate and caring, and she let him talk it out. As Lee had been, she was a gift, and she saved his life.

In December 1994, ten years on, Anderson, now ninety-seven, but looking seventy, visited Calgary. I met him at the inn where he stayed, and we talked into the night. He told me of his last hours with Lee, her poem which he had memorized—things I still needed to hear. When it was near midnight, I looked at him with all his years and reminded him of one of the gifts he had given me—a book by Elbert Hubbard.

*A last portrait of the Fra,
aged 59, aboard the* Lusitania,
*New York harbor.
From* The Selected Writings of
Elbert Hubbard.

Hubbard, I dare say, affected me deeply in time, for he understood misfortune. "Life is a voyage, and we are all sailing under sealed orders," he once said. "We plan, plot, scheme and arrange, and some fine day Fate steps in and our dreams are tossed into the yeasty deep."[24]

In Spring 1915, in New York, Hubbard and his wife Alice boarded the *Lusitania*, steaming for Liverpool. Just past lunch on May 7th, at 2:10 PM, the liner was torpedoed by a German U-Boat. Right after the explosion, the Hubbards emerged from their suite on the portside and came upon the boatdeck. Neither seemed perturbed, and they stood, arm in arm, wondering what to do.

As the ship heaved and settled fast by the bow, frantic crewmen and passengers sped by with women and children, while others strained at the lifeboats.

"What are you going to do?" a friend asked.

Elbertus shook his head, but Alice smiled and said, "There does not seem to be anything to do."

Then the Fra wheeled and the two paced directly to a room on the top deck and closed the door behind them.

They would die together, holding each other.[25]

The horror of the next moments is hard to shut out—the ship listing, turning, tumbling, tipping, nose downward, the water rushing up decks, stairways, passageways, then under that door....

"The thought of getting safely out of the world has no part in the life of an enlightened man," the Fra once wrote— "to live fully while he is here is his problem—one world at a time is enough for him."[26]

These things I learned later, through Anderson's gift, given six or seven years after Lee's death. I was interviewing Carl at Brooks then, where he lived alone, pressing him again for the meaning of his life, when he strolled across the living room to a bookcase. There he pulled out two of Hubbard's works, the *Note Book* and the *Scrap Book* and bade me choose which I would have. Deeply moved, though Hubbard was new to me then, I chose the former.[27]

Now as we finished our talk in the inn at Calgary, I said, "Carl, I never told you this before, but Lee gave me that book."

He looked at me and whispered, "I know."

The memory of a great love
can never die from out the
heart. It affords a ballast
'gainst all the storms that
blow. And although it lends
an unutterable sadness,
it imparts and
unspeakable peace.[28]

Fra Elbertus

Notes

PROLOG

1. The title, *Feasting on Misfortune*, was inspired by *The URANTIA Book* which asserts "[All great souls] have learned to feast upon uncertainty, to fatten upon disappointment, to enthuse over apparent defeat, to invigorate in the presence of difficulties, to exhibit indomitable courage in the face of immensity, and to exercise unconquerable faith when confronted with the challenge of the inexplicable." (p. 291).

2. Christiaan N. Barnard, quoted in Mitzi Chandler, *Reminders for Co-Dependents* (Deerfield Beach, FL, Health Communications, 1989), p. 186.

3. Bruce A. White, *Elbert Hubbard's The Philistine: A Periodical of Protest (1895–1915)* (New York: University Press of America, 1989), pp. 125–26.

4. Elbert Hubbard, *Selected Writings of Elbert Hubbard*, Vol. I, Pamphlets, "A Message to Garcia" (New York: William H. Wise and Co., 1922), pp. 254–58.

5. Elbert Hubbard, *Selected Writings of Elbert Hubbard*, Vol. IX, Philistia, "A Great Compliment" (New York: William H. Wise and Co., 1922), p. 277.

6. Freeman Champney, *Art & Glory: The Story of Elbert Hubbard* (New York: Crown Publishers, 1968), pp. 37–38.

7. Mary Hubbard Heath, *The Elbert Hubbard I Knew* (East Aurora, NY: The Roycrofters, 1929), p. 211.

8. Ibid., p. 212.

9. Ibid., p. 134.

10. Elbert Hubbard, *Selected Writings of Elbert Hubbard*, Vol. IV, Preachments, "A Thousand and One Epigrams" (New York: William H. Wise and Co., 1922), pp. 388, 393, 430, 441, 458, 461; Elbert Hubbard, *The Note Book of Elbert Hubbard* (New York: William H. Wise and Co., 1927), pp. 39, 198; Elbert Hubbard, *Selected Writings of Elbert Hubbard*, Vol. XII, An American Bible (New York: William H. Wise and Co., 1923), pp. 280, 361; Elbert Hubbard, *Selected Writings of Elbert Hubbard*, Vol. XIII, The Legacy, "Roycroft Dictionary" (New York: William H. Wise and Co., 1923), p. 405.

11. Elbert Hubbard, *Selected Writings of Elbert Hubbard*, Vol. VI, Fra Elbertus (New York: William H. Wise & Co., 1922), pp. 98–99.

I BURNSITES

1. "Truax Trial," Nov. 27, 1893, Methodist Church, General Council, Court of Appeal, United Church Archives, Victoria University Archives, University of Toronto.

2. Ibid., quoting *The Expositor of Holiness*.

3. Ron Sawatsky, "'Unholy Contentions about Holiness': The Canada Holiness Association and the Methodist Church, 1875–1894," paper for the Annual Conference of the Canadian Society of Church History, June 8, 1982.

4. Ibid., quoting Nelson Burns, *Divine Guidance or the Holy Quest* (Brantford, ON: The Book and Bible House, 1889), p. 63.

5. *The Doctrine and Discipline of the Methodist Church* (Ottawa: William Briggs, 1891), pp. 4–8.

6. Beth Sheehan, "The Bull Outfit," in Isabel Campbell, ed., *Pioneers of the Peace* (Grande Prairie and District Old Timers' Association: Friesen, 1975), pp. 34–39.

7. W.D. Albright to Mrs. J.M. Sherk, Jan. 21, 1928, f3, box 2, W.D. Albright Papers (hereafter WDA Papers), Glenbow Alberta Archives (hereafter GAA).

8. Ibid.; Biographical Notes, W.D. Albright for "Who's Who in American Education"; "W.D. Albright, Aug. 15, 1881—Notes as at Mar. 31, 1945," WDA Papers, f3, box 1, GAA.

9. Eileen Albright Ross, telephone interview, Aug. 28, 1990.

2 THE APOSTLE

1. See David W. Leonard and Victoria L. Lemieux, *The Lure of the Peace River Country, 1872–1914* (Calgary: Detselig, 1992).

2. For population losses in the early twenties, see R.G. Moyles, ed., *Challenge of the Homestead: Peace River Letters of Clyde and Myrle Campbell, 1991–1924* (Historical Society of Alberta/Alberta Records Publication Board, 1988), pp. 313–14. From 1921 to 1926 the town of Peace River lost 41 percent of its population; 85 townships in census divisions 15 and 16 lost at least 50 percent of their population. *Census of the Prairie Provinces*, 1936 (Ottawa: King's Printer, 1938), pp. 887–994.

3. "Settlers are Pouring into the Peace River Country in Thousands," *The Edmonton Journal* (hereafter *Journal*), July 7, 1928, p. 3.

4. Ibid.

5. "Strong Argument Presented in Behalf of Edmonton's Claim for Chamber of Commerce Convention," *Journal*, Sept. 13, 1928, p. 13.

6. H.F. Mullett, "120 Elevators Erected Where only 22 in 1923 for Peace River Grain," *Journal*, May 25, 1929, Immigration and Land Settlement—Peace River District, GAA, clippings.

7. George Murray, "Peace River Expects to Market 17,000,000 Bushels This Year," *Journal*, June 2, 1930, Immigration and Land Settlement—Peace River District, GAA, clippings.

8. George Murray, "'Second Edmonton' Envisioned in Fertile Peace River Region," *Journal*, June 10, 1930, Immigration and Land Settlement—Peace River District, GAA, clippings.

9. George Murray, "Peace River Yearns for Maps When Province Gets Resources," July 2, 1930, *Journal*, Immigration and Land Settlement—Peace River District, GAA, clippings.

10. Letters Selected from Dr. Percy Jackson's Letters written from Notikewin, WDA Papers, f27, box 4, GAA.

11. W.D. Albright, "A Sane Land Settlement Policy," sent to *Canadian Comments*, June 6, 1930, f1, box 1, WDA Papers, GAA.

12. C.A. Dawson and R.W. Murchie, *The Settlement of the Peace River Country, A Study of a Pioneer Area* (Toronto: MacMillan, 1934), p. 237.

13. Ibid., p. 237–38.

14. Albright, "A Sane Land Settlement Policy."

15. E.C. Stacey, *Peace Country Heritage* (Saskatoon: Western Producer, 1974), p. 56

16. Ibid., pp. 82–83.

17. Albright, "Trials of the Pioneer," address to Sudeten Settlers at Tupper, B.C., WDA Papers, f9, box 2, GAA.

18. Stacey, *Peace Country Heritage*, p. 63.
19. Ibid.
20. Ibid., pp. 50, 46.

3 THE DISORDER

1. E.C. Stacey, *Peace Country Heritage* (Saskatoon: Western Producer, 1974), p. 1.
2. Ibid., p. 23.
3. Ibid., p. 20.
4. I.C. Shank to D.C. Jones, Nov. 25, 1990.
5. Eileen Albright Ross, telephone interview, Aug. 28, 1990.
6. R.G. Moyles, ed., *Challenge of the Homestead: Peace River Letters of Clyde and Myrle Campbell, 1919–1924* (Calgary: Historical Society of Alberta, 1988), pp. 247–48.
7. Gordon Albright, interview by D.C. Jones, Calgary, Oct. 3, 1990.
8. Ibid.
9. Eileen Albright Ross to D.C. Jones, Sept. 12, 1990.
10. Gordon Albright, interview, Oct. 3, 1990.
11. Eileen Albright Ross to D.C. Jones, Aug. 29, 1990.
12. Eileen Albright Ross, telephone interview, Aug. 28, 1990.
13. Madelon Flint Truax and Beth Flint Sheehan, *People of the Pass: A Human Interest Story of the Monkman Pass* (Grande Prairie: Menzies Pinters, 1988), pp. 272–75; Beth Sheehan to D.C. Jones, Oct. 4, 1994.
14. Bruce sent assignments home regularly from his RCAF pay, and his father collected what he could from Bruce's debtors. Bruce's last assignment had just cleared his debt, though he did not receive written notification of that fact before he died. (Eileen Albright Ross to D.C. Jones, Nov. 5, 1990.)
15. W.D. Albright, "Notes as at Mar. 31, 1945," WDA Papers, f3, box 1, GAA.
16. Gordon Albright interview, Oct. 3, 1990.
17. Albright to Sherk, Jan. 21, 1928.
18. W.D. Albright to Editor, *The Family Herald & Weekly Star*, n.d., WDA Papers, f1, box 1, GAA.
19. Hubbard, *Selected Writings of Elbert Hubbard*, Vol. XII, An American Bible, p. 356.
20. Hubbard, *The Note Book of Elbert Hubbard*, p. 159.

4 BIRTH OF A GHOST TOWN AND DESPAIR

1. Wemyss Cotter to Teddie, Aug. 19, 1908, 91.86, f2, Provincial Archives of Alberta (hereafter PAA).
2. Arthur Cotter to Miss Mason, Sept. 20, 1908, 91.86, f2, PAA.
3. W. Cotter to Charlotte, May 14, 1909, 91.86, f3, PAA.

4. W. Cotter to Charlotte, May 18, 1909, f3, PAA.

5. W. Cotter to Charlotte, June 8, 1909, f3, PAA.

6. J.S. Dennis to W. Cotter, July 7, 1909, f3, PAA.

7. W. Cotter to Charlotte, July 21, 1909, 91.86 f3, PAA.

8. Ibid.

9. W. Cotter to Charlotte, July 29, 1909, f3, PAA.

10. W. Cotter to Charlotte, July ? 1909, f3, PAA.

11. W. Cotter to Charlotte, July 29, 1909, f3, PAA.

12. W. Cotter, speech on citizenship, July 1, 1910, f4, PAA.

13. Elbert Hubbard, *Selected Writings of Elbert Hubbard*, Vol. XIII,
    "Saskatoon," Short Stories and Index (New York: Wiliam H. Wise and
    Co., 1928), p. 121–22. Hubbard was impressed with the growth of
    Saskatoon, however, and he did estimate the population of that city,
    Moose Jaw, Edmonton, Calgary and Medicine Hat to be "one hundred
    thousand to five hundred thousand" each in twenty-five years, or by
    1939. Edmonton was closest at 86,000; Medicine Hat farthest at 9,600.

14. David C. Jones, *Empire of Dust — Settling and Abandoning the Prairie
    Dry Belt* (Edmonton: University of Alberta Press, 1987), p. 243.

15. David C. Jones, *"We'll All Be Buried Down Here" — The Prairie Dryland
    Disaster, 1917–1926* (Calgary: Historical Society of Alberta, 1986), pp.
    136–37.

16. Ibid., p. 131.

17. Ibid., p. 143.

18. Arlene Cooper, interview of Mrs. Leah Slater, Medicine Hat, Alberta,
    Sept. 30, 1984.

19. Ibid., p. 86.

20. Tracy Anderson to David C. Jones, Nov. 23, 1989.

21. Lois Valli, "Empty Land," in *Prairie Wool* (St. Joseph, Ill.: L & L Printing,
    1991), p. 9.

22. Valli, "Nine Bar Ranch—1935," *Prairie Wool*, p. 45.

23. L. Valli, interview by David C. Jones, Brooks, Alberta, July 11, 1989.

5 A WOMAN FOR ALL SEASONS

1. Lois Valli interview by D.C. Jones, Brooks, Alberta, July 11, 1989.

2. Lois Valli to David C. Jones, Feb. 4, 1991; M.A. Valli interview by David
   C. Jones, Brooks, Alberta, June 6, 1984.

3. Lois Valli to David C. Jones, Feb. 18, 1991.

4. Valli to Jones, Feb. 18, 1991.

5. V.E. Valli to David C. Jones, Dec. 11, 1990.

6. Ibid.

7. V.E. Valli to Jones, Dec. 11, 1990.

8. Ibid.; Lois Valli to David C. Jones, Feb. 21, 1991.

9. Lois Valli, interview by David C. Jones, Brooks, Alberta, Mar. 18, 1991.

10. L. Valli, interview, July 11, 1989.

11. V.E. Valli to Jones, Dec. 11, 1990.

12. Lois Valli to David C. Jones, Dec. n.d. 1989.

13. L. Valli interview.

14. Ibid.

15. L. Valli to Jones, Feb. 4, 1991.

16. A.W. (Tony) Cashman, *The Vice-Regal Cowboy: Life and Times of Alberta's J.J. Bowlen* (Edmonton: Institute of Applied Art, 1957), p. 53, 56, 60, 68, 74, 123, 133, 159.

17. *Tilley East Commission Report*, p. 17.

18. L. Valli interview; Gilda Valli to David C. Jones, Dec. 27, 1990.

19. MA Valli interview by David C. Jones, Brooks, Alberta, June 6, 1984.

20. Ibid.

21. Carl J. Anderson to David C. Jones, Feb. 14, 1991.

22. MA Valli, Diary, Jan. 31, 1937.

23. L. Valli interview, Mar. 18, 1991.

24. Elbert Hubbard II, ed., *The Philosophy of Elbert Hubbard* (New York: William H. Wise & Co., 1934), p. 116.

25. Angela Valli, "Lois & 'Buck' Valli," Apr. 9, 1991.

26. L. Valli interview.

27. MA Valli interview.

28. G. Valli to Jones, Dec. 27, 1990.

29. T.L. Duncan, Onefour, to Premier Brownlee, July 6, 1926, 69.289 f345, PAA.

30. G. Valli to Jones, Dec. 27, 1991.

31. L. Valli interview.

32. Ibid.

33. Cashman, *The Vice-Regal Cowboy*, pp. 164–65.

34. V.E. Valli to Jones, Dec. 11, 1990.

35. L. Valli, "Depression Help—1932," *Prairie Wool* (St. Joseph, Illinois: L & L Printing Service, 1991), p. 41.

36. L. Valli, "Sheepherder's Code," *Prairie Wool*, p. 31.

37. L. Valli, "Ranch Work," *Prairie Wool*, p. 27.

38. Lois Valli, miscellaneous poetry, in author's possession.

39. L. Valli, "A Lesson From A Flower," *Prairie Wool*, p. 131.

40. L. Valli to Jones, Feb. 18, 1991.

6 WATER

1. C.W. Peterson, "Irrigation and Rural Industries," *Farm and Ranch Review*, Feb. 1936, p. 10.

2. "Eastern Banker, Quoted by Attorney-General, Is Not Irrigation Enthusiast," *The Edmonton Journal*, Feb. 14, 1922, Scrapbook Hansard (hereafter SH), GAA.

3. W.H. Childress, "History of the Lethbridge Northern Irrigation Project," [1934c], 73.307, f100, PAA.

4. Ibid.; M.L. Wilson, chair, *Report of the Commission Appointed to Report on the Lethbridge Northern and other Irrigation Districts in Alberta*, Oct. 1930, p. 6; J. Sutton to L.C. Charlesworth, Aug. 4, 1928, 73.307, f98, PAA.

5. John A. Widtsoe, "An Examination into Conditions on the Lethbridge Northern Irrigation District, Alberta Canada," Feb. 1925, 73.307 f111, PAA.

6. L.C. Charlesworth to V.W. Smith, Feb. 25, 1932; Charlesworth to Smith, Mar. 2, 1932, 73.307, f99, PAA.

7. Childress, "History of the Lethbridge Northern Irrigation Project."

8. Ibid.

9. Wilson, *Commission*, p. 22.

10. L.C. Charlesworth to V.W. Smith, Feb. 1, 1923; Charlesworth to J.E. Brownlee, Nov. 21, 1933, 73.307 f95, PAA.

11. L.C. Charlesworth to F.S. Grisdale, Apr. 9, 1935, 73.307, f96, PAA.

12. Mr. McDougall memorandum, "The Bow River Project," Aug. 8, 1923, 69.289, f474, PAA.

13. V. Meek et al., *Committee Report, Canada Land and Irrigation Project*, 1925, 69.289 f474, PAA.

14. Canada Land and Irrigation Company Ltd., *Annual Report*, July 19, 1923, box 150, f1276, Canada Land and Irrigation Company Papers, GAA.

15. McDougall, "The Bow River Project."

16. Meek, *Committee Report*.

17. S.G. Porter to C.J. McGavin, Oct. 29, 1934, box 28, f340, CPR papers, GAA.

18. A. Griffin to S.G. Porter, Jan. 12, 1934, box 37, f559, CPR papers, GAA.

19. Ibid.

20. "Alberta's South Country," *The Edmonton Journal*, Sept. 14, 1922, clipping.

1. Minutes of Mass Meeting, Nolan's Hall, Calgary, Oct. 30, 1923, box 44, f 510, CPR Papers, GAA.

2. Frank Kelly, Committee Representing 200 Settlers on CPR Irrigated Lands, to Mr. Doughty, Apr. 24, 1923, box 44, f510, CPR papers, GAA.

3. Joseph S. Bonham to Governor General, Feb. 27, 1923, RG89, vol. 309, f5026, Public Archives of Canada (hereafter PAC).

4. P.L. Naismith to Dear Sir, June 27, 1923, box 44, f511, CPR papers, GAA.

5. Minutes, Oct. 30, 1923.

6. Ibid.

7. "CPR Contract Holders Reject the Latest Plan," clipping, box 44, f510, CPR papers, GAA.

8. P.L. Naismith to Sir Augustus Nanton, Oct. 31, 1923, telegram, box 44, f510, CPR papers, GAA.

9. W.D. Trego to Executive Committee, CPR, Nov. 2, 1923, box 44, f510, CPR papers, GAA.

10. "If Farmers Stand Solidly Together, We Believe They Will Obtain All They Demand From Company," *CPR Contract Holders' Bulletin*, n.d., box 44, f510, CPR papers, GAA; Memo [1923], box 44, f510, CPR papers, GAA.

11. "If Farmers Stand Solidly Together...."

12. Ibid; J.S. Dennis to P.L. Naismith, Nov. 12, 1923, private, box 44, f510, CPR papers, GAA.

13. Memo [1923], box 44, f511, CPR papers, GAA.

14. F.L. Trego to David C. Jones, Jan. 25, 1991.

15. Frank Brown, interview by David C. Jones, Calgary, Alberta, Dec. 7, 1994.

16. Ibid.; also F.L. Trego to David C. Jones, Mar. 7, 1991, and Apr. 26, 1991.

17. "Irrigation A Success!" *The Farmers' Tribune* (Carlstadt), Oct. 6, 1914.

18. A. Griffin to P.L. Naismith, Dec. 28, 1923, box 44, f510, CPR papers, GAA.

19. P.L. Naismith to Augustus Nanton, Dec. 19, 1923, box 44, f510, CPR papers, GAA.

20. "No Relief Beyond New Contract of Thirty-Four Years," *Calgary Albertan*, Dec. 19, 1923, box 44, f510, CPR papers, GAA. Some settlers deemed Trego a Moses, others disagreed. O.N. Gilbert, spokesman for over fifty plowmen from the Rosebud, Rockyford and Standard areas, charged that Trego's knocking was a direct blow against his own property and against immigration itself. Like the railway, Gilbert equated criticism with treason. See "CPR Land Contract Holders Strongly Favor New

Amortization Plan," *Calgary Herald*, Jan. 12, 1924, box 44, f 510, CPR papers, GAA.

21. Ibid.; "If Farmers Stand Solidly Together..."; "No Relief Beyond New Contract..."; Griffin to Naismith, Dec. 28, 1923; Don Bark to P.L. Naismith, Dec. 28, 1923, box 44, f510, CPR papers, GAA.

22. "Mr. Trego Tells Previous Experience," *The Farmers' Tribune* (Carlstadt), Oct. 6, 1914.

23. "Irrigation a Success!"

24. "If Farmers Stand Solidly Together...."

25. "Irrigation A Success!" italics Trego's.

26. W.D. Trego, "Misrepresenting Dry Farming Crops," *The Farmers' Tribune* (Carlstadt), Oct. 6, 1914.

27. Chas. W. Peterson to Henry Sorensen, Dec. 17, 1909, RG89, v.37, f15, vol. 1, PAC.

28. Henry Sorensen to E.F. Drake, Dept. of the Interior, Apr. 16, 1913, italics in the original, RG89, v.37, f15, vol. 1, PAC.

29. A.L. Blunt to Minister of Interior, Apr. 30, 1913, RG89, v.37, f15, vol. 1, PAC.

30. J.B. and B.W. Hall to Minister of Interior, July 21, 1913, RG89, v.37, f15, vol. 1, PAC.

31. "To the Subscribers of the Fighting Fund organized by the Irrigation Farmers of the United Farmers of Alberta," quoting Dennis's letter, Feb. n.d., 1913, RG89, v.37, f15, vol. 1, PAC.

32. Ibid., quoting Sorensen's letter, Mar. 1, 1913, and Sorensen to G. Zimmerman, Mar. 10, 1923.

33. Ibid., quoting G. Zimmerman to H. Sorensen, Feb. 20, 1913.

34. Memorandum of an interview between the Minister of the Interior and the Irrigation Committee of the United Farmers of Alberta, Calgary, Sept. 1, 1913, RG89, v.37, f15, vol. 1, PAC.

35. E.F. Drake to W.J. Roche, June 25, 1913, RG89, v.37, f15, vol. 1, PAC; memo showing irrigable acreage being farmed in 1922 in Alberta, Mar. 1923, RG89, v.58, f30B, PAC.

36. "If Farmers Stand Solidly Together...."

8 BLOODY BOLIVIA!

1. For an illustration of the Department's attitude, see E.F. Drake to Deputy Minister of the Interior, Mar. 27, 1923, RG89, vol. 209, f5026, PAC.

2. Griffin to Naismith, Dec. 28, 1923.

3. "CPR Contract Holders Taking Steps to Move," *Calgary Albertan*, Mar. 26, 1924, box 44, f510, CPR papers, GAA.

4. "Will the CPR Force Settlers to Leave the Country," *CPR Contract Holders' Bulletin* (Calgary), [1924] no. 4, box 44, f510, CPR papers, GAA.

5. "H.B.Co.'s Land Occupants Are Not Worrying," *Calgary Herald*, Mar. 26, 1924, box 44, f510, CPR papers, GAA.

6. "Bolivia The Land Of Opportunities," *CPR Contract Holders' Bulletin*, [Apr.? 1924], box 44, f510, CPR papers, GAA.

7. Ibid.

8. "Alta. Farmers Buying Land In Far-Off Bolivia," *Calgary Albertan*, Apr. 3, 1924, box 44, f510, CPR papers, GAA.

9. "Beware of Bolivia Advises Farmer Who Made Trip," *Calgary Herald*, Apr. 3, 1924, box 44, f510, CPR papers, GAA.

10. S.G. Porter to D.W. Hays, Dec. 22, 1930, box 24, f290, CPR papers, GAA.

9 HELL AND THE SAGE

1. Carl J. Anderson to David C. Jones, Mar. 31, 1989.

2. Eastern Irrigation District Annual Report 1926, box 4, CPR papers, GAA.

3. Untitled history of efforts to form EID, July 1, 1935, 73.307, f91, PAA; Anderson to Jones, Mar. 31, 1989.

4. Minutes of Meeting of Department of Natural Resources, Dec. 12, 1935, f539, box 50, CPR papers, GAA.

5. Renie Gross and Lea Nicoll Kramer, *Tapping the Bow* (Brooks: Eastern Irrigation District, 1985), p. 177.

6. "Settlers' Taxes," [1935] f539, box 50, CPR papers, GAA.

7. Gross and Kramer, *Tapping the Bow*, pp. 88–91.

8. Yogananda dedicated his *Autobiography of a Yogi* (Los Angeles: Self Realization Fellowship, 1946), a spiritual classic, to Luther Burbank, whom he called "an American saint."

9. *Scandia Since Seventeen* (Scandia, AB: Scandia Historical Society, 1978), p. 9.

10. Gross and Kramer, *Tapping the Bow*, p. 161.

11. Ibid., p. 160.

12. Ibid., p. 174.

13. *Scandia*, p. 41.

14. Carl J. Anderson interview, Brooks Alberta, by David C. Jones, 1984.

15. Ibid.

16. Carl J. Anderson interview, Brooks, Alberta, by David C. Jones, 1988.

17. Personal communication; also, Anderson to Jones Sept. 18, 1990; Anderson to Jones, July 2, 1991.

18. Hubbard, *The Note Book of Elbert Hubbard*, pp. 12, 23, 26, 33.

19. Ibid, p. 26.

20. Hubbard, *Selected Writings of Elbert Hubbard*, Vol. IX, Philistia, p. 191.

21. Ibid., pp. 38–40.
22. Elbert Hubbard, *Selected Works of Elbert Hubbard*, Vol XI, The Man of Sorrows (New York: William H. Wise & Co., 1922), p. 39.
23. Ibid., p. 27.
24. Hubbard, *Selected Writings of Elbert Hubbard*, Vol. IX, Philistia, p. 193.
25. David Arnold Balch, *Elbert Hubbard: Genius of Roycroft: A Biography* (New York: Frederick A. Stokes Co., 1940), p. 170.
26. Elbert Hubbard, *Selected Writings of Elbert Hubbard*, Vol. V, The Elect, White Hyacinths (New York: William H. Wise, and Co., 1922), pp. 397, 401–2, 405.
27. Balch, *Elbert Hubbard: Genius of Roycroft* , p. 204.
28. Champney, *Art & Glory: The Story of Elbert Hubbard*, p. 101.
29. How closely did Hubbard approach his own ideals? The answer is beyond the scope of this book. Readers may consult Hubbard's biographers Albert Lane, Felix Shay, Mary Hubbard Heath, David Arnold Balch, Freeman Champney, Charles F. Hamilton, and Bruce A. White for their opinions— but probably only Hubbard himself knew. My assessment of him is more than favorable—though everyone is inconsistent until he reaches the exalted level Hubbard sought. For every foe Hubbard retained till his death, he had five hundred or a thousand friends.
30. *Elbert Hubbard's Scrap Book* (New York: William H. Wise & Co., 1923), pp. 30, 40.
31. Anderson to Jones, Sept. 18, 1990.

10 THE BARGAIN

1. Renie Gross and Lea Nicoll Kramer, *Tapping the Bow* (Brooks: Eastern Irrigation District, 1985), p. 164.
2. L.C. Charlesworth to F.S. Grisdale, Mar. 4, 1935, 73.307, f91, PAA. This lengthy collection regarding the EID take-over contains numerous statements from all sources about the problems of the Eastern Section.
3. Charlesworth to Grisdale, Mar. 4, 1935.
4. Anderson interview, 1984; Anderson to Jones, Mar. 31, 1989.
5. Ibid.
6. Untitled history of EID.
7. Charlesworth to Grisdale, Mar. 4, 1935.
8. Gross and Kramer, *Tapping the Bow*, p. 167.
9. William Sheldrake to F.S. Grisdale, Dec. 4, 1934, 73.307, f91, PAA.
10. "Minority Commit'e[sic] Report," *Brooks Bulletin*, Jan. 31, 1935, p. 1.
11. S.G. Porter to W.M. Neal, Jan. 30, 1935, box 28, f341, CPR Papers, GAA.
12. S.G. Porter confidential memo, Dec. 5, 1934, box 28, f337, CPR Papers, GAA.

13. Porter to Neal, Jan. 30, 1935, italics in next paragraph mine.
14. "Counter Petition Re New Irr. District," *Brooks Bulletin*, Jan. 24, 1935.
15. "Open Letter from Contract Holders' Committee," *The Brooks Bulletin*, Feb. 7, 1935.
16. Porter to Neal, Jan. 30, 1935.
17. Ibid.
18. Small committee to S.G. Porter, Feb. 25, 1935, 73.307, f91, PAA.
19. Anderson, 1984 interview.

11 THE LEGACY

1. Small committee to S.G. Porter, Feb. 25, 1935 in L.C. Charlesworth to F.S. Grisdale, Mar. 4, 1935, 73.307, f91, PAA.
2. Carl J. Anderson interview, Brooks, Alberta, 1984, by David C. Jones.
3. Untitled history of EID, July 1, 1935, 73.307 f91, PAA.
4. S.G. Porter to W.M. Neal, Feb. 26, 1935, CPR papers, box 28, f341, GAA. Porter wrote, "While I do not wish to state just now that we should accept these terms, at the same time if an agreement were made on the basis of the figures named in this letter, we would still be much better off than to continue operating the project ourselves."
5. Ibid.
6. Carl J. Anderson interview by David C. Jones, Brooks, Alberta, 1988.
7. See Jones, *Empire of Dust*, ch. 9, and p. 271.
8. *Scandia Since Seventeen* (Scandia, AB: Scandia Historical Committee, 1978), pp. 50–55.
9. Ibid., p. 55; Anderson, interview by phone, Nov. 14, 1994.
10. Anderson interview, Brooks, Alberta, Nov. 26, 1994.
11. Anderson to Jones, July 29, 30, 31, 1991.
12. Anderson to Jones, Sept. 18, 1990.
13. Ibid.
14. Ibid.
15. Anderson to Jones, Mar. 31, 1989.
16. Hubbard II, ed., *The Philosophy of Elbert Hubbard*, p. 109.

12 UNCONSCIOUS OF THEIR NOBILITY

1. Department of Public Works, Annual Report 1914, A.A. Carpenter, Report of the Commission Appointed to the Investigation and Enquiry into the Cause and Effect of the Hillcrest Mine Disaster, pp. 166–67.
2. Investigation and Enquiry into the Cause and Effect of the Hillcrest Mine Disaster, pp. 164–65.
3. "Hope Abandoned for the Recovery of Any More Bodies from Hillcrest," *The Calgary Daily Herald* (hereafter *CDH*), June 20, 1914, p. 30.

4. "Survivors Tell of Their Escape from Hillcrest Mine," *The Morning Albertan* (Calgary), June 22, 1914, p. 9.

5. "Forty-Eight Men Saved," *CDH*, June 22, 1914, p. 1.

6. "Survivors Tell of Their Escape," p. 5.

7. "Nearly Two Hundred Dead," *The Coleman Bulletin*, June 25, 1914, p. 1.

8. Lorry William Felske, "Studies in the Crow's Nest Pass Coal Industry from its Origins to the End of World War 1," unpublished Ph.D. thesis, University of Toronto, 1991, pp. 238–39.

9. "Hope Abandoned...," p. 16.

10. "217 Miners Entombed," *The Blairmore Enterprise*, June 19, 1914, p. 1.

11. "225 Men Entombed in Hillcrest Mine," *Lethbridge Daily Herald*, June 19, 1914, p. 8.

12. "Forty–Eight Men Saved in Hillcrest Disaster Out of a Total of 237," *CDH*, June 22, 1914, p. 1.

13. A.C. Yokome, "Survivors Tell of Their Escape From Hillcrest Mine," *The Morning Albertan* (Calgary), June 22, 1914, p. 5.

14. "Forty-Eight Men Saved...."

15. "217 Miners Entombed," p. 1.

16. "Hope Abandoned...," p. 30

17. "Survivors Tell of Their Escape from Hillcrest Mine," *The Morning Albertan* (Calgary), June 22, 1914, p. 9.

18. "Terrible Disaster in the Hillcrest Mines," *The Morning Albertan* (Calgary), June 20, 1914, p. 16.

19. "The Victims of Hillcrest Disaster Laid to Rest Amid Scenes of Grief," *CDH*, June 22, 1914, p. 7.

20. "Inquest Into Colliery Disaster at Hillcrest Formally Opened Today," *CDH*, June 20, 1914, p. 1.

21. "Hope Abandoned...," p. 20.

22. "195 Men Perish in the Worst Mining Disaster That Has Ever Occurred in Canadian History," *The Morning Albertan* (Calgary), June 20, 1914, p. 1.

23. "Nearly Two Hundred Dead," *The Coleman Bulletin*, June 25, 1914, p. 8.

24. "Forty-Eight Men Saved," p. 1

25. *The Blairmore Enterprise*, June 26, 1914, n.t., n.p.

26. "Survivors Tell of Their Escape from Hillcrest Mine," *The Morning Albertan* (Calgary), June 22, 1914, p. 9.

27. "Nearly Two Hundred Dead," *The Coleman Bulletin*, June 25, 1914, p. 8.

28. "Undertaker Davies' Tremendous Task," *The Coleman Bulletin*, June 25, 1914, p. 1.

29. "The Victims of Hillcrest Disaster...," p. 7.

30. Hubbard, *Selected Writings of Elbert Hubbard*, Vol. IV, Preachments, p. 419.

1. Hubbard, *Selected Writings of Elbert Hubbard*, Vol. IV, Preachments, p. 455.

2. *Canadian Annual Review* (hereafter *CAR*), 1919, p. 449.

3. David J. Bercuson, *Fools and Wisemen* (Toronto: McGraw Hill Ryerson, 1978), p. 48; A. Ross McCormack, *Reformers, Rebels, and Revolutionaries: The Western Canadian Radical Movement* 1899–1919 (Toronto: University of Toronto Press, 1977), pp. 60–61.

4. McCormack, *Reformers, Rebels, and Revolutionaries*, pp. 26, 54.

5. Ibid., pp. 58–59.

6. *CAR*, 1919, p. 456.

7. Ibid., p. 492.

8. *Report of the Royal Commission Respecting the Coal Industry of the Province of Alberta 1935* (Edmonton: King's Printer, 1936), p. 7; *Report of the Alberta Coal Commission 1925* (Edmonton: Acting King's Printer, 1926), p. 1. Estimates of the percentage of world resources were steadily adjusted downward to 3 percent.

9. *Report of Alberta Coal Commission 1925* (Edmonton: Acting King's Printer, 1926), pp. 1, 58.

10. Warren Caragata, "The Labour Movement in Alberta: An Untold Story," in David Leadbeater, ed., *Essays on the Political Economy of Alberta* (Toronto: New Hogtown Press, 1984), p. 116.

11. Charles Allen Seager, "A Proletariat in Wild Rose Country: The Alberta Coal Miners, 1905–1945," Ph.D. Thesis, York University, 1981, p. 169.

12. David Jay Bercuson, ed., *Alberta's Coal Industry 1919* (Calgary: Historical Society of Alberta, 1978), p. 117.

13. Ibid., pp. 114–16.

14. "Scalding Criticism of Bunkhouse System By Coal Miners Working in District 18," *The Morning Albertan* (Calgary), Feb. 19, 1919, p. 6.

15. Bercuson, *Alberta's Coal Industry*, p. 88.

16. Ibid., pp. 185–86.

17. Ibid., pp. 191, 194.

18. Ibid., pp. 191–98.

19. Ibid., p. 118.

20. Ibid., pp. 198–99.

21. Ibid., p. 221.

22. Ibid., pp. 198–200, 118.

23. Ibid., p. 118.

24. "Record Crowd Present at the Rosedale Trial," *Drumheller Review*, Feb. 15, 1918; "Frank Moodie Fined, Brother Dismissed," *Calgary Daily*

Herald, Feb. 14, 1918, p. 1. The United mine workers were furious that Moodie later appealed the conviction and won.

25. Bercuson, *Alberta's Coal Industry*, pp. 121–22.

26. Report, Apr. 22, 1918, Moodie Papers, box 1, f4, GAA.

27. Report, Apr. 23, 1918.

28. Report, Apr. 24, 1918.

29. Report, Apr. 25, 1918.

30. Report, June 5, 1918.

31. Bercuson, *Alberta's Coal Industry 1919*, p. 104.

32. Reports, June 12, 15, 1918.

33. Report, June 21, 1918.

34. J.F. Moodie to Major Fitz Horrigan, Oct. 7, 1918, Moodie Papers, box 1, f1, GAA.

35. Report, Aug. 3, 1918.

36. Report, Oct. 3, 1918.

37. Report, Aug. 3, 1918.

38. Report, Aug. 26, 1918.

39. Report, Sept. 6, 1918.

40. Report, June 5, 1918.

41. Report, Aug. 28, 1918.

42. Bercuson, *Alberta's Coal Industry*, p. 125.

43. Report, Nov. 13, 1918.

44. Report, Nov. 27, 29, 1918.

45. "Stories of Trial by Onlooker," *One Big Union Bulletin*, Dec. 27, 1919, p. 2.

46. Report, Sept. 16, 1918.

47. Report, Jan. 4, 1919.

48. Report, Nov. 27, 1918.

49. Report, Nov. 12, 1918.

50. Report, Dec. 2, 1918.

51. Report, Dec. 10, 1918.

52. Report, Dec. 14, 1918.

53. Report, Dec. 17, 1918.

54. Report, Dec. 17, 1918.

55. Bercuson, *Alberta's Coal Industry*, p. 98.

56. Report, Oct. 18, 1918.

57. Howard Palmer with Tamara Palmer, *Alberta: A New History* (Edmonton: Hurtig, 1990), p. 188.

58. Canada, *1936 Census*, p. 833; "Well Organized to Battle the 'Flu,'" *The Drumheller Mail*, Oct. 31, 1918; "Epidemic Spreading in Rural District," *The Drumheller Mail*, Nov. 7, 1918.

59. Heather MacDougall, "The Fatal Flu," *Horizon Canada*, 8:88 (Nov. 1986): 2090–91.

60. Report, Oct. 28, 1918.

61. Report, Oct. 24, 1918.

62. Report, Oct. 29, 1918.

63. Report, Nov. 11, 1918.

64. Bercuson, *Alberta's Coal Industry*, p. 124.

65. Seven signatories to F. Moodie, Dec. 28, 1918, Moodie Papers, box 1, f2, GAA.

66. Reports, Dec. 22, 26, 27, 1918.

14 THE BROTHERS' WAR

1. "Tip Blaine, Well Known Citizen Shot and Killed By a Hun," *Drumheller Review*, Nov. 15, 1918; "Peace Celebration Ends in Tragedy," *The Drumheller Mail*, Nov. 14, 1918; "Inquest and Preliminary Trial," *The Drumheller Mail*, Nov. 14, 1918; "Popular Oldtimer Victim of Tragedy," *The Drumheller Mail*, Nov. 14, 1918.

2. Alberta Provincial Police Annual Report 1919, Cases, p. 10, 72.370, f1, PAA; "Albert Arnold, Ex-Officer of German Army, Acquitted on Charge of Murder of Blaine, Drumheller Victory Bond Seller," *The Morning Albertan* (Calgary), Jan. 21, 1919, p. 12. "Killing of E.A. Blaine Described," *Calgary Daily Herald*, Jan. 20, 1919, pp. 1, 11; "A Otto Arnold is Acquitted of Blaine's Murder," *Calgary Daily Herald*, Jan. 21, 1919, p. 12.

3. Report, Jan. 6, 1919.

4. Report, Jan. 7, 1919.

5. Report, Jan. 8, 1919.

6. Report, Jan. 10, 1919.

7. Report, Jan. 8, 1919.

8. Report, Jan. 8, 1919.

9. Report, Mar. 2, 1919.

10. Report, Mar. 13, 1919.

11. Report, Mar. 15, 1919.

12. UMW Convention, verbatim report, 1919, pp. 127, 128, UMW Papers, GAA.

13. UMW Convention, verbatim report, 1919, p. 75.

14. Quoted in Leonard Louis Levinson, *The Left Handed Dictionary* (London: Collier Macmillan, 1963), p. 48.

15. Report, Jan. 11, 1919.

16. Hubbard, *The Note Book of Elbert Hubbard*, p. 119.

17. *Report of the Alberta Coal Commission 1925* (Edmonton: Acting King's Printer, 1926), pp. 2, 13, 41, 326.

18. Lorry William Felske, "Studies in the Crow's Nest Pass Coal Industry from Its Origins to the End of World War 1," Ph.D. thesis, University of Toronto, 1991, pp. 306–8.

19. Ibid., pp. 188–89, 194, 196, 199, 205, 207, 210, 212, 243, 257, 260–63.

20. Sixteenth Annual Convention, District 18, United Mine Workers of America, verbatim report, 1919.

21. *Alberta Coal Commission 1925*, pp. 306–7.

22. Bercuson, *Alberta's Coal Industry 1919*, pp. 234–35.

23. Seager, "A Proletarian in Wild Rose Country," p. 331.

24. Report, Nov. 14, 1918.

25. Report, Apr. 10, 1919.

26. Report, Apr. 27, 1919.

27. Report, Feb. 1, 1919.

28. Report, May 4, 1919; Seager, " A Proletarian in Wild Rose Country," p. 335.

29. Report, May 9, 1919.

30. Report, May 11, 1919.

31. Report, May 27, 1919.

32. Report, June 2, 1919.

33. Reports, June 3, 5, 1919.

34. Report, June 9, 1919.

35. Report, June 10, 1919.

36. Report, June 16, 1919.

37. Report, June 16, 1919.

38. Report, June 20, 1919.

39. Report, June 26, 1919.

40. Report, July 6, 1919.

41. Report, July 7, 1919.

42. Report, July 8, 1919.

43. Report, July 10, 1919.

44. Report, July 16, 1919.

45. Report, July 17, 1919.

46. Report, July 23, 1919.

47. Report, Aug. 1, 1919.

48. Reports, Mar. 7–8, 1919.

49. Report, Aug. 6, 1919.

50. Seager, " A Proletarian in Wild Rose Country," p. 341.

51. "Law and Order Dead in Drumheller," *One Big Union Bulletin*, Nov. 29, 1919, p. 6.

52. "Returned Vets Treat O.B.U. Men to A Ride," *The Drumheller Mail*, Aug. 14, 1919.

53. Hubbard, *Selected Writings of Elbert Hubbard*, Vol. I, Pamphlets, p. 30; Hubbard, *Selected Writings*, Vol. VI, Fra Elbertus, p. 253.

15 THE CAT'S ANTIDOTE

1. "The Office Cat," *Medicine Hat News* (hereafter *News*), Apr. 13, 1926. Several parts of this chapter appeared in David C. Jones, *A Funny Bone That Was—Humor Between the Wars* (Calgary: Detselig, 1992).

2. *News*, Apr. 23, 1923.

3. *News*, Jan. 14, 1933, with an adjustment of the second phrase.

4. *News*, Mar. 6, 1933.

5. *News*, May 2, 1929.

6. *News*, June 11, 1930.

7. *News*, June 17, 1926.

8. *News*, Oct. 17, 1928.

9. *News*, Dec. 1, 1922, usually attributed to Benjamin Franklin.

10. *News*, Oct. 4, 1927.

11. *News*, Feb. 14, 1923.

12. *News*, June 10, 1933.

13. *News*, Mar. 31, 1938.

14. *News*, Aug. 28, 1935.

15. *News*, Mar, 9, 1936.

16. Mary Bellamy, Medicine Hat, telephone interview, Oct. 8, 1991 by David C. Jones; "Pay Final Tribute to Late A.J.N. 'Alf' Terrill," *News*, Mar. 8, 1947, p. 3.

17. Alberta Provincial Police (hereafter APP), *Annual Report* 1920, p. 68.

18. A.L. Marks to A.G. Browning, Mar. 21, 1919, f412, 83.192, PAA.

19. W.F. Gold to A.G. Browning, June 26, 1917; July 26, 1917; July 13, 1917, Aug. 17, 1917, f408, 83.192, PAA.

20. W.F. Gold to A.G. Browning, July 4, 1917; Rev. T. Taylor to Rev. W.F. Gold, Sept. 21, 1917, f408, 83.192, PAA.

21. *News*, Aug. 15, 1924.

22. *News*, Nov. 25, 1921.

23. *News*, Apr. 17, 1923.

24. *News*, Nov. 30, 1922.

25. APP, *Annual Report* 1920, p. 61; APP, *Annual Report* 1921, p. 12; APP, *Annual Report* 1922, p. 3; APP, *Annual Report* 1918, n.p.

26. APP *Annual Report* 1918, D. Division, n.p.

27. APP *Annual Report* 1920, Liquor Control Branch, p. 6.

28. APP *Annual Report* 1921, C. Division, p. 28.

29. APP *Annual Report* 1921, Liquor Branch, p. 10.

30. APP *Annual Report* 1922, Liquor Branch, p. 12.

31. *News*, Jan. 10, 1922.
32. *News*, May 6, 1922.
33. *News*, Aug. 12, 1929.
34. *News*, May 30, 1923.
35. *News*, Feb. 27, 1922.
36. John Herd Thompson with Allen Seager, *Canada, 1922–1939; Decades of Discord* (Toronto: McClelland and Stewart, 1985), p. 64; W.H. Smith, Board of Home Missions and Social Service, Presbyterian Church of Canada, "The Liquor Traffic in British Columbia," Sept. 1922, f97d, 69.289, PAA.
37. APP *Annual Report* 1920, pp. 19, 28.
38. *News*, Dec. 13, 1922.
39. APP *Annual Report* 1922, Liquor Branch, p. 13.
40. *News*, June, 28, 1928.
41. *News*, July 25, 1936.
42. Hubbard, *The Note Book of Elbert Hubbard*, p. 134; Hubbard, *Selected Writings of Elbert Hubbard*, Vol. IV, Preachments, p. 394.
43. Terrill, editorial, "The Beauty That Remains," *News*, Aug. 9, 1922, p. 2.
44. *News*, Aug. 24, 1923.
45. *News*, Feb. 27, 1922.
46. *News*, Mar. 13, 1928.
47. *News*, Mar. 4, 1924.
48. *News*, Feb. 14, 1926.
49. *News*, Apr. 19, 1926. Like the Cat's other utterances, some of these maxims may have been brainchildren of great thinkers, but most were brief enough to have been coined by many.
50. *News*, July 5, 1930.
51. *News*, Aug. 18, 1925.
52. *News*, Mar. 1, 1922.
53. *News*, Aug. 10, 1926.
54. *News*, May 3, 1926.
55. *News*, Dec. 26, 1924.
56. *News*, Feb. 14, 1924.
57. *News*, Dec. 8, 1933.
58. *News*, Jan. 28, 1927.
59. *News*, Oct. 24, 192.
60. *News*, Oct. 8, 1924.
61. David C. Jones, L.J. Roy Wilson and Donny White, *The Weather Factory: A Pictorial History of Medicine Hat* (Saskatoon: Western Producer, 1988), pp. 14–17.
62. *News*, June 26, 1935.

63. Lois Valli, Brooks, Alberta, interview by David C. Jones, 1988.

64. Joke heard verbally from a survivor of the Depression.

65. Neil Rutherford, Bowell, interview by David C. Jones, 1984.

66. *News*, Mar. 28, 1922.

67. *News*, May 13, 1922.

68. Thompson and Seager, *Canada, 1922–1939*, p. 351; see also, Palmer and Palmer, *Alberta: A New History*, ch. 9.

69. Gerald Friesen, *The Canadian Prairies: A History* (Toronto: University of Toronto Press, 1984), p. 388.

70. David R. Elliott, *Aberhart: Outpourings and Replies* (Calgary: Alberta Records Publication Board/Historical Society of Alberta, 1991), p. 151; Arthur M. Schlesinger, Jr., *The Age of Roosevelt: The Coming of the New Deal* (Cambridge, MA: Riverside Press, 1958), pp. 62–63.

71. *News*, June 12, 1933.

72. *News*, Jan. 2, 1930.

73. *News*, Mar. 18, 1935.

74. *News*, Apr. 12, 1923.

75. *News*, Oct. 26, 1934.

76. *News*, June 1, 1932.

77. *News*, Nov. 18, 1933.

78. *News*, June 11, 1931.

79. *News*, Mar. 26, 1928.

80. *News*, Aug. 28, 1934.

81. *News*, Dec. 17, 1926.

82. *News*, Dec. 14, 1928.

83. *News*, Feb. 27, 1922.

84. Hubbard, *Selected Writings of Elbert Hubbard*, Vol. IX, Philistia, p. 108.

16 FATHER LOUIS

1. Culerier, Divers Ecrits, Oct. 6, 1945, f7926, 71.220, PAA.

2. *Dictionnaire Biographique Des Oblats De Marie Immaculée au Carrière* (Ottawa: L'Université D' Ottawa, 1976), pp. 96, 240–41.

3. Culerier, "Report of Trip To Whitecourt," May 11?, 1915, f7919, 71.220, PAA.

4. Maurice Legris, "Saint of the Coal Branch," *Alberta History* 37, no. 1 (Winter 1989): 2.

5. Ibid., pp. 4–5.

6. Culerier, Diaries June 18, 1934, f6347, 71.220, PAA; Jules Le Chevallier, "Le R.P. Culerier, OMI" [1946], f7924, 71.220, PAA.

7. A.A. den Otter, "A Social History of the Alberta Coal Branch," M.A. thesis, University of Alberta, 1967, p. 40.

8. *Report of the Alberta Coal Commission, 1925* (Edmonton: King's Printer, 1926), pp. 59–60.

9. den Otter, "Social History," p. 174.

10. Toni Ross, *Oh! The Coal Branch* (Edmonton: Friesen, 1974), p. 131.

11. *Prairie Census*, 1936, p. 873.

12. "Celebration at Mountain Park," *The Edson Herald*, July 13, 1917, p. 1.

13. "Mountain Park Banquet Great Social Affair," *The Western Leader* (Edson), Apr. 21, 1917, p. 1.

14. Ross, *Coal Branch*, pp. 219, 189.

15. Ibid., p. 30.

16. Ibid., pp. 201–202.

17. den Otter, "Social History," p. 189, *Prairie Census* 1936, pp. 873, 881.

18. Ross, *Coal Branch*, p. 74.

19. Ibid., p. 80.

20. Ibid., p. 72.

21. Ibid., pp. 232, 215.

22. Ibid., p. 124.

23. den Otter, "Social History," p. 100.

24. Ross, *Coal Branch*, pp. 300–301.

25. Ibid., p. 223.

26. Ibid., p. 92.

27. Ibid., pp. 111, 116–18.

28. Hubbard, *Selected Writings of Elbert Hubbard*, Vol. IV, Preachments, "A Thousand and One Epigrams," p. 400.

29. Legris, "Saint," p. 2.

30. Culerier, Diaries, Mar. 22, 1918, f6349, 71.220, PAA.

31. Culerier, Diaries, "Bootlegger," [1945], f6349, 71.220, PAA.

32. Ross, *Coal Branch*, p. 48. Snovitch is a pseudonym, no name being given in the source.

17 A CHURCH RAT

1. Culerier, Diaries, Feb. 18, 1940, f6347, 71.220, PAA.

2. Culerier, Diaries, Jan. 25, 1904, f6349, 71.220, PAA.

3. Culerier, Diaries, Apr. 20, 1903, f6347, 71.220, PAA.

4. Culerier, Diaries, Oct. 6–7, 1902; Dec. 5, 1903, f6349, 71.220, PAA.

5. Culerier, Diaries, Apr. 20, 1903, f6347, 71.220, PAA.

6. Culerier, Diaries, Oct. 12, 1901, f6349, 71.220, PAA.

7. Culerier, Diaries, April 14, 1902, f6341, 71.220, PAA.

8. Culerier to Père Provincial, Feb. 25, 1934, f7920, 71.220, PAA; Culerier, Diaries, Mar. 9, 1901, f6347, 71.220, PAA.

9. Culerier, Diaries, Sept. 14, 1903, f6349, 71.220, PAA.

10. Culerier, Diaries, Feb. 18, 1940, f6347, 71.220, PAA.

11. Culerier to Desnoyers, Aug. 6, 1935, f6349, PAA. Culerier constantly rewrote his diaries.

12. Culerier, Diaries, Nov. 1, 1904, f6349, 71.220, PAA.

13. Culerier, Diaries, Dec. 28, 1935, f6349, 71.220, PAA.

14. Culerier, edit of diary, Feb. 1905; Dec. 28, 1935, f6349, 71.220, PAA.

15. Culerier, Diaries, Aug. 28, 1933, f6349, 71.220, PAA.

16. Ibid.

17. Culerier, edit of diary Feb. 1905, Dec. 28, 1935, f6349, 71.220, PAA.

18. Culerier to Reverend Père General, June 18, 1934, f6349, 71.220, PAA.

19. Culerier, Feuille Volant, 1921, n.p., n.f., PAA.

20. Culerier to Père Provincial Langlois, June 3, 1936, f7922, 71.220, PAA.

21. Culerier to Langlois, Dec. 17, 1933, f6349, 71.220, PAA.

22. Culerier to Père Provincial Lacombe, Sept. n.d. 1924, f7925, PAA.

23. Culerier, Diaries, Aug. 4, 1903, f6349, 71.220, PAA

24. Culerier, Diaries, Mar. 14, 1904, rewritten Dec. 23, 1935, f6349, 71.220, PAA.

25. Culerier, Diaries, Feb. 11, 1940, f6343, 71.220, PAA.

26. Ibid.

27. Culerier, Diaries, Jan. 21, 1934, f6349, 71.220 PAA.

28. Culerier to Père Provincial Langlois, Jan. 25, 1933, f7920, 71.220, PAA.

29. Father Langlois to Culerier, Feb. 4, 1933, f7920, 71.220, PAA.

30. Culerier to Reverend Père General, Dec. 9, 1933, f6349, 71.220, PAA.

31. Culerier to Father Auclair, Aug. 28, 1937, f7923, 71.220, PAA.

32. Culerier to Père Provincial, May 9, 1934, f7921, 71.220, PAA.

33. Culerier to Father Moulin, Mar. 27, 1934, f6347, 71.220, PAA.

34. Culerier, Diaries, Dec. 29, 1939, f6347, 71.220, PAA.

35. Culerier to Archbishop O'Leary, Oct. 4, 193, f6349, 71.220, PAA.

36. Culerier, Diaries, June 24, 1934, f6347, 71.220, PAA.

37. Ibid.

38. Culerier to Archbishop O'Leary, Dec. 9, 1933, f6349, 71.220, PAA.

39. Culerier to Reverend Père General, Nov. 27, 1933, f6349, 71.220, PAA.

40. Culerier to Reverend Père General, June 18, 1934, f6349, 71.220, PAA.

41. Culerier, jottings, to Archbishop O'Leary, Dec. 8–9, 1933, f6347, 71.220, PAA.

42. Culerier, Diaries, Dec. 3, 1933, f6349, 71.220, PAA.; Culerier to Father Langlois, Dec. 15, 1933, f6349, 71.220, PAA.

43. Culerier, Diaries, Aug. 27–28, 1936, f6347, 71.220, PAA.

44. Culerier, Diaries, Jan. 16, 1934, f6349, 71.220, PAA.

18 THE CROSS BEARING

1. Culerier, Diaries, Mar. 9, 1901, f6347, 71.220, PAA.
2. Culerier, "The Nature of the Religious Life," Sept. 14, 1926, f6353. These lectures are in English.
3. Culerier, "Humiliations," Feb. 14, 1928, f6354.
4. Culerier, "The Cross in the Life of a Religious," [1929], f6355.
5. Culerier, "The Cross in the Life of a Religious."
6. Mother Catherine Thomas, *My Beloved: The Story of a Carmelite Nun* (New York: Image Books, 1959), p. 136.
7. Culerier, "Humility," Jan. 31, 1928, f6354.
8. Culerier, "Humiliations," Feb. 14, 1928, f6354.
9. Culerier, "Fidelity to Little Things," Apr. 10, 1928, f6354.
10. Elbert Hubbard, *Little Journeys to the Homes of Great Orators* (New York: William H. Wise and Co., 1923), p. 130
11. Hubbard, *Selected Writings of Elbert Hubbard*, Vol. XII, An American Bible, p. 321.
12. Hubbard, *The Note Book of Elbert Hubbard*, p. 15.
13. Culerier, "Scruples," [1928?], f6354.
14. Ibid.
15. Culerier, "How to Accept and Take Corrections," May 25, 1937, f6354.
16. Culerier, "Obedience," Mar. 30, 1926, f6353.
17. Ibid.
18. Culerier, "Obedience," Nov. 24, 1925, f6353.
19. Culerier, "Charity."
20. Culerier, "Obedience," [1926], f6353.
21. Culerier, "Obedience," June 12, 1926, f6353.
22. Culerier, "Obedience," [1929].
23. Ibid.
24. Ibid.
25. Ibid.
26. Culerier, "Dangers of Our Vocation," Feb. 24, 1937, f6353.
27. Ibid.
28. Ibid.
29. Ibid.
30. Culerier to Monsignor Breynat, Oct. 16, 1936, p. 347, f6349.
31. Culerier to Père Provincial Langlois Oct. 17, 1933, f7920.
32. Culerier to Père Provincial Langlois, Oct. 17, 1933, correspondence 1933, f7920, 71.220, PAA.
33. Culerier, Diaries, Feb. 18, 1935, f6349.

34. Culerier to Father Langlois, Jan. 16, 1934, f6349.

35. Samuel H. Sandweiss, *Spirit and Mind* (San Diego: Birthday Publishing, 1985), p. 27.

36. Culerier, "Education," [1929], f6355.

37. Culerier, "Faults Against Charity," Mar. 13, 1928, f6354.

38. Culerier, "Education," [1929?], f6355.

39. Ibid.

40. Ibid.

41. Culerier, "Education," cont., [1929?].

42. Ibid.

43. Culerier to Père Provincial, Dec. 5, 1933, f7920.

44. Hubbard, *Selected Writings of Elbert Hubbard*, Vol. IV, Preachments, p. 469.

EPILOG

1. Louis Culerier, Diaries, May 8, 1945, f6349, 71.220, PAA.

2. Jules Le Chevallier, "Le R.P. Louis Culerier, O.M.I.," [1946], f7924, 71.220, PAA.

3. Ibid.

4. Gordon Albright, interview, by David C. Jones, Calgary, Oct. 3, 1990.

5. Eileen Ross to D.C. Jones, Aug. 29, 1990; Gordon Albright, interview, Calgary, Alberta, Oct. 3, 1990.

6. F.D. Trego to D.C. Jones, Apr. 26, 1991.

7. "Predicts Huge Oil Yield for Alberta," *Calgary Herald*, Apr. 4, 1936, clippings, GAA.

8. *A Report on Alberta Elections, 1905–1982* (Edmonton: Queen's Printer, 1983?), p. 55.

9. "Moodie," obituary, *Calgary Albertan*, Jan. 25, 1943, clippings, GAA.

10. United Mine Workers' Convention, Jan. 7, 1933, UMW Papers, box 6, f28, GAA.

11. Hubbard II, ed.,*The Philosophy of Elbert Hubbard*, p. 92.

12. Hubbard, *The Note Book of Elbert Hubbard*, p. 89.

13. J.F. Miller to J.F. Moodie, Sept. 29, 1919, box 1, f4, Moodie papers, GAA.

14. Hubbard II, ed., *The Philosphy of Elbert Hubbard*, p. 154.

15. "Pay Final Tribute to Late A.J.N. 'Alf' Terrill," *Medicine Hat News*, Mar. 8, 1947, p. 3.

16. Lois Valli to D.C. Jones, Aug. 6, 1990.

17. Angela Valli to D.C. Jones, Apr. 9, 1991.

18. Lois Valli, "January 1988," *Prairie Wool* (Champagne, Ill.: V.E. Valli, 1991), p. 109.

19. Valli, "February 1988," *Prairie Wool*, p. 121.

20. Elbert Hubbard, *Little Journeys to the Homes of Great Philosophers*, (New York: William H. Wise & Co., 1928), p. 321.

21. Lois Valli to D.C. Jones, Aug. 6, 1990.

22. Lois Valli, interview, Brooks, Alberta, by David C. Jones, May 23, 1994.

23. Ibid.

24. Hubbard, *The Note Book of Elbert Hubbard*, p. 88.

25. Hubbard, *Selected Writings of Elbert Hubbard*, Vol. I, Pamphlets, pp. 16–17. A superb account of the sinking occurs in A.A. Hoehling and Mary Hoehling, *The Last Voyage of the Lusitania* (New York: Dell, 1974).

26. Hubbard, *Selected Writings of Elbert Hubbard*, Vol. IX, Philistia, p. 41.

27. Carl J. Anderson, interview, Calgary, Alberta, Dec. 9, 1994. Later, Anderson gave me the *Scrap Book* too.

28. Hubbard II, ed., *The Philosophy of Elbert Hubbard*, p. 119.

Comment on Sources

THIS VOLUME REPRESENTS A TENTATIVE STEP toward relating the metaphysical literature to the past. There is a vast lore on the spiritual fulfillment of the self and on the role of suffering in that fulfillment. My own primary influences are *The URANTIA Book* (1981, 1 volume, 2100 pages), *A Course in Miracles* (1976, 3 volumes, 1200 pages), the *Selected Writings of Elbert Hubbard* (1922, 14 volumes), the Silver Birch and other books of the British spiritual tradition, and the many works by and about Paramahansa Yogananda, J. Donald Walters, and Sathya Sai Baba. There are five hundred books just in English on Baba alone.

Elbert Hubbard is my exemplar of this general literature. The best sources of the Sage's wisdom and philosophy are *An American Bible* (1911), *The Motto Book* (1909 and 1914), *The Note Book of Elbert Hubbard* (1927), *The Philosophy of Elbert Hubbard* (1930) and "A Thousand and One Epigrams" in Volume IV, Preachments, of his *Selected Writings* (1922). The epigrams and their original application are sprinkled throughout his works.

From 1908 to 1915, Roycroft published what are now rare and costly editions of *The Complete Writings of Elbert Hubbard* in twenty volumes. The best study of Roycroft books is Paul McKenna's *A History and Bibliography of the Roycroft Printing Shop* (1996).

Hubbard's *Little Journeys to the Homes of the Great* (1916, 14 volumes), available in many editions, are mixed in quality, episodic and impressionistic, but containing pockets of genuine insight, later reassembled and reissued many times.

One great need in a study of the relationship between adversity and self-awareness, misfortune and self-definition, is an inquiring, introspective personality to examine. An individual who bares a soul in writing or speaking, or who seeks peace or self-realization—and who leaves a track of the endeavor.

The Albert Truax-Nelson Burns revolt was part of the irrepressible gnostic tradition in Christianity and of the equally irrepressible search for human potential. The essential claims of Truax and Burns are in the "Truax Trial" the United Church Archives, Toronto, and in Burns's *Divine Guidance or the Holy Quest* (1889). *The Doctrine and Discipline of the Methodist Church* (1891) dictates the contending Methodist creed.

Other sources were chosen to set the scene of struggle or to reveal individual odysseys.

The effusions of H.F. Mullet and George Murray capture the enthusiasm of the late twenties influx into the Peace River country. *The Settlement of the Peace River Country: A Study of a Pioneer Area* (1934) by C.A. Dawson and R.W. Murchie is the landmark piece on the settlement. Two other books deepen the background—R.G. Moyles, *Challenge of the Homestead: Peace River Letters of Clyde and Myrle Campbell, 1919–1924* (1988) and David W. Leonard and Victoria L. Lemieux, *The Lure of the Peace River Country, 1872–1914* (1992).

Donald Albright's struggle to reshape the environment is in the Albright papers, Glenbow, and his relations with family are in my communications with his son and daughter.

The letters of Wemyss Cotter, recently unearthed, and now in the Provincial Archives of Alberta, bear the fond hopes of drybelters.

Sources for Lois Valli's journey are mostly oral—a 1984 interview with Buck, correspondence with Valli's son and daughters, and my long and valued communication with Lois. Her poetry she shared, before a goodly portion appeared in *Prairie Wool* (1991).

The context of irrigation is in the commissions of John A. Widtsoe (1925) and M.L. Wilson (1930). The Canada Land and Irrigation Company papers and the Canadian Pacific Railway papers are at Glenbow, and the role of the Alberta government is in the provincial archives.

Willet Trego's dispute with the Canadian Pacific, including copies of *The Contract Holders' Bulletin*, are carefully filed in the CPR papers. Both F.L. Trego, Willet's son, and Frank Brown, his grandson, related memories of Trego. Copies of the trenchant *Farmers' Tribune*, Carlstadt, are in the Glenbow Library.

The farmer takeover of the Eastern Irrigation District is in Renie Gross and Lea Nicoll Kramer, *Tapping the Bow* (1985) and in the CPR and provincial irrigation records. In examining Carl Anderson's role and nature, *Scandia Since Seventeen* (1978) helps, but nothing can replace Anderson's tireless and thoughtful response to my many questions.

Several commissions analyzed the floundering coal industry, and one spotlit the Hillcrest mine disaster. The most vivid and heartfelt accounts of that horror were penned by reporters on the scene. Two superb dissertations about coal mining in Alberta stand out—Allen Seager's "A Proletariat in Wild Rose Country" (1981), a model of how to *write* a thesis, and Lorry Felske's "Studies in the Crow's Nest Pass Coal Industry" (1991), a model of how to achieve *balance* of perception. For Frank Moodie and Operative 3, my primary source is the fascinating reports of the spy, a swatch of which augments the original accession at Glenbow.

The humor columns of The Office Cat run daily in the *Medicine Hat News* for more than two decades after 1921. The background and administration of prohibition appears in the Alberta Provincial Police reports.

The long diaries, numerous letters, and careful lectures of Father Louis Culerier are in the Oblate collection of the Provincial Archives. Only the lectures are in English.

My most valued lessons on perception appear in *A Course in Miracles* (1976) which declares, "Many are at odds with the world they perceive because they think it is antagonistic to them. The problem is not out there; it is inside the perceiver." (pt. 1, p. 206) "Everything you perceive is a witness to the thought system you want to be true." (pt. 1, p. 191) "It is impossible not to believe what you see, but it is equally impossible to see what you do not believe." (pt. 1, p. 192) What you choose to find in the world is your evaluation of yourself. "Choose littleness and you will not have peace, for you will have judged yourself unworthy of it." (pt. 1, p. 285)

Index

and Alice Moore, 7
on another's troubles, 41, 43
background, 4
and Bertha Hubbard, 7
and Billy Sunday, 6, 8
on caste, 200
on cosmic consciousness, 112
on creeds, 7
criticism of churches, 234
criticism of lawyers, doctors,
    teachers and professors, 112–13
death, 262
on divinity in humanity,
    233–234, 239
divorce, 7
on duplicity, 7, 255
on Emerson, 9
epigrams, 6-7
"Essay on Silence," 113
on genius and difficult
    environments, 137
on hate, 113, 175, 187
and humor, 7, 207
literary output, 5, 291–92
on loneliness, 65
on love, 7, 243, 263
Man of Sorrows, The, 6
"A Message to Garcia," 5
on misery and self-expression,
    258
on missionaries, 218
on Momus, god of laughter, 207
Note Book, 110, 115, 262
opposition to doctrine of
    depravity, 6
on oppression, 6
on peace, 263
The Philistine, 5

on power of sub-conscious, 9
on real self, 206
on reformers, 200
on religion, 111
Roycroft, 5
Scrap Book, 116, 262
on self-respect, 6
on separation, 7
on spiritual law, 110
on spying, 253
on suffering, 7, 243
visiting Prairie West at boom
    time, 49
on the wise man, 111–12
White Hyacinths, 113
Hudson's Hope, 24
humor, importance of, 205
Hutchinson, W., 155

Iron Springs, AB, 76
Imrie, John, 24
Industrial Workers of the World
    (IWW), 152, 173
irrigation, 4, 73–80, 87, 100, 122,
    127–37
isolation, 226

Jack the Frog, 217–20
Jackson, Dr. Mary Percy, 25–27
Jansenism, 248
Jewel Mine, 183
Jones, Harry, 123, 127–28
Jones, Robert "Klondike," 96–97
Jorawsky, 68
"Journal of Tonton Meric, The,"
    218